1 & 2 PETER
and JUDE

BELIEF

A Theological Commentary
on the Bible

GENERAL EDITORS

Amy Plantinga Pauw
William C. Placher[†]

1 & 2 PETER and JUDE

CATHERINE GUNSALUS GONZÁLEZ

WESTMINSTER
JOHN KNOX PRESS
LOUISVILLE • KENTUCKY

© 2010 Catherine Gunsalus González

First edition
Published by Westminster John Knox Press
Louisville, Kentucky

11 12 13 14 15 16 17 18 19 20—10 9 8 7 6 5 4 3 2 1

Scripture quotations from the New Revised Standard Version of the Bible
are copyright © 1989 by the Division of Christian Education of the National Council
of the Churches of Christ in the U.S.A. and are used by permission.

Book design by Drew Stevens
Cover design by Lisa Buckley
Cover art: © David Chapman/Design Pics/Corbis

Library of Congress Cataloging-in-Publication Data

González, Catherine Gunsalus.
    1 & 2 Peter and Jude : a theological commentary on the Bible / Catherine
Gunsalus González. — 1st ed.
        p. cm. — (Belief)
    Includes bibliographical references (p.   ) and indexes.
    ISBN 978-0-664-23202-3 (alk. paper)
    1. Bible. N. T. Peter—Commentaries. 2. Bible. N. T. Jude—Commentaries.
I. Title. II. Title: 1 and 2 Peter and Jude.
    BS2795.53.G66 2011
    227'.907—dc22

                                                                    2010034952

PRINTED IN THE UNITED STATES OF AMERICA

Contents

Publisher's Note

William C. Placher worked with Amy Plantinga Pauw as a general editor for this series until his untimely death in November 2008. Bill brought great energy and vision to the series, and was instrumental in defining and articulating its distinctive approach and in securing theologians to write for it. Bill's own commentary for the series was the last thing he wrote, and Westminster John Knox Press dedicates the entire series to his memory with affection and gratitude.

William C. Placher, LaFollette Distinguished Professor in Humanities at Wabash College, spent thirty-four years as one of Wabash College's most popular teachers. A summa cum laude graduate of Wabash in 1970, he earned his master's degree in philosophy in 1974 and his Ph.D. in 1975, both from Yale University. In 2002 the American Academy of Religion honored him with the Excellence in Teaching Award. Placher was also the author of thirteen books, including *A History of Christian Theology*, *The Triune God*, *The Domestication of Transcendence*, *Jesus the Savior*, *Narratives of a Vulnerable God*, and *Unapologetic Theology*. He also edited the volume *Essentials of Christian Theology*, which was named as one of 2004's most outstanding books by both *The Christian Century* and *Christianity Today* magazines.

Series Introduction

Belief: A Theological Commentary on the Bible is a series from Westminster John Knox Press featuring biblical commentaries written by theologians. The writers of this series share Karl Barth's concern that, insofar as their usefulness to pastors goes, most modern commentaries are "no commentary at all, but merely the first step toward a commentary." Historical-critical approaches to Scripture rule out some readings and commend others, but such methods only begin to help theological reflection and the preaching of the Word. By themselves, they do not convey the powerful sense of God's merciful presence that calls Christians to repentance and praise; they do not bring the church fully forward in the life of discipleship. It is to such tasks that theologians are called.

For several generations, however, professional theologians in North America and Europe have not been writing commentaries on the Christian Scriptures. The specialization of professional disciplines and the expectations of theological academies about the kind of writing that theologians should do, as well as many of the directions in which contemporary theology itself has gone, have contributed to this dearth of theological commentaries. This is a relatively new phenomenon; until the last century or two, the church's great theologians also routinely saw themselves as biblical interpreters. The gap between the fields is a loss for both the church and the discipline of theology itself. By inviting forty contemporary theologians to wrestle deeply with particular texts of Scripture, the editors of this series hope not only to provide new theological resources for the church, but also to encourage all theologians to pay more attention to Scripture and the life of the church in their writings.

We are grateful to the Louisville Institute, which provided funding for a consultation in June 2007. We invited theologians, pastors, and biblical scholars to join us in a conversation about what this series could contribute to the life of the church. The time was provocative and the results were rich. Much of the series' shape owes to the insights of these skilled and faithful interpreters, who sought to describe a way to write a commentary that served the theological needs of the church and its pastors with relevance, historical accuracy, and theological depth. The passion of these participants guided us in creating this series and lives on in the volumes.

As theologians, the authors will be interested much less in the matters of form, authorship, historical setting, social context, and philology—the very issues that are often of primary concern to critical biblical scholars. Instead, this series' authors will seek to explain the theological importance of the texts for the church today, using biblical scholarship as needed for such explication but without any attempt to cover all of the topics of the usual modern biblical commentary. This thirty-six-volume series will provide passage-by-passage commentary on all the books of the Protestant biblical canon, with more extensive attention given to passages of particular theological significance.

The authors' chief dialogue will be with the church's creeds, practices, and hymns; with the history of faithful interpretation and use of the Scriptures; with the categories and concepts of theology; and with contemporary culture in both "high" and popular forms. Each volume will begin with a discussion of *why* the church needs this book and why we need it *now*, in order to ground all of the commentary in contemporary relevance. Throughout each volume, text boxes will highlight the voices of ancient and modern interpreters from the global communities of faith, and occasional essays will allow deeper reflection on the key theological concepts of these biblical books.

The authors of this commentary series are theologians of the church who embrace a variety of confessional and theological perspectives. The group of authors assembled for this series represents more diversity of race, ethnicity, and gender than any other commentary series. They approach the larger Christian tradition with a critical respect, seeking to reclaim its riches and at the same time to acknowledge its shortcomings. The authors also aim to make available to readers a wide range of contemporary theological voices from many parts of the world. While it does recover an older genre of writing, this series is not an attempt to retrieve some idealized past. These commentaries have learned from tradition, but they are most importantly commentaries for today. The authors share the conviction that their work will be more contemporary, more faithful, and more radical, to the extent that it is more biblical, honestly wrestling with the texts of the Scriptures.

William C. Placher
Amy Plantinga Pauw

Abbreviations

ACCSNT   Ancient Christian Commentary
             on Scripture: New Testament

ANF   *Ante-Nicene Fathers*

BECNT   Baker Exegetical Commentary on
             the New Testament

LCC   Library of Christian Classics

NICNT   New International Commentary
             on the New Testament

NPNF   *Nicene and Post-Nicene Fathers*

NRSV   New Revised Standard Version

THNTC   Two Horizons New Testament
             Commentary

PART 1
1 PETER

Introduction:
Why 1 Peter? Why Now?

We will study three brief letters in this book. Of them, this first one is by far the most familiar to Christian audiences. Many passages from this epistle appear in the Revised Common Lectionary. Many phrases will seem familiar to those who have a basic knowledge of Scripture. At the same time, 1 Peter is probably far less familiar than Paul's Letters and the four Gospels. Since we will deal with the theological implications of this letter rather than with the details of authorship and setting that are usual in commentaries, we begin with a few of the historical issues that are basic to any interpretation.

This little jewel of Christian teaching is well worth the time spent studying it. It is brief, to the point, and gentle in its advice, with a clear sense of the difficulty Christians have in being part of the society in which God has placed them and at the same time being part of the new creation that challenges so much of that society's assumptions. It also challenges several of our own assumptions. First, it demonstrates how essential the Hebrew Scriptures were for the early church. They are not simply an historical introduction to the New Testament. Second, it shows that the church is absolutely basic for the Christian. Contrary to contemporary thought, the church is not an optional gathering for those who enjoy it, leaving many who call themselves Christians generally ignoring the church. Third, actual participation in a congregation is essential for a Christian. It is not enough to learn its teachings. Finally, the Christians to whom this letter was written faced the possibility of persecution in a way that most of us do not. This gave them a perspective on the church that we need to see. Though at first glance we may decide the letter has little to teach us because we are not new Christians and rarely experience the kind of persecution that could lead to death or imprisonment, a more thorough look at the letter may show us otherwise.

Some Technical Matters

Before we begin a theological study of 1 Peter we need to mention a few basic issues about the letter with which biblical scholars have dealt. These issues impinge on the theological interpretation to some degree.

The question of who wrote 1 Peter and to whom it was written would seem to be answered quite readily by the opening verse of the letter. Indeed, before modern critical scholarship it was usual to hold that the apostle Simon Peter was the author, and the audience was made up of Jewish Christians, since "exiles of the Dispersion" was taken to mean Diaspora Jews. In addition, since it was generally held that Paul was the missionary to the Gentiles while Peter concentrated on the Jews, it was easier to assume that the recipients were Jewish Christians.

Such a view has changed radically in the last two centuries, as to both the author and the audience. Most now assume that the author is not the apostle, but a writer a generation after Peter, whose death is usually given in the time of Nero in the 60s. There is great difficulty explaining a masterful use of Greek by a Galilean fisherman, as well as the author's reliance on the Greek version of the Old Testament. Both of these could be accounted for if Peter gave the general ideas and someone else wrote the letter. But there is also much evidence of a later date in the character of the persecution and how well established churches are in the area of the Roman Empire near the Black Sea, for the provinces mentioned are in the interior of what is today Turkey, then part of the Roman Empire. All of this means that modern scholarship usually dates the letter in the late first century, by an author other than the apostle.

In addition, there is general agreement that the intended audience is largely Gentile Christians. This is clear from the description of the previous life these new Christians had led, a life that was like that of their pagan neighbors, who now question what has happened to them.

We may not know the name of the author, but when we read the message within the letter it is clear that it is a message to us by someone who was not only a faithful Christian but was also able to encourage others to be faithful. That is a word we also need to hear. That it was written mainly to Gentile Christians also means we probably have more in common with that ancient audience than we would have had they indeed been Jews of the Diaspora.

The Necessity of the Hebrew Scriptures

If we assume that the majority of those to whom this letter was addressed were Gentile Christians, it is astonishing that the letter is filled with quotations from and allusions to the Hebrew Scriptures. The Old Testament here is not being used to prove that Jesus is the fulfillment of the promises to Israel, as might have been the case were it written to Jews. Rather, the Old Testament is a major source for helping these Christians understand who they are. This means that both in their preparation for baptism and in their continued growth thereafter, there must have been great stress on learning significant portions of those Scriptures. These references come from the Pentateuch, the Prophets, Psalms, and Proverbs. It is clear that for the earliest church the term "Scripture" meant the Hebrew Bible. Not until the second half of the second century was the term applied to Christian writings.

In our own churches today, there is often the sense that the Old Testament is merely an historical introduction to the real story, and an introduction that can be ignored

[R]ecalling that Peter's audience is primarily Gentile, and so unskilled in rehearsing the story of God's dealings with Israel, Peter works to form them through a particular way of construing their history that is deeply rooted in the eternal plan of God and that takes seriously the formation and nurture of God's people, Israel, through Passover, exodus, and the pattern of reconciliation through sacrifice.

—Joel B. Green

1 Peter, THNTC (Grand Rapids: Eerdmans, 2007), 201.

to some degree. It is a word to Israel and not to us. That is hardly the opinion here. A study of 1 Peter is an opportunity to discover how the early church interpreted the Hebrew Scriptures as applying to itself in a profound way. Christians really interpreted themselves in the light of those ancient writings.

The Essential Character of the Church

Much that is essential to the biblical view of the nature of the church is to be found in this brief letter, and much of it is unintelligible without a clear understanding of what Israel was called to be. What is often lacking in the view of the church of many Christians today is precisely to be found here, retained from Israel's calling. It is a sense of the corporate, the calling of the church rather than of individual Christians who agree to join together in a congregation. We live in such an individualistic culture that the notion that the church is essential to the Christian is difficult for many to understand. We may say in the Creed that we believe in the "holy catholic church," but that is often far from the reality we live, or else we interpret it to mean that we can be part of this "spiritual" church without belonging to any particular one. It is hard for us to fathom that the Bible is written to congregations, to gatherings of God's people, and not to individuals. It is a word to us because we are part of such a gathering. The Bible is not a book of good advice to the world in general. It is God's word to God's people. It has authority because the people to whom it is written believe that God has called them and made a covenant with them. Whether Israel or the church, we acknowledge Scripture as our authority because we acknowledge God as our God. It is a word to us individually because we are part of the people to whom it is written.

The individualistic character of our culture is seen clearly in the writing of the famous nineteenth-century Reformed theologian Friedrich Schleiermacher. Early in that century he wrote that the major distinction between Protestant Christianity and its Roman Catholic counterpart was that, for Protestants, "the individual's relationship to the Church is dependent upon his relation to Christ, while the latter [Roman Catholicism] contrariwise makes the individual's relation to Christ dependent on his relation to the Church."[1] Schleiermacher explained that the Protestant reformers had no intention of creating a new church, but only of reforming the existing one; and yet he sees the result as a truly new understanding of the relation of the individual to the church. The church, for him, is a collection of those who believe and join together, but their primary relationship is individually to Christ rather than to the organic body of believers. The original readers of 1 Peter would not have understood how one could be related to Christ but not to the church, nor would they have viewed the church as a hierarchical body, an institution through which one reached Christ. The early church would have found both the Protestant and the Catholic sides of Schleiermacher's division inadequate.

The individualism of our current culture is, in many ways, the result of the Industrial Revolution. The developing industrial economies, strong earlier in European Protestant countries than in Catholic, allowed and often compelled people to move from their extended families to the cities, now earning their living through wages. The earlier feudal economies depended on families staying in the same place for generations, tied to a place and to a strong hierarchical social structure. The Protestant churches in the nineteenth century and later picked up on this individualism, while the Catholic Church retained the earlier feudal form for much longer. So Schleiermacher may be quite right in his description of the two churches at the time when he wrote, but this was the understanding neither of the early church nor of the Reformers.

In fact, John Calvin, in the sixteenth century, preserved much of the earlier understanding:

> But because it is now our intention to discuss the visible church, let us learn even from the simple title "mother" how useful, indeed how necessary, it is that we should know her. For there is no other way to enter into life unless this mother conceive us in her womb, give us birth, nourish us at her

1. Friedrich Schleiermacher, *The Christian Faith*, trans. H. R. Mackintosh and J. S. Stewart (Edinburgh: T.& T. Clark, 1928), 103.

breast, and lastly, unless she keep us under her care and guidance until, putting off mortal flesh, we become like the angels.[2]

In this regard, Calvin quite agrees with Cyprian's statement in the
third century that a person "can no longer have God for his Father,
who has not the Church for his mother."[3] This is not a sentiment
that many today would understand. Both Cyprian and Calvin were
speaking of the organized, fully human church that meets physically, not some ethereal idea of the church. The actual congregations
within which the church lives its life in history are absolutely essential for the Christian.

Therefore, one of the major problems today's readers of 1 Peter
may face is its emphasis on the church, both the local congregation
and the church catholic. For those early Christians, the church was
no ordinary human institution. Rather it was both the body of Christ
and the community in which the Holy Spirit dwelled. It was holy
because the Holy Spirit held it together. It was the body of Christ
because it linked us with our Head.

The Role of the Congregation in Christian Life

Christians today, even those who are quite active in a congregation,
are in a very different situation than those to whom this letter was
addressed. For the first hearers of the letter, the congregation had
become a new family. Even though they might still be living with
unbelieving relatives, the church had now become their primary
relationship. They usually met at least once a day, often for a meal.
They were mostly relatively poor tradespeople who had left the
countryside and moved to the booming economy of the cities, leaving their extended families behind. Others had lived all their lives
in the city but were household slaves of rich members of the society. A few were the wives of these well-to-do men, but probably the
only members of the family to be part of the church. For all of these

2. John Calvin, *Institutes of the Christian Religion* 4.1.4; ed. John T. McNeill, trans. Ford Lewis
Battles, LCC 20–21 (Philadelphia: Westminster Press, 1960), 2:1016.
3. Cyprian, "On the Unity of the Church" 5 (*ANF* 5:422–23).

people, the congregation was essential. The gatherings were their lifeblood, the constant reinforcement of their new identity.

For us, the situation is very different. Most likely everyone in our families is a church member, however active he or she may be. Many if not most of our friends are Christians, or at least have had some connection to a church in the past. They belong to many different congregations. A few friends may be of other faiths or avowedly secular. Our congregation is not the primary source of our identity. We may go to church once a week, or even a few times more for meetings. But this is very different from the daily gatherings, somewhat clandestine, in a private home or outdoors, that marked the early church. We do not assume that others in the congregation will help us financially if we are in trouble, or raise our children if something were to happen to us. We do not experience the congregation as our new family.

In many places in the world even today, however, some of that early sense of the church remains. This is largely in areas where Christians are a minority and to be baptized may mean that your birth family will disown you and that your faith will be a serious impediment in the society. Christians then need to depend upon one another for friendship, for social life, for assistance in all sorts of problems of daily life. The missiologist Bishop Lesslie Newbigin wrote of his experience in South India:

> The position in an ordinary Indian village or small town is completely different. The whole of a man's life—his work, his recreation and his religion—is lived in relation to the same set of people. Whichever way he turns, he meets the same people. . . . And even the Church—the one fellowship which stands in the village in the Name of Christ—insists that it is the place where all men are to be at home. . . . It is not really surprising that quarrels are frequent and bitter, or that they are generally eventually healed. They are essentially quarrels between people who know that they cannot finally repudiate one another.[4]

4. James Edward Lesslie Newbigin, *That All May Be One* (New York: Association Press, 1952), 109–10.

This is quite a contrast to our situation, where people often leave one congregation and join another in the same town, or stop going to church altogether, while still considering themselves Christians.

The Possibility of Persecution

Though the church was essential to the identity of these early Christians, the very support and joy they found in the congregation put them at odds with the wider society. Though they might have been marginal to the society before their conversion because of their economic or social status, as Christians they were even more marginal. Though the church gave them a new sense of their own value, the world around them could be quite suspicious. Persecution was an ever-present possibility, and Christians had to weigh the new identity with its security against the opposition of the surrounding culture. Paradoxically, the closer together they grew as a church the stronger the external opposition to them grew. As John Elliott writes:

> Conversion to Christianity at first appeared to offer a "place of belonging," fraternal assistance, and participation in a community of equals—benefits which were denied these strangers in the larger society indifferent to their needs and suspicious of their presence. The vehemence, however, with which the local communities had reacted to the Christian sect had made increased suffering rather than security the lot of these believers.[5]

That is far from our experience. In the next few chapters we shall see that though this letter was written to congregations living in very different circumstances than ours, with different ideas of what the church is, it has a great deal to say to Christians today.

As you begin this study, it would be helpful to keep a list of the Old Testament passages that are referred to or whose images are borrowed. These passages will be mentioned and discussed, but

---

5. John H. Elliott, *A Home for the Homeless: A Social-Scientific Criticism of 1 Peter, Its Situation and Strategy*, 2nd ed. (Minneapolis: Fortress, 1990), 101.

having a list showing how frequent such references are will help in understanding how vital a knowledge of the Hebrew Scriptures is for Christians. That could in turn nurture a greater desire to read and study the Old Testament.

It would also be helpful constantly to remember that this letter is written to congregations, not to individual Christians. Modern English has lost the distinction between the singular and plural "you." In the Greek original, most of the verb forms translated "you" were in the plural form. We easily read them as singular, and lose the congregational context. The King James Version was written while there still was a clear distinction between "thou" and "ye," the first being singular and the second plural. It would be interesting to read that translation of 1 Peter, looking precisely for the plural character of most of the terms of address. It is cumbersome reading for many people today precisely because we have lost the verb forms that were common in the seventeenth century. But we have also lost the sense that the letter was written to a gathered group of Christians and spoke about their common life, rather than to individual Christians about their personal lives.

A final word: For many Christians the doctrine of the Trinity is a strange item of Christian thought that has little relevance to the Christian life. In studying this letter, make note of how the relationship of God the Father, the Son Jesus Christ, and the Holy Spirit is described, or how the various persons are understood to affect the life of the congregation and the Christian.

1:1–12

We Are Heirs of a Great Salvation

Human beings always have the task of understanding their identity. They may identify themselves by who their parents are, what tribe or nation they belong to, who their spouses or children are, what their occupation is, and so forth. Some may even claim they themselves have created their own identity—they are "self-made"—and however limited or even false such a view is, it is still a way of understanding who they are, what their identity is. At the very beginning of this letter, the task of the writer is to show the readers who they are, what their identity is in God's eyes. Whatever that identity is should be their own view as well. No matter what they think of themselves—slave or free, rich or poor—they are God's redeemed people. This is not something they need to strive to become; it is who they are right now because they are part of the church, and their task is to live on the basis of this identity.

Dietrich Bonhoeffer, shortly before he was executed in a Nazi prison in 1945, wrote a poem entitled "Who Am I?" In this poem he compares how others around him saw him as a strong and brave man whereas in his own feelings, which were much more negative, he was afraid and weak. He concludes with these words:

> Who am I? They mock me, these lonely questions of mine,
> Whoever I am, Thou knowest, O God, I am thine!
>
> —Dietrich Bonhoeffer

Letters and Papers from Prison, ed. Eberhard Bethge, trans. Reginald H. Fuller (London: Fontana, 1953), 173.

1:1–2
Chosen, Destined, and Sanctified

The letter opens with an address to a wide group of churches, calling them part of the Dispersion. Everyone would have understood the reference to the Jewish Diaspora that had begun with the Babylonian captivity centuries earlier, when many Jews were taken from Judea. Over the years Jews had been scattered throughout the Roman Empire and beyond. In spite of this scattering there was a strong sense that they were still one people, united by the worship of the God of Israel, no matter where they lived. It was many of these Diaspora Jews who had been present at Pentecost, as recorded in Acts 2. Now there are churches in some of these far-flung areas, churches that may have been begun by those Diaspora Jews who had become Christians in Jerusalem and then returned home.

Regardless of their origin, when this letter was written these churches were made up largely of Gentile Christians. And yet the term "Dispersion" or "Diaspora" also applied to them. In the same sense that Jews are part of the one community of faith no matter where they live, and are set apart from their neighbors both by their faith and by their practices, so too Christians form one church no matter where they live. They too have one faith, and one lifestyle, a life of holiness and love. It is this unity of the whole church throughout the world, regardless of the language Christians speak or the culture in which they live, that the ancient creeds mean when they affirm belief in the "one holy catholic church." Christians may be divided into millions of separate congregations, organized into thousands of denominations, and yet we affirm there is only one church, one body of Christ. In Ephesians and Revelation the church is called "the bride of Christ" (Eph. 5:25–32; Rev. 19:9). A friend once said that Christ has only one bride—not a harem! His bride is the one church, however divided it appears to the world.

If the letter was written from Rome, which many suppose, then the reference to churches in the Dispersion would be a way of assuring these Christians at the edges of the empire that they are truly part of the one church and they have not been forgotten by those in the centers of Christianity, small as such centers were at the time. These distant Christians are as much a part of Christ's church as those in Rome or Antioch or any of the other big cities. They are far from the centers of imperial power, but they are not far from the major centers of the church. If they are suffering, then the whole church is aware of this and supports them. They have not been forgotten.

We often do not think about the oneness of the church throughout the world. We are so divided by denominations and by nationalities that other Christians are often thought of as being part of a different church. Yet we still say the words of the Creed. Perhaps on World Communion Sunday we consider our unity. If we imagine the churches that are now suffering persecution or other difficulties, what would it mean to them to hear from other Christians, showing that they have not been forgotten, that they are remembered in our prayers? Some of the new books of daily prayer include prayers for Christians in different parts of the globe. The use of such prayers can remind us that we are part of the one church, living in all sorts of conditions, throughout the entire world. As we read the newspaper or listen to the news on the media, we can picture Christians in

---

For the Christians are distinguished from other men neither by country, nor language, nor the customs which they observe. For they neither inhabit cities of their own, nor employ a peculiar form of speech, nor lead a life which is marked out by any singularity.... But, inhabiting Greek as well as barbarian cities, according as the lot of each of them has determined, and following the customs of the natives in respect to clothing, food, and the rest of their ordinary conduct, they display to us their wonderful and confessedly striking method of life. They dwell in their own countries, but simply as sojourners. As citizens, they share in all things with others, and yet endure all things as if foreigners. Every foreign land is to them as their native country, and every land of their birth as a land of strangers....

[W]hat the soul is in the body, that are Christians in the world. The soul is dispersed through all the members of the body, and Christians are scattered through all the cities of the world. The soul dwells in the body, yet is not of the body; and Christians dwell in the world, yet are not of the world.

—*Epistle to Diognetus*, 5–6

(*ANF* 1:26–27).

those places and pray for them. That does not mean we do not pray for non-Christians, but we have a special responsibility to remember suffering parts of the body of Christ. If there is any way to let them know of our concern, that would be an added blessing.

These scattered Christians are called to remember who they are. In their local communities they may be of no account or viewed with suspicion, but they are chosen by God. The verbs are very strong: they have been chosen, destined, and sanctified. There is a clear Trinitarian emphasis here: God the Father has chosen them; their obedience is to Jesus Christ their Savior; they are sanctified by the Holy Spirit in order to be obedient. Often the Trinity is presented as a puzzle to be solved, a doctrinal statement that is necessary intellectually but irrelevant to the Christian life. Here we have a clear statement that relates the Trinity to the lives of believers: God the Father chose them. God the Spirit sanctified them and gave them the strength to be obedient to Jesus Christ. And Christ is the Son, whose work of redemption centers on the cross and resurrection. All three statements are true, yet it is only one God at work in our lives. Though the Common Lectionary does not use these verses, they could be a very useful text for Trinity Sunday.

> **Although it would be anachronistic to call this a reference to the Trinity, surely such verses as this one later issued in the orthodox doctrine of the Trinity at the First Council of Nicaea (AD 325).**
> —Karen H. Jobes
>
> *1 Peter*, BECNT (Grand Rapids: Baker Academic, 2005), 68.

The people have been "sprinkled with his blood" and now, because of Christ's resurrection, they have gained untold riches: salvation, hope, joy, which by the power of God they begin to experience even now, though the full inheritance will be only in the life to come. Now they are called to be faithful, to live as those who are part of this new people. They probably gathered at least once a day and took some of their meals together. All of their gatherings included worship, and at least once a week, on Sunday, they celebrated Communion, feeling themselves to be in the presence of the risen Christ, renewing their sense of the future to come when he returns. The mention of a "sprinkling of blood" points to the covenantal character of baptism and the Christian life. For ancient Israel, the covenant at Sinai was sealed by the blood of sacrificed young bulls that Moses sprinkled on the people (Exod. 24:3–8). The covenant established the people as God's own people, and the people agreed that God was their only Lord. The covenant was with the people, and new members of the community—either by birth or by conversion—were added to the people by a covenantal sign. In Israel the sign is circumcision. In the church, it is baptism. (Paul shows the relationship between the two signs in Col. 2:11–12.)

We can imagine what these words might mean to those ancient Christians, who had to make great changes in their lives in order to be part of this people. But it is more difficult to understand their import when we are part of a society that assumes most people grow up as Christians, whether or not they go to church. For the ancient church, it was not a matter of not drinking or dancing, not playing cards, or avoiding some forms of entertainment. Surely they were forbidden to go to the dramas about the gods, and drunkenness was viewed negatively. But for them, not being able to worship the gods of the city probably meant they were separated from their families and from their traditional work, since families and the guilds of various trades both had gods that were worshiped in the home and in the workplace. Also, Christians needed to live their lives acknowledging only God as the Lord, which meant Caesar was not their lord. This in itself would mark them as suspicious enemies of the state. They could not abandon unwanted children, nor could they hate their enemies or be unfaithful in marriage. All of these actions were quite common in the wider society's understanding of normal human life. The sense of being part of a new people is much more difficult for us, and we probably do not experience the joy and hope that came with the realization of the dramatic change that the early church knew.

It would be interesting in a contemporary congregation to ask what marks of a Christian life would set a congregation apart from the rest of the society. Such a discussion could be a learning experience for a congregation, even if it could reach no agreement. The lack of agreement on a common lifestyle for Christians is a characteristic of our day, and one of the problems in seeking the visible unity of the church. But if we get away from much of the traditional list of what Christians do not do and concentrate on what positive actions and attitudes would mark Christians as distinct from their neighbors, we might have a very enlightening discussion. Are there any actions that distinguish Christians from good, upright citizens and neighbors? Are Christians only distinguished by what they do *not* do?

In these few opening verses, we have seen several parallels between Israel and the church: they are a people chosen by God; a people that remains one though separated and scattered in Diaspora; a people with whom God has established a covenant through the shedding of blood; they have a covenant that points to the holiness that God expects from the people. These are not accidental parallels, but they are there because the early church truly believed that God had taken actions in the past that showed the character of God's interaction with the creation, and therefore what happened in Israel points to God's actions in the life of the church. It is the same God in both Testaments, a God who acts in history in certain ways. This intentional parallelism is known as "typology."

FURTHER REFLECTIONS
Typology

Typology as a form of biblical interpretation holds that certain central events in the life of God's people—both Israel and the church—are keys to understanding God's actions in the later life of the people. This is seen in the Old Testament itself: The exodus is a key event showing God's rescue of the people from bondage and leading them to a place where they can worship God appropriately and live out God's commands. The return from exile many centuries later is understood by the prophets to be a new exodus, freeing the people from a new bondage. (This is especially true in Isa. 40–55, the writings of the one referred to as Second Isaiah. See Isa. 43:14–21.) The early church understood the work of Christ as the ultimate exodus, freeing people from bondage to sin and death, and allowing them to worship God and lead holy lives. As we saw in the Exodus passage, the purpose of God's freeing people is not simply liberty from an oppressor, however significant that is. The purpose of freedom from bondage is to allow them space for the proper worship of God. It is as though freedom from bondage is not secure if there is no proper relationship to God. If true worship is lacking, there will be a new bondage to new idolatry. Permanent true freedom depends upon the worship of God, the creator and redeemer.

In 1 Peter we will encounter many typological interpretations, and these will be pointed out as we come to them. But it is useful to see how typology is used here to relate the Old Testament to the New. The Old Testament is not simply a collection of prophecies about Jesus, so that when Jesus comes the prophecies are fulfilled and because of their fulfillment the Old Testament is no longer necessary—as though, since we have the fulfillment, the prophecy can be checked off the list and has no further import. First Peter does not deal with the Old Testament in terms of prophecy and fulfillment but in terms of a typological relationship in which the Old Testament remains the absolutely necessary source for our interpretation of God's action in Christ as well as in our own times and in our own lives. Granted, once Christ has come, we understand the actions of God in the past in a new and fuller form, but we would not understand the work of God in Christ without the record of God's work in ancient Israel.

In this opening passage of 1 Peter the event of God's establishing a covenant with Israel after freeing them and giving them the law is seen as the interpretive key for the work of Christ, whose death was the covenantal sacrifice that calls the new people to live in obedience. Both the exodus and the cross were historical events, but the earlier one helps us understand the full meaning of the later one. Without the exodus and the covenant under Moses, Christians would not have truly understood what Jesus was accomplishing. Just as Israel was freed from slavery in Egypt, led safely across the Red Sea, given a covenant with God, and ultimately led into the promised land, so Christians in baptism are led through the water, made part of the covenant, and ushered into a new life that is the foretaste or down payment of the kingdom itself. The promised land is the type of the kingdom. For Christians, crossing the Jordan into the promised land becomes a type of death leading to entrance into the fullness of the kingdom. That the establishment of the covenant at Sinai involved a bloody sacrifice is very important for the interpretation of the death of Christ as the establishment of a new covenant. This epistle is filled with typological interpretations, many woven together with the overarching exodus event, as well as the Suffering Servant of Isaiah 53 and the great flood through which a few were saved.

> A famous hymn, "Guide Me, O Thou Great Jehovah," uses typology in a beautiful way:
>
> When I tread the verge of Jordan,
> Bid my anxious fears subside;
> Death of death, and hell's destruction,
> Land me safe on Canaan's side.
> —**William Williams**
>
> *The Presbyterian Hymnal* (Louisville: Westminster/John Knox Press, 1990), no. 281.

This opening section of two verses concludes with a brief benediction. The writer blesses the readers, asking that God's grace and peace may be with them. The letter will close with an even longer benediction. To enclose the letter with such blessings is typical of the period. We find this form in Paul's Letters as well as others. The word "benediction" means "a good word." Its opposite is "malediction," "a bad word." Those are the Latin-based words. In the Germanic words that have come into English, the terms are "blessing" and "curse." In these letters, as well as in worship itself, the blessing is significant. It is not the writer's or the pastor's blessing that is given, but God's blessing. In many traditional cultures that have been strongly influenced by Christianity it is typical for parents to bless the children as they go to bed, or go on a journey. The parent puts a hand on the child's head and blesses the child. This shows the goodwill of the parent toward the child; the forgiveness of any wrongs or anything else that could limit the love for them. It shows that the parent wishes only the best for the child. Yet it is more than the parent's goodwill: within the faith community, parents are vehicles by which God's goodwill—God's grace and peace—is given to the child. It is the sign that all is well in the relationship. In worship, the pastor gives God's blessing to the people as they are ready to leave the service. The raised arms are a long-distance, group form of the hand on the head. The letter blesses the people before they read it and then again at the conclusion. These letters were read to the congregation in the midst of worship, and it was as though the writer, even from a long distance, was blessing the people so they know all is well in the relationship of this church with all the others in the Dispersion.

1:3–7

A New Birth

The passage speaks of a "new birth" that opens the converts to their new family and its inheritance. In contemporary churches there is great discussion of this "new birth" or being born again. Some churches believe that the experience of accepting the lordship of Jesus is the necessary preparation for baptism, and therefore do not accept the baptism of infants. The experience of the new life is first, and becoming part of the church by baptism is second. For other churches, baptism provides the covenantal promise to which faith clings. The promise is always before faith, and without the promise of God for forgiveness there is no faith. Therefore, the promise can come first, and faith builds on this promise, which means infant baptism is possible, when given to infants who will grow up in the church and in a devout family, hearing again and again God's promise to them. In both cases, however, baptism and the new life associated with it are viewed individualistically.

For the early church, baptism was the actual incorporation into the body of Christ, this new people, and therefore it was the moment that God adopts those whom God the Father had chosen. It was the time of the gift of the Holy Spirit, who would now strengthen them to lead holy lives. Again, we can see the Trinitarian structure of the meaning of baptism: brought to baptism by the Father, incorporated into the Son, and strengthened by the Holy Spirit—a structure used by the baptismal formula itself. Imagine a ten-year-old child, poor and orphaned, whose future is dim indeed. Then the child is adopted into a well-to-do and loving family. In the days and weeks before the adoption occurs, the child may fantasize about the new future that will be possible, but the actual moment of adoption is what changes everything. In the same manner, the newly baptized believed the actual baptism itself was the new birth into a new family, a new family that had an astonishing inheritance, and a new life that began now but extended even after death. That is what is meant by the inheritance kept in heaven, an inheritance that cannot waste away like many on earth, nor can it be destroyed by anything. It is what Jesus spoke of in the Sermon on the Mount: "store up for yourselves treasures in heaven, where neither moth nor rust consumes and where thieves do not break in and steal" (Matt. 6:20).

For adults who wished to enter this new family, there had to be a time of discovering if they were ready to make the transition and the commitment necessary. This period of time was called "the catechumenate." It could last a few years. There were teachers and older Christians who helped those who desired to enter the church. The catechumens studied the teachings of the church, but they also practiced the lifestyle that was required. Only after the church was convinced that they were ready to become part of this new society were they baptized. If they had young children they also were baptized, for they were now growing up in this new people, which included their parents as well as the whole congregation. It was rather like the current practice of naturalization: if parents from another country decide to become citizens here, their young children also become citizens, and future children will also be citizens and understand the culture in which they grow up.

The early church could not have separated baptism and the community of faith. Baptism was the essential point of entrance into this new people, a people who formed a new culture, a new society. It was as much a corporate event as an individual one.

FURTHER REFLECTIONS
The Catechumenate

The catechumenate was an essential part of the early church's baptismal practice. It was in its early stages of development when this letter was probably written, but became universally established in the early second century. Although in the New Testament many people were baptized immediately after they came to the belief that Jesus was indeed the Christ, the Messiah, that practice changed when most of the people to be baptized were Gentiles unacquainted with the faith of Israel. In the New Testament those who are so quickly baptized are either Jews or what are termed "God-fearers," such as Cornelius (Acts 10) and the Ethiopian eunuch (Acts 8:26–38). These "God-fearers" attended synagogue and temple worship, and held to the monotheism of Judaism and to its ethical teachings. They did not become part of Israel, however, largely because they did not wish to abide by the laws of separation that forbid interaction with Gentiles, by the food laws, or by circumcision. The Ethiopian eunuch could not have become a Jew because the Law forbids the addition of a eunuch to the people of Israel (see Deut. 23:1). He was reading Isaiah and had been to Jerusalem to worship, so he obviously was acquainted with the faith of Israel. As the church grew, many who wished to join were Gentiles who had no such connection with Israel. They needed a great deal of training so that the church could be sure they were not simply adding Jesus to the gods of the household they already worshiped, and that they truly understood the ethical practices required of God's people. For these Gentiles, a period of two or three years was soon established, with teachers who guided them and older Christians who could be their sponsors. Most catechetical teaching was about ethics and required clear changes in the lives of the catechumens. These changes were not easy, and could lead to rejection by families and friends who did not understand why they could not participate in festivals in honor of the various gods of the city.

As congregations began experimenting with catechetical forms, they often relied on teachers who offered themselves for carrying out the necessary training. However, it took a generation or so before the church gained full control of these teachers. People might go to a famous teacher, perhaps paying them, and then appear before the church as a candidate for baptism. The "false teachers" we encounter in 2 Peter and Jude may have been such people.

In our own day, missionaries in traditionally non-Christian areas usually develop similar practices in their own congregations, even if the denomination does not have such a practice in this country. It would be difficult to baptize a Hindu who accepts Jesus but then simply adds Jesus to the number of gods already worshiped in that household. There needs to be evidence that the candidate has abandoned the former worship practices. Also, customs that are quite acceptable in the society may not be in accord with Christian teaching, such as the taboos of the caste system, so the church needs to be clear that the candidate has put into practice the needed changes.

The catechumens were under the guidance of the teacher until shortly before Easter, when those deemed ready for baptism were presented to the bishop for examination. It was at this point that they learned the statement of faith, similar to our Apostles' Creed, which would be their baptismal confession of faith.

In our own day, as our own society becomes more secular and the church cannot assume that those who seek baptism as adults really know much about the faith, contemporary forms of the ancient cat-echumenate are being reinvented. The Roman Catholic Church took the lead in this. At the request of the Second Vatican Council, the church developed the "Rite for the Christian Initiation of Adults." This involves training laity to become sponsors of candidates for bap-tism, as well as providing a structured path, lasting several months, in which the person learns what the church does in mission, how it lives its life, and the faith upon which such a life is based. Such a program requires the involvement of the whole congregation and has been a point of significant renewal in the life of many congrega-tions. The same is true for Protestant churches that have developed similar programs. Many congregations, however, still assume that anyone who asks to be baptized probably knows enough about the gospel, and there is little training. This may indicate that the con-gregation itself does not want newcomers who are more enthu-siastic, more informed, and more involved than they themselves are. The reality is, however, that there are many unbaptized adults whose families of origin did not participate in the church at all, and who now wish to become part of the church. They may have very confused ideas about what it is the church teaches, but have been transformed by the actions of some Christians outside the church or by what they see in the life of the congregation and wish to be part of it. This is very much parallel to the experience of the early church, and the reason why they began the catechumenate.

The resurrection of Jesus is central to this astonishing inheritance. He has opened the way to new life, conquering death itself, and freeing us from the power of sin that leads to death. Therefore, our inheritance is this new, resurrection life, which gives us hope now, no matter what happens. Our new life is joined to Christ's risen life, and it cannot be taken away as long as we are joined to Christ. Many Christians think that the promised new life is only after death, but much of the New Testament points out that the new life in Christ begins now. Even now we have died with Christ in baptism and have been raised with him. We have only the beginning of that new life now, but we are assured that it continues forever. These few verses mean exactly what Paul says in longer and more poetic form in Romans 8. Our new life is safely in Christ, and therefore nothing can destroy it.

A famous second-century theologian, Irenaeus, the bishop of Lyons, used wonderful imagery for the meaning of this new life. If by baptism we have become part of the body of Christ, and if the head of that body has risen, then we know that there is life in the rest of the body and we too shall be raised with him (*Against Heresies* 3.3). It is as though we are at a funeral, and suddenly the supposedly deceased's head begins to rise. We can be sure the rest of the body is also alive and will begin to show this new life. The resurrection of Christ shows that the head of the body that is the church has been raised from the dead, and has begun the process of the whole body receiving this new life. Through the work of the Holy Spirit this new life has begun in us, but this is a process that will be completed only after the dying to the old life has been completed.

The letter assumes that the final revelation of the new life, the full dawning of the kingdom of God, and the return of Christ are in the near future. That is "the salvation ready to be revealed in the last time." Much of the New Testament holds to that view, though by the late first century the church began grappling with the delay of the end times and the fulfillment of the work of Christ. Without the expected return of Christ in the near future, other understandings, many taken from the Greek world, began to be combined with

Christian teaching. Christians started thinking that the whole of the new life began for each individual only after death. It was an individual end time, rather than one for the whole of history. When in the fourth century Christianity was favored by the Roman Empire and almost everyone was baptized, the expectation of the experience of new life was drastically weakened. This was a significant change that allowed a more individualistic interpretation of the faith, losing much of the significance both of baptism and of the role of the community of faith in the Christian life.

1:8–9

Faithful Suffering

These distant Christians are commended for the faith that they have. Their faith is based on the message they have heard, on the proclamation of the gospel that caused them to seek baptism. They had never seen Jesus in the flesh. They were far removed from those first disciples who had followed Jesus from Galilee or heard him preach. These people had only the words of those evangelists who had preached the gospel to them.

We often think that it would have been far easier to have faith if we had been with Jesus during his earthly life. If we had heard his words and seen his deeds, then of course we would have understood who he was and followed him. But was it really easier for those people who heard him? Clearly, most of those who saw him in the flesh did not believe. They saw only a human being. His teachings were difficult for many to consider. Think of the rich young ruler. Would we have stayed with Jesus if he had spoken those words to us? Even the disciples decided to go back to their earlier lives after the crucifixion. It was the encounter with the risen Christ that transformed them into believers who could spread the message of the gospel. Later believers hear the words of the gospel proclaimed to them. These too are merely human words and can be readily dismissed, especially if they require much from us. But the astonishing work of the Holy Spirit lets us see in them more than human words: we hear the Word of God.

The letter assumes that these congregations are currently suffering difficulties or soon will be. We need not think of official persecution, but rather that their neighbors are becoming suspicious of them
and they are having problems that may lead to being taken before
the authorities. If they were taken before Roman officials they could
face death if they did not renounce their faith. At the time of this letter most Christians were not arrested, and yet it always remained a
threat if the people around them felt they were causing trouble. The
trouble might be rumors about their worship—did they actually eat
bodies and drink blood?—or their refusal to worship the gods of
the city. Perhaps if there was a natural disaster the people felt the
traditional gods were angry because not everyone worshiped them,
and this could lead to reporting the Christians as unpatriotic and
the cause of the trouble. Much of the rest of the epistle will be advice
about how to act in these dangerous circumstances.

The suffering these Christians may have to endure will strengthen
their faith. It is like gold being purified by fire. The writer says that
they will be protected by God's power, but that power does not
keep them from suffering. How strong their faith is, how genuine,
will be discovered in the midst of trials. The early church was very
clear that no Christian should seek suffering. They were not to go
out and seek persecution. The Lord's Prayer, which they repeated

Søren Kierkegaard, a philosopher and theologian in the early nineteenth
century, wrote about the similarity between those first disciples and those of
us in later generations:

The testimony of the contemporary provides an occasion for the successor,
just as the immediate contemporaneity provides an occasion for the
contemporary. And if the testimony is what it ought to be, namely the
testimony of a believer, it will give occasion for precisely the same ambiguity
of the aroused attention as the witness himself has experienced. . . . There is
no disciple at second hand. The first and the last are essentially on the same
plane, only that a later generation finds its occasion in the testimony of a
contemporary generation, while the contemporary generation finds this
occasion in its own immediate contemporaneity.

—Søren Kierkegaard

Philosophical Fragments, trans. David F. Swenson (Princeton: Princeton University Press, 1936), 87–88.

daily, included the petition that they not be led into a time of trial and temptation. They could leave town and try to avoid the officials. They could explain their beliefs and actions to their neighbors. But if they were called before the magistrates, they should confess their faith without fear. God's power would protect them even in the midst of martyrdom. This power of God is not an impersonal force. Many of the martyrs and those who suffered for their faith said that they believed that at the time when they should have felt great pain somehow Christ had entered into their pain and suffered it for them and with them. This experience was the cause of joy, and the awareness of God's presence with them in suffering assured them that their salvation was actually occurring. In the midst of suffering they were closer to Christ, directly experiencing their redemption. In Hebrews 11:32–39 there is a list of the faithful within Israel. The list includes those who were saved from terrible deaths as well as those who, equally faithful, died terrible deaths. They were equally faithful even though their lives were very different. Christians knew that the same was true for them.

> After speaking of the suffering and persecution of Paul, Athanasius writes:
>
> The other saints also, who had a like confidence in God, accepted a like probation with gladness. . . . [T]hey perceiving the cleansing and the advantage resulting from the divine fire, were not discouraged in trials like these, but they rather delighted in them, suffering no injury at all from the things which happened, but being seen to shine more brightly, like gold from the fire.
>
> —Athanasius
>
> *Letter* 13.3 (*NPNF* 4:540).

In our own day, some Christians seem to believe that their faith should protect them from suffering. If there are difficulties, this proves that their faith is not strong enough. These verses make very clear that faith does not protect us from trouble; indeed, it may cause us more. These Christians could have avoided suffering if they only were willing to deny their faith. The strength and power that they are promised is given in the midst of suffering, not as a means to avoid it.

Verses 3–9 are used in the Revised Common Lectionary for the first Sunday after Easter in Year A. When read on this day, the text is a call to Christians to renew their identity as part of the people who know the power of the risen Christ to bring them through all the difficulties they face, even persecution. We have been born again into this Easter people. This new creation into which we have entered is not seen or understood by the world around us, and so we are tempted to lose our faith in what God has accomplished for us in Christ. The faithful know by experience that the risen Christ is with them, and his power is sufficient for them in all circumstances.

1:10–12

Glimpsing the Future

This section of the letter closes with a reference to the prophecies in Israel that pointed to Christ. It was Christ's spirit in those prophets that let them glimpse the future salvation God had prepared. These prophets realized that they were seeing a future where God's promises to Israel would be fulfilled beyond their wildest imagination. That is to say, they saw that God would redeem not only Israel, but also the whole of creation that had been under the power of sin and decay ever since the fall at the beginning of history. It is not that these prophets were given a date and time, or a list of all the events to come. However, in the midst of their own time, with all of its pain and faithlessness, God showed them that a time was coming when God would put an end to sin. God would act in human history in such a way that the creation would no longer turn away from God, but would finally be the good creation God had intended from the beginning. These prophets also understood that they themselves would not see this redemption in their own lifetimes. Yet they were joyful at the realization that it would come, and their own faithfulness meant that they could live in the knowledge of God's ultimate faithfulness to the promises given to Abraham and to Moses. These prophets were like Moses, whom God allowed to see the promised land, although he himself would not enter it (Num. 27:12–14). In Hebrews we find a similar understanding. After listing examples of the faithful over the centuries, the writer said: "Yet all these, though they were commended for their faith, did not receive what was promised, since God had provided something better so that they would not, apart from us, be made perfect" (Heb. 11:39–40).

This idea of redemption is far different than the individualistic one we often encounter. Moses could not enter the promised land himself, and yet his eyes beheld it. Did this mean that he had no joy because he himself did not set foot in the land? No, for the sight of the land made clear to him that what he had worked for all his life, following the will of God, was not in vain. There was joy in seeing that the future of the people was secure, that the exodus from slavery in Egypt would be completed. God's work of redemption is not for separate individuals, one here, another there, but rather it is for the whole of creation. Those who are given a glimpse into that astonishing future have their full measure of joy, even though they must wait for the completion of God's work. In fact, all of us still wait for that fulfillment. None of us, no matter how faithful we are, no matter how hard we work, will live long enough to see in this life the fulfillment of the tasks God has given us. We are part of a long line of those who work with joy because we trust that our work, given us by God, is part of the whole enterprise of bringing the creation to God's goals.

The passage about Moses' death was used typologically by Martin Luther King Jr. in his famous last speech, shortly before his assassination, when he said that he was not afraid to die because he had been to the mountaintop; he had been allowed to glimpse the promised land of freedom for his people. King was applying in his own day the sense that the work he was doing was God's work, and that though he himself would not live to see the full accomplishment of it, he had, by faith, seen that God would indeed bring to full fruition what King had labored for. Faith is the assurance that God's work, in our own lives and in the whole creation, will be completed in God's own time, and that our work for God is not in vain, no matter how far short of the goal we seem to be.

In a culture that views success on the basis of goals achieved, this is a difficult concept to understand. We are involved in God's mission, and we do not expect it to be accomplished in our own lifetimes. Yet if we are faithful in the tasks we are given as part of that mission, we have the joy of knowing that the goal will be achieved, and we can participate in that joy even now. The ancient prophets rejoiced because of what they glimpsed, even though it had not yet come to pass.

This passage in 1 Peter makes clear that the ancient prophets were inspired by Christ—by the preincarnate Son of God—so that when the prophets studied the Scriptures they could see the shape of the future work of God in history. It is on this basis that they spoke of the role of Israel in enlightening the Gentiles, so that the promise that Abraham's seed would be a blessing to the whole world would be fulfilled. They did not know the time or the exact character of the future work of God in Christ, but their own prophecies pointed to it. As we will see later in this letter, one of the prophetic passages that is central for this writing is that of the "Suffering Servant" in Isaiah 53. That text may be what lies behind the statement that the prophets "testified in advance to the sufferings destined for Christ and the subsequent glory" (1 Pet. 1:11). These few verses again have a Trinitarian character. It is God the Father's mission, proclaimed to the prophets by the Son, and communicated to these later believers by the power of the Holy Spirit that accompanied the preaching of the gospel.

As mentioned above, in this text it is the second person of the Trinity, the preincarnate Christ, working within the ancient proph-

---

John Calvin wrote about the importance of human beings in relation to angels as follows:

But as [God] did not entrust the ancient folk to angels but raised up teachers from the earth truly to perform the angelic office, so also today it is his will to teach us through human means. As he was of old not content with the law alone, but added priests as interpreters from whose lips the people might ask its true meaning . . . , so today he not only desires us to be attentive to its reading, but also appoints instructors to help us by their effort. This is doubly useful. On the one hand, he proves our obedience by a very good test when we hear his ministers speaking just as if he himself spoke. On the other, he also provides for our weakness in that he prefers to address us in human fashion through interpreters in order to draw us to himself, rather than to thunder at us and drive us away.

—John Calvin

Institutes of the Christian Religion 4.1.5; ed. John T. McNeill, trans. Ford Lewis Battles, LCC 20–21 (Philadelphia: Westminster Press, 1960), 2:1017–18.

ets that let them see God's work of redemption in the future. In the Nicene Creed, however, the church affirms that it is the third person, the Holy Spirit, that "spoke through the prophets." This difference at least needs to be noted, though we probably should not make too much of it. It is the Spirit who inspires both the prophets and the later readers who also need the work of the Holy Spirit to understand and believe what they read. It is Christ who is the fulfillment of those promises and who therefore opens to us the future God had always intended, a future known to us through the ancient writings.

The prophets who had a glimpse of this glorious future saw something that even the angels had not seen. This probably seems a very strange statement to us, but angels did play a significant part in the early church's theology. What may surprise us is that angels are understood to be heavenly creatures, servants of God, who assist human beings; yet, ultimately, human beings are to be superior to the angels. The glorious future mentioned here is the restoration of human beings to the place God intends, as children of God, brothers and sisters by adoption of the Son of God. We find a similar thought in Hebrews 2:5–13. There Psalm 8 is quoted, a psalm that looks back to the creation story in Genesis 1:26–27, which declared that human beings were the pinnacle of God's creation. All of the work of redemption leads to the final restoration of the place of human beings in God's plan for creation.

In these few opening verses the author has set forth many of the themes that will be elaborated throughout the letter. There is a possibility of suffering, and therefore these Christians should remember who they are: part of the body of Christ, heirs of a great future. Suffering also is a means of purification, and should not be dreaded. They should remember that their new life is a foretaste of that future, and it is to such a degree better than the old life they lived that even suffering pales in comparison. And though they are far from other Christians, those other Christians remember and pray for them. They have been called by God, redeemed by the Son of God, and given the power of this new life by the strengthening of the Holy Spirit.

1:13–2:3

Therefore We Are Called to Holiness

The epistle began with a recounting of the great things God had done in calling this people to be God's own. Now the focus turns from what God has done to what the people are to do in response. They have been called not simply to have a new status but to be a new people, a people related to the true God, who is holy. Therefore they too are to be holy. This means a change in behavior as well as a new understanding of who God is. The true God is not like the idols whom they previously worshiped, and therefore their relationship to the true God is a different sort of relationship than they had earlier with the idols, whom they could placate with offerings. It is for this reason that the church took time to make sure new converts understood how this new relationship to the true God was very different from their previous relationship to the idols. This God cannot be bribed. This God is holy. This God calls them by name and seeks to be related to them in bonds of love.

We need to remember that what they are called to be is totally based on what God has already done for them. Just as Israel was formed by being called out of Egypt and

> And what does it mean that a man is said to treat money ... "as if it were God"? What has the lust of grabbing and of laying up treasure in common with the joy in the presence of the Present One? Can the servant of Mammon say *Thou* to his money? And how is he to behave towards God when he does not understand how to say *Thou*? He cannot serve two masters—not even one after the other: he must first learn to serve *in a different way*.
>
> —Martin Buber
>
> *I and Thou*, trans. Ronald Gregor Smith, 2nd ed. (New York: Scribner's Sons, 1958), 106.

Israel's new life was to be shaped by the law that God gave them after their release from bondage, so also these Gentiles have been called out of their bondage under sin and death, and on the basis of what God has already done for them, they are to respond in holiness of life.

1:13–17

Grace and Works

"Therefore." With this word a new section of the letter begins, showing that it is tied closely to what went before. *Because* these Christians have been chosen by God the Father, *because* by baptism they have been joined to Jesus Christ the Son and redeemed by him, and *because* they have been strengthened by the Holy Spirit, *therefore* they are to be holy. On their own, by their own strength, without the involvement of the triune God, they could not be holy. Since they have been called, redeemed, and strengthened by God, *therefore* they are to be holy.

Holiness cannot be achieved passively. It requires hard work. Though these Christians are to "set all their hope" on Jesus, this does not mean that they simply wait until his return. There are things for them to do now, and the task that is given them is to transform their minds, their actions, their attitudes, their whole lives, so that they are holy. These newly born Christians are urged now to engage in the kind of training that will let them develop and mature. How mature they are depends on how holy they are.

This process of becoming holy is what is known as sanctification. All Christians agree that we are to become holy. However, there has been some conflict between those who are afraid that too much stress on sanctification causes Christians to think their salvation is completely up to them and those who believe that justification must be accompanied by a growth in holiness. An emphasis on sanctification is labeled "salvation by works" by the first group, while the lack of an emphasis on holiness is often termed "antinomianism"— that is, lawlessness—by the second group. At the Reformation, this was clearly a major issue. Martin Luther and the Protestant leaders who followed him agreed that the medieval Catholic Church had led people to believe that their salvation depended upon how many good works they did. What the Protestants wished to restore was an understanding that our salvation hinges solely on what God in Christ has done for us, a view termed "salvation by grace." John Calvin agreed with Luther that salvation is completely due to the action of God, but still stressed the need for Christians to spend their energy on becoming holy, not as the cause of their salvation, but as the result of the salvation they have been promised. Luther, though he agreed that Christians should be holy, feared that this emphasis on our own holiness would lead directly back to salvation by works.

This tension has existed throughout the history of the church. For instance, in the fourth century the debate between Augustine and Pelagius was about the same issue in an even stronger form than in the Reformation. It is easy to slip from an emphasis on becoming holy to the thought that it is all up to us, that we must work to become holy in order to receive the salvation God has promised. In this passage, however, the order is clear: first we know that God has chosen, redeemed, and strengthened us. It is only on that basis that we can then begin to work on our own lives in order to make them more holy.

There is a fascinating correspondence between John Wesley and William Law in the eighteenth century. Law had written a book, *A Serious Call to a Devout and Holy Life*, which Wesley and his companions used while students at Oxford. The book outlines what is needed for a holy life, a very demanding set of directions. Wesley tried to follow this counsel, and increasingly felt that it was hopeless, that he never could do enough. Law wrote that God's grace only came to those who first did their best on their own strength. In the midst of his despair Wesley wrote to Law, saying that he should have put in his writing that all of his ideas about a disciplined life only apply once a person had experienced the grace of God, not as a means of obtaining that grace. Wesley had found that any attempt to do enough to warrant God's saving grace was bound to failure, because by ourselves we never could be holy enough. On the other hand, Wesley was very clear that those who have experienced the forgiving grace of God are to pursue a holier life very actively.

All of this tension and debate is clarified by this little word "therefore." Grace comes first. The experience of grace not only gives us the understanding that our sins are forgiven, but also shows us that we have been called by God—and in our baptism we are called by name. We have been redeemed by Christ Jesus and made part of his body, and made joint heirs with him of the future that he has made possible. We have been strengthened by the Holy Spirit, who has joined us to these other believers who will be essential in our growth in holiness. The first twelve verses of this letter are all there as we begin verse 13. There is grace already, but the full measure of the grace of Christ will only be known to us when the full inheritance we have been promised is revealed. Until then, we are to be

> John Wesley was very clear about the relationship of faith and works:
>
> [B]oth repentance, and fruits meet for repentance, are, in some sense, necessary to justification. But they are not necessary in the *same sense* with faith, nor in the *same degree* . . . for those fruits are only necessary *conditionally*; if there be time and opportunity for them. Otherwise a man may be justified without them, as was the *thief* upon the cross . . . but he cannot be justified without faith; this is impossible.
>
> —John Wesley
>
> "Sermon XLIII. The Scripture Way of Salvation," in *The Works of John Wesley*, 3rd ed. (1872; repr., Grand Rapids: Zondervan, 1958), 6:48.

disciplined, striving to become holy. This requires a change not only in actions but also in our thinking, which is why we are called to prepare our minds.

The imagery of a new birth continues here. Birth is only the beginning. After a child is born it needs to grow up in a community, not only to be nourished and kept from harm, but also to be socialized. The task of a family is to guide the children born into it to become part of the wider society. The children need to know how to act, how to deal with others, what is judged to be right and wrong. Children who grow up without such socialization will have a difficult time when they are adults. They may be physically mature, but emotionally and culturally they are still children. The newly baptized are still children—indeed, newly born infants—and they require the family of which they are now members to guide and direct them, to help them become mature Christians. The early church called those who had just been baptized "neophytes," from the Greek, meaning "newly planted." The neophytes have been planted in the church, and now that community is to help them grow into healthy, mature members. This is one of the reasons early Christians could not imagine a Christian without the church. It would be like a newly born baby left to fend for itself. The result would be death, not mature life.

This view of the church as family has several important consequences. First of all, the church is not so much made up of families as it is itself one family. It is for this reason that traditionally the last name—the family name—is not used in baptism. The last name of all the baptized is "Christian." The baptismal service itself often asks the existing members if they pledge to help the newly baptized grow as a Christian.

As a family, the congregation has the task of socializing new members. For churches in our own day this may be a difficult assignment, since the congregation is often together only a few hours a week. The early church had an easier time fulfilling this task because the members were so dependent on one another that they met at least once a day. We need to find ways to accomplish this task in our own time. Because we have lived for many generations in a culture we assumed to be sufficiently Christian that the church did not need to do much in this regard, we have many baptized people who have no idea that the Christian life is anything other than being a good citizen. This makes the task of socializing the next generation very difficult. It requires thoughtful consideration as to how to fulfill this task of socializing current adult members of the congregation so that they can contribute to the development of the next generation. This may involve helping individual families train their own children as well as providing small groups or mentors for adults. Many parents who are active members of a congregation long for help in knowing how to establish family customs of prayer. They themselves were raised in homes that did not pray at meals or at bedtime, and they need resources and assistance to make such family practices appropriate for themselves and their children.

Finally, the epistle reminds these Christians that the whole congregation calls on God as "Father"—most likely a reference to the

Lord's Prayer, which Christians recited several times a day. All Christians are the children of one Father, as well as brothers and sisters of the Son of God. Above all, this means that they are one family.

Christians will be judged on their behavior just as others will be. Again, this does not mean that they are saved by their works but rather that, having received the grace of God, they are to seek a holy life. They are to seek holiness while they are in exile. This exile refers back to verse 1. Just as Israel was in exile because of the Dispersion, so Christians are scattered, separated from other Christians, and yet all are one church. Each congregation is to carry out the task of becoming a mature Christian family. To do this requires a certain "reverent fear" of God. There is nothing here of the cozy "Man Upstairs" theology. God is God, and, though God is loving and graceful, we are never to think of God as a pushover who will let us do anything we wish with no consequences, a kind of heavenly bellhop whose task is to fulfill our wishes, whose job it is to forgive us and let us go on sinning. "Reverent fear" combined with loving thankfulness is the mark of a mature Christian who is seeking to become holier, day by day.

1:18–21

The Price of Your Redemption

One of the reasons for their "reverent fear" is the realization of how costly was their opportunity for a new life, a second birth. Just as a slave might be freed by the payment of gold or silver, these Christians had been freed from the power of sin by a payment of blood: the price was the cross of Christ. It is not clear from this passage to whom the payment was made. The tradition that has been dominant in the Western church for centuries would assume that it was a payment to God, demanded because human sin offended God, especially God's justice. But for the early church, it was much more likely that this was understood as the price of the freedom paid to Satan, the power of evil, for those whom he had held captive since the fall. That view is more probable because the term "ransom" is used, which means the price paid for freedom from bondage, from slavery or prison, rather than a debt owed because of a crime committed.

Gustav Aulén described this view as held by Irenaeus and others in the early church:

The work of Christ is first and foremost a victory over the powers which hold mankind in bondage: sin, death, and the devil. ... In Irenaeus' thought, the Incarnation is the necessary preliminary to the powers which hold man in bondage, and man is helpless. The work of man's deliverance is accomplished by God Himself, in Christ.

—Gustav Aulén

Christus Victor, trans. A. G. Herbert (New York: Macmillan, 1957), 20.

One of the reasons for assuming that the recipients of this letter were Gentile rather than Jewish Christians is the reference to the futility of their former lives, the lives they lived before becoming part of the church. Their behavior then included all sorts of things that now they reject. Jewish Christians had little new to learn from the moral teachings of the church. They had already been guided by the law of Moses. It was the Gentiles for whom the life the church expected was very different than what had been perfectly acceptable in the Greco-Roman world in which they lived and into which they had been socialized. These ways had been learned from their ancestors. Now they were learning new ways from their new "family," the church.

The reference to Christ as the "lamb without defect or blemish" has overtones of the Passover celebration. This is a major typology (see pp. 17–20, "Further Reflections: Typology") throughout the New Testament. At the original Passover, in each household a lamb without blemish was sacrificed and its blood placed on the doorposts, a sign that death would not strike that family, while God's judgment was executed upon the households of the Egyptians, killing their firstborn (Exod. 12:21–28).

The blood of Christ now frees those of Christ's household, the church. God's fierce judgment is not exercised on them. Because they have been so rescued—or ransomed—they are to be God's people and live according to God's will. In the same way that Moses led the people of Israel from bondage in Egypt to freedom in the promised land, a life that was to be lived according to the laws of the covenant, so Christians are freed from bondage to sin and called to be God's people, living according to the laws of the new covenant, which bear a great resemblance to the laws of the covenant under Moses.

Verse 20 has had a variety of interpretations throughout the history of the church. What does it mean that Christ "was destined before the foundation of the world"? For some, it has meant that the sacrificial death of Christ was always intended, or that, at least, when God foresaw that there would be human sin, God planned for a means of redemption, all of this occurring before anything was created. For others, notably Irenaeus, the second-century theologian, the incarnation of the Son, the second person of the Trinity, was always intended, even had there been no sin. His death became necessary because of sin, but there would have been an incarnation even if human beings had never sinned. The coming of the Son of God in human form was always necessary in order for human beings to develop and mature beyond the ability they had in themselves. It was only at the right time, when the population was large enough, when the arts of communication and travel had reached a certain point, that the incarnation would occur in order to lead humanity to a new level of existence, preparing them for a future life in the presence of God. God's initial creation, as seen in the early chapters of Genesis, was indeed perfect, but it was the perfect beginning of creation, a creation destined to grow and mature.[1]

This view is also hinted at in Paul's Letter to the Romans, where he compares the first and second Adam, indicating that though Adam was first, he was the "type" of Christ who was to come, and this expectation was there at the beginning (Rom. 5:12–14). The modern theologian who has explored a similar theology is the French Jesuit Pierre Teilhard de Chardin. The incarnation was always intended so that human beings could come closer to God. Because of human sin, however, the Incarnate One, Jesus Christ, had to ransom those who were in captivity to sin and death before this always intended new growth and maturity could occur.

Though the incarnation of the Son, the Lord Jesus Christ, was intended from before creation even began, the revelation of that plan,

---

1. Irenaeus, *Proof of the Apostolic Preaching*, trans. Joseph P. Smith, Ancient Christian Writers 16 (New York: Newman, 1952), 55.

the incarnation itself, occurred only at the end of the ages, in the time of the writing of this letter. How can we make any sense of that when we live so many centuries after the supposed end of the ages?

Though the early church clearly believed that the end of all history was indeed at hand, we know that it was not. In another sense, however, the end of the ages did arrive in Jesus. Within Judaism at the time of Jesus there was a clear division between the Sadducees, who did not believe in the resurrection of the dead, and the Pharisees, who held to such a resurrection. However, the Pharisees believed that the resurrection of the dead would occur at the end of history when the Messiah would come to bring in the kingdom. The Jewish Christians of the first generation believed that in Jesus the end of the ages had indeed dawned, even though, surprisingly, the old creation continued. Those who recognized Jesus as the Messiah believed that in him the kingdom had dawned, though in a fashion hidden from the world and known only to faith. Those who were baptized became part of this new age that had begun, even though they still were part also of the old world that continued. They lived in both the new creation and the old.

This view was made easier by the fact that Jesus rose from the dead on the first day of the week. There was a belief in Judaism of the time that the end of the old creation would occur on the "eighth day." That is, the weeks would continue throughout history, the seventh day, the Sabbath, being followed by the first day of the next week. But one day the Sabbath would not end. The day after that last Sabbath would be an eighth day, the dawning of the eternal Sabbath, not the beginning of a new week like all the previous ones. Jesus rose on the first day of the week, but to faith it was also the eighth day, the beginning of the eternal Sabbath, the kingdom of God. Christians live in both worlds, trying to live the life of the new creation with its mores in the midst of the old world.

It is because of the coming of Christ that these Gentiles have learned to trust the one, true God. Again, this would not be the case for Jews, since it was through the covenant with Moses that they learned to trust God and place their hope in the God of Israel. Granted, they did not always live up to this belief, even as Christians have not always lived up to their belief in a trustworthy God who gives them hope. But particularly a reading of the Psalms and the Prophets makes clear that Israel knew that God was the ultimate source of all of their hope, and that God was indeed trustworthy. These Gentile Christians had no way to know this God until the resurrection of Jesus sent forth this new mission of God, a mission that seeks to include all nations in this covenant. The covenant with Moses was the necessary beginning of God's plan—the revelation of God to a particular people, training them to hear and obey God's Word. At the right time, that plan continued in the incarnation of Christ, and with his death and resurrection this covenant is extended to all peoples. We read in Hebrews 1:1–2: "God spoke to our ancestors in many and various ways by the prophets, but in these last days he has spoken to us by a Son, whom he appointed heir of all things, through whom he also created the worlds."

To have faith in this God is to have hope. The two cannot be separated. Faith that has no hope is not faith, nor is hope a real hope if it is not based on faith in the God who alone gives us true hope. We may have wishful thinking, desires for the future, but real hope that does not disappoint, hope that is assured of the future, is a gift from God. This is the hope that faith knows.

1:22–25

Faith and Hope Lead to Holiness

The call to holiness that began in 1:13 now is defined more fully: it is genuine love. These Christians have been "purified," which in this context probably means that they have been baptized, so that their sins have been forgiven, and they have been shown the truth of how God wishes them to live. All this has been done so that they can begin to love one another, not simply in the way they act, but in the way that they actually feel. They are now enabled to love genuinely, from the heart.

Often Christians assume that their *actions* should change, and that they should *act* as though they forgive another person or *act* as though they loved the poor, but this is hard work because it goes against what they truly feel. Rarely do we pray that God may change our hearts so that such love is genuine and requires no effort at all. This is what is meant by genuine love: love from the heart. Such a dramatic transformation is humanly impossible, but what we are promised in our baptism is the power of the Holy Spirit and the example of the new family into which we have been born to help us pray diligently for such a transformation. This means, however, that the congregation needs to be such a helpful model, not of perfection, but of fellow travelers on the path to sanctification. It is difficult, for instance, if a congregation has the same attitude toward enemies of the state as does the wider society—that such enemies are to be despised or at least not prayed for. In such a congregation, how could the new convert learn a different set of attitudes that are based on love for enemies as well as for friends?

Cyprian was the bishop of Carthage in the mid-third century and a martyr. He was converted as an adult and wrote about his experience of baptism:

[A]fter the life-giving water of Baptism came to my rescue and washed away the stain of my former years and poured into my cleansed and purified heart the light which comes from above, . . . what previously had seemed impossible now seemed possible. What was in me of the guilty flesh now confessed it was earthly. What was made alive in me by the Holy Spirit was now quickened by God.

—Cyprian

Quoted in *The Journey Toward God: In the Footsteps of the Great Spiritual Writers*, ed. Benedict J. Groeschel with Kevin Perrotta (Ann Arbor: Charis, 2000), 30.

Saint Benedict, called the father of Western monasticism, wrote his *Rule* in the sixth century. He believed that a monastery should be a school of holiness, and that the efforts of all should be directed toward forming a holy, loving community. If members sought only their own holiness, this would not lead to a holy community but rather to members who kept measuring themselves against others, feeling that they were holier than the others, or despairing because they were not as holy as others. The same thing applies in a congregation. Our desire should be to form a holy, loving community. The congregation is not there simply to help us on our journey; rather, we are there to help the whole community become more holy.

Throughout the history of the church, the marks of holiness have been love and humility. These are virtues that cannot be learned alone. By ourselves we may think that we are very loving, very humble. But put us in a gathering of difficult people and our love and humility will disappear very quickly. Real holiness is impossible to learn alone. It is for that reason that our baptism is not only about us. It joins us to others in a specific gathering of God's people. It makes us part of the body of Christ that is seeking to become holy even as its head is holy.

The image of the new birth appears again in verse 23. In contrast to our first birth that was of perishable seed that would die, our second birth is of imperishable seed. (We need to realize that until modern times it was assumed that the seed of the father was what produced the child; the mother was like the field in which the seed was planted.) This imperishable seed is the Word of God. There is a similar idea in the prologue of the Gospel of John: "To all who received him, who believed in his name, he gave power to become children of God, who were born, not of blood or of the will of the flesh or of the will of man, but of God" (John 1:12–13).

This is a very important concept. The Word of God is active, not merely words on a page. When the Word penetrates the heart, it creates the new person. The term "Word of God" is used in several senses in the Bible. It is the message God gave to the prophets, and it is all of the Hebrew Scriptures, as well as the New Testament. It is the second person of the Trinity who became incarnate as Jesus of Nazareth. It is the message of the gospel that is proclaimed in preaching throughout the centuries. Many medieval paintings of the annunciation show Mary reading, and an infant on a beam of light from heaven enters her ear. In other words, when we say that Mary conceived Jesus by the Holy Spirit, it means that in hearing the Word of God from the angel Gabriel, her heart was open to that Word and she conceived the Word of God in the flesh.

The author quotes Isaiah 40:6–8 to show this power of the Word of God to produce the new creation, and then applies it to the congregation hearing this letter, and to us as well. Because we have heard the word of the gospel that has been proclaimed to us, and because we have responded to that word through the power of the Holy Spirit, we have been born again, we have been made into a new people, forming a congregation, a beachhead, a colony of the new creation, hidden in the midst of this old world, a reality known only to faith.

Verses 17–23 are the lectionary's Epistle selection for the third Sunday of Easter in Year A. These words are a reminder of the cost of our salvation and the life of holiness we are able to lead because Christ has ransomed us and freed us from the power of sin. This passage would be particularly helpful to show the meaning of baptism for the congregation's understanding of itself. Indeed, the Sundays after Easter would be very appropriate for an in-depth look at the nature of the church based on the meaning of baptism, especially if there have been baptisms at Easter following preparation during Lent.

The early church generally baptized all candidates at Easter. If that had not been possible for someone, Pentecost and Epiphany provided two other occasions. This is very different than the practice of most churches in the past several centuries, when baptisms have been celebrated more at the convenience of families and scattered throughout the year. What this has meant is that often a Sunday service begins, and then a baptism is performed, with little connection to the rest of the service. When baptisms are grouped at a time that makes sense in the liturgical year, it becomes possible to connect the meaning of baptism to the central message of the gospel and make it an occasion for the whole congregation to learn more about the meaning of their own baptism and what it means to be the church. Originally, Lent developed out of the final preparation of candidates who were to be baptized at Easter. The Scripture readings and sermons for that time stressed the meaning of Christian discipleship as following the way of the cross, dying with Christ to the old life. Easter was a celebration of Christ's resurrection and also of our own birth into a new life in him. The Sundays after Easter can continue the meaning of this new life for both the individual and the church as a whole. We miss a great opportunity for strengthening the discipleship of the congregation if we focus the celebration of a baptism only on the individual or on families, or a brief ceremony that interrupts the usual Sunday worship, which then continues as though nothing had happened. The new services for the renewal of baptism developed by many denominations can also be used during this season.

2:1–3

Ridding Ourselves of the Old Ways

The imagery of the new birth continues, again with overtones of the Passover. In the Passover celebration all the old yeast in a household was thrown out, and only unleavened bread was used, in remembrance that the Hebrew people left Egypt so quickly that they had no yeast in the desert. (Only cooks today who use a sourdough pot will understand this reference. Yeast was not in neat packages, but the new bread had to use a starter from a previous batch of dough, a starter that was fed each time new bread was made, but was itself never baked.) In the same way that a householder had to throw out the old yeast, newborn Christians had to throw out their old ways, their old attitudes and habits. This is a very helpful reminder to us, because so often we think that we can simply add new virtues to our old lives, whereas the more difficult task may be ridding ourselves of the old attitudes. After the Passover, we have a new beginning, a new "starter." (In bread making this meant capturing wild yeast bacteria that are often in the air. In some areas, like Alaska and San Francisco, bakeries or cooks pride themselves on the sourdough starters they have kept going for decades because of the excellent wild yeast found there.)

So these new Christians have to rid themselves of the old and develop the new at the same time. That means that whenever they face a situation in which their old life leads them to a certain action or response, they must stop, realize that this is one of the points of conflict between their old and their new lives, and consciously choose the new way. The recognition of the conflict is the first step, and perhaps the most difficult. It is a task to which we also are called: sensitizing ourselves to recognize the conflict between our normal way of doing things—the culturally acceptable way—and the demands of the gospel. Paul wrote to the Corinthians: "our paschal lamb, Christ, has been sacrificed. Therefore, let us celebrate the festival, not with the old yeast, the yeast of malice and evil, but with the unleavened bread of sincerity and truth" (1 Cor. 5:7b–8).

The specific attitudes denounced in 1 Peter 2:1 are malice, guile, insincerity, envy, and slander. To be mad at people and wish that they would "get what's coming to them"; to be jealous of others because they seem to have all the luck; to tell others what someone we do not care for is really like—these are human reactions that are so common we would hardly think of them as temptations, yet that is precisely what is meant here. Perhaps if the text had spoken of murder and bodily harm, or stealing and false testimony in court, we could understand it more easily. We would probably recognize the sinfulness of such actions quite easily, and most likely avoid committing them. But these ancient Christians are called to the harder task of rooting out of their lives the attitudes and actions that come long before what we would call serious sins. Envy and malice, insincerity and slander all would ruin a small, intimate community. They would prevent the love that is to be the hallmark of the church. If these new Christians are to be socialized into loving habits, the long-time members are going to have to exhibit them in their lives and not just preach about them. These Christians are called to be loving toward one another in order to show the world a new kind of community, a new kind of society that is truly the life of the new creation. No one is expected to change overnight, but what is expected is that they will learn to recognize the old ways when they appear, and learn to practice the new ways that they are being taught.

When we remember that these small communities are made up of people who would probably not be together in the wider society, we can see how hard the task was for them. Here are slaves and some slave masters, people from different ethnic backgrounds, of different social strata, differing levels of education. How can they develop new attitudes in such a diverse community, and overcome long-held stereotypes about one another? In our often monolithic congregation, one race, one socio-economic level, we can avoid such difficult learning.

In many ways, those early Christians had an easier task than we might have, since the line between the old life and the new life was sharp. They were prepared to judge their old life because they knew they were entering a new way. We, however, live in a culture that for generations has been assumed to be Christian, and therefore the line is blurred. Much of what is culturally accepted is in reality opposed to the gospel, and much that is condemned by society may well be the cutting edge of the Christian life. What do we do with the idea of loving our enemies when we are part of a military superpower? How do we get ahead if we are humble and willing to live simply? How are we part of a loving and sharing community if we meet only one hour a week and then have little personal interaction? How do we represent the one body of Christ when we are divided into many groups, often fighting one another? These are questions we face that those early Christians did not.

Verses 2 and 3 have references to the Lord's Supper that early Christians would have understood, but may escape us because of our different practices. These newborn Christians are to be hungry for milk—the milk of the gospel—just as infants hunger for their mother's milk. The early practices of the first Communion service included giving the newly baptized a cup of milk and honey, to show that they had entered the promised land. The words of Psalm 34:8: "O taste and see that the LORD is good," also were frequently used in Communion. For a new Christian the meaning was clear: to continue to grow in the faith required being part of the body of Christ that was constantly nourished at the Lord's Table and in the common life of the body.

FURTHER REFLECTIONS
Early Baptismal Practices

Late in the nineteenth century an ancient manuscript, the *Rite of Hippolytus*, was discovered that proved to be a description of second-century worship practices in the city of Rome. This, along with other discoveries, has given us a far better picture of baptisms in the early church. Though it is later than the writing of 1 Peter, there are so many similarities that we can say the theology behind the ceremonies is similar to the theology of 1 Peter. No matter whether these practices occurred in earlier decades or writings such as 1 Peter influenced the development of these ceremonies in the second century, at least we can say these later ceremonies help us understand 1 Peter better.

Baptisms were generally held on the night before Easter, so that the newly baptized could be part of their first Communion service on Easter itself. Candidates had been catechumens (see pp. 21–25, "Further Reflections: The Catechumenate") and now were deemed ready to become part of the church. Baptisms were held in a separate room or building from where the congregation was gathered. The candidates were separated by gender and baptized naked, to emphasize that this was indeed a new birth. Children were baptized, even those who were so young that an adult had to answer the questions for them. These were probably children whose parents were becoming part of the church. Before they were baptized the candidates were asked to reject the powers of sin and evil under which they had lived. This is called "the renunciations." There was a clear sense that one could not simply add Jesus to the beliefs already held. Elements of the previous life had to be rejected. Then candidates entered the baptismal font, where they were asked if they believed in God the Father, with the words similar to the first part of what we know as the Apostles' Creed, and then water was poured over them. A second time they were asked to confess their faith in Jesus Christ, using the words of the second part of the Creed, and a second pouring of water occurred. A third time they were asked if they believed in the Holy Spirit, and there was a third and final pouring of water. They were completely wet, but they may not have been immersed, since the remnants of fonts that have been discovered are not sufficiently deep for that. Following the baptism they were given a white robe to wear, and taken to the bishop, who anointed the candidate's head with oil, naming them Christians. The white robes were probably rare new clothes for many of the poorer candidates. The book of Revelation mentions the white robes that the redeemed around the heavenly throne are wearing (Rev. 7:9). Also, the image of taking off the old clothes and putting on new is frequent in the New Testament (see Col. 3:9–10; Eph. 4:22–24).

The anointing with oil was an important part of the ceremony. Oil was used in ancient Israel for the anointing of kings and priests. Those who were baptized were part of the royal and holy people of God, and this would be very important in their self-understanding. The term "Christ" means "the anointed one." Christians were anointed—or "christed"—with oil, marking them as "Christian."

When all the candidates had been baptized and anointed they entered the congregation. The church had been gathered in prayer and singing, awaiting the arrival of the newly baptized—now called "neophytes" or newly born—and with their entrance, Easter began. When the white-robed group entered the worship of the congregation, they appeared as those who had died to the old life and were now born anew. They also were those who had died with Christ and had been raised with him. These images mixed together in the ceremonies, reminding the older members of their own baptismal character.

Those just baptized had never before been present at a Eucharist. Until now they had been dismissed before the Communion part of the weekly gathering occurred. Now they received the bread and then, only on this occasion, they received two extra chalices to drink from: the first was water, so that they could be baptized on the inside as well as the outside; a second of milk and honey mixed, to show that not only had they been part of the exodus from sin and death but they had also crossed the Jordan and entered the promised land, at least with a foretaste of the milk and honey there. (See pp. 17–20, "Further Reflections: Typology.")[2]

For new Christians, it was very clear that their baptism was only the beginning, the actual moment of their new birth. Ahead of them—and of the whole congregation—lay the task of growing in faith, in love for one another, in holiness in all of life, in word, in deed, and in thought. Such holiness could not be completed in this life. Always there would be room for greater growth. A Christian or a congregation that believes it has arrived at sufficient holiness and needs only to hold on to what it has does not understand the nature of the Christian life. Development in faith and life is not just for children. It is for all Christians throughout their whole lives.

2. Hippolytus, *The Apostolic Tradition*, trans. Burton Scott Eaton (Ann Arbor: Archon Books, 1962), 43–49.

2:4–17

Called to Be God's Priestly People

We have seen in the previous section that holiness is not only an individual goal, but above all it is a goal for the community. Now that is spelled out dramatically. The building of a loving community is compared to the creation of a house, where everything depends upon the proper foundation and the fitting together of all the parts. This is no ordinary house, however. It is a house in which God is to be found.

2:4–8

Being Built Together

The holiness of God's people makes it possible for them to be "a spiritual house," a space in which God is not only worshiped but also present. The image shifts rapidly from the Christians as stones being built into the house to them as the priests offering spiritual sacrifices within the house. The mention of priests has often led readers to assume that what is being built is a temple, a house for God in the cultic sense. However, John Elliott, in his study of 1 Peter, *A Home for the Homeless*, makes clear that what is intended here is the building of a house, with the ancient meaning of house as household.[1] In the Greco-Roman culture of the time, a household was a basic structure of society. It included the *paterfamilias*, who was the head of

---

1. John H. Elliott, *A Home for the Homeless: A Social-Scientific Criticism of 1 Peter, Its Situation and Strategy*, 2nd ed. (Minneapolis: Fortress, 1990), 220–37.

the household but the physical father of only a few. The household included blood relatives of many generations, slaves, clients dependent upon the link to this household, and a variety of others. The household provided the basic sense of identity within the society. And within ancient Judaism one spoke of "the house of David" or "the house of Benjamin," meaning the tribe and the people associated with it, such as slaves. The alien was one who had no "household" affiliation.

Many of those who joined the church in its early centuries were without such a household membership. Some were new to the city, having grown up in the countryside and now seeking a living as a worker in the city, often going from one city to another. They might work in leather or be potters or tent makers. They were low in the social stratification of the city. Others in the church had clear household membership: household slaves, masters, or the wives of a well-to-do citizen.

If many of those attracted to the church were without clear connections in the wider society, and if the church presented itself as an alternate household, headed by God the Father, we can understand its appeal. The language that we have already seen in 1 Peter is based on such an emphasis. In baptism we are born again into a new household, the household of God—an entrance made possible by the death and resurrection of Jesus Christ. By baptism we are made brothers and sisters of the Son of God, and siblings of one another. The household refers both to the small gatherings in each city, and to the one household of God throughout the world. It is wider than the household of Caesar, which included all those dependent upon the emperor. In fact, the letter itself is written to show that these small groups in Asia are part of the same household as those in Rome and the rest of the empire. Baptism therefore involves leaving one household—if one is already part of one—and becoming part of another. We must note the continued Trinitarian reference that we saw in the earlier part of the letter: the head of the household is God the Father, who, by action of the Spirit, has added adopted children to the family through the work of the Son.

We live in a culture that is not based on belonging to households in the classic sense. We are highly individualistic. Yet several points of this passage apply to us as well. First, if the congregation functions as it should, there is a sense of belonging, of being a part of a family that belongs to God. The church is not a service agency that simply responds to individual needs. It is a community, a family. Even if we go far away from home, when we enter a church we are part of the family. When we meet Christians from other countries, there is a sense that, though we have never met them before, we are part of the same family. At least, these are the understandings that need to be fostered in our congregations. Second, though we may not have to reject the previous household to which we belonged, it is true that we cannot simply add Christian faith to our lives without rejecting ways of life we held before. The "renunciations" of the early baptisms still apply today. (See pp. 47–49, "Further Reflections: Early Baptismal Practices.")

It is this whole household that has the priestly role. They are to offer spiritual sacrifices. What is the role of a priest? A priest stands between the people and the god to whom the priest owes service. He may offer physical sacrifices of animals or other elements on others' behalf. He may pray to the god on behalf of the people, since the people may not be able to approach the god directly. He is an intermediary between the people and the god. Israel had priests who functioned in the temple; but as we shall see in a few verses, all Israel was to be a priestly people.

The whole Christian community is a priestly people. All believers are directly related to God, the God of Israel, because he is now the father of the family into which they have been born. For whom are they to intercede? For whom are they priests? As we study the worship practices of the early church we discover that the prayers of intercession, the prayers of the people, occurred within the Communion service, where only the baptized were present. These prayers included prayers for the whole world, for peace and tranquility, for the emperor—even when there was official persecution—for the sick and dying, even those who were not part of the community of faith. In other words, the prayers of this priestly people were for the whole world, all of which was the property, the creation, of God. In a sense they prayed for the whole, wider household of God who created all things and all peoples, even those parts of that household that did not know or acknowledge God, who did not know that they were part of that household. Christians were the priestly people for the whole world.

The concept of "the priesthood of all believers" is based on passages like this in the New Testament. That phrase has often been used to mean we do not need one another because each one of us can approach God directly. The phrase, though true, has lost much of its meaning. We need the whole community in order to be the priestly people, interceding for the whole world. It is not a matter that we each are our own priests and therefore do not need the community of faith. It is the community that is the priestly people, and it is in its gathered form—as a community—that its priestly power is exhibited. Even when we are praying alone, it is because that community exists that we can approach God.

The author continues the theme of stones and buildings, using three passages from the Old Testament. The first reference is to Isaiah 28:16, and the author of 1 Peter places Jesus as the promised cornerstone. When buildings were constructed almost completely of stone, the cornerstone played an extremely important role. The walls that were built on it needed to be level and true. If the cornerstone was faulty, then the walls built upon it would not be true. The higher the walls, the more obvious the fault: the walls would tilt in one direction or another and not meet. This Isaiah passage speaks of a true cornerstone promised in Zion so that the renewed people, the household of God, would be faithful. If Jesus is the true cornerstone of this house, then as we are built upon him the house that we become will be God's house.

This passage from Isaiah 28 is artfully connected to two others. The first of these is Psalm 118:22, quoted many times in the New Testament, which shows that the cornerstone that was rejected by the builders—those who were trying to build up God's people in the wrong way—is the cornerstone God has chosen. In its original setting in Isaiah it referred to those who tried to build up Israel on false understandings of God's commandments. In the mind of the author of Peter this could refer to the Jews who rejected Jesus, or it could refer to those Christian contemporaries who build on false understandings of the gospel. In our own day, it can mean those

> Jesus said to them, "Have you never read in the scriptures: 'The stone that the builders rejected has become the cornerstone; this was the Lord's doing, and it is amazing in our eyes'? Therefore I tell you, the kingdom of God will be taken away from you and given to a people that produces the fruits of the kingdom."
>
> —Matthew 21:42–43

who profess Christ and yet build their lives on a different basis, or churches that build themselves up on the basis of preaching a gospel of prosperity or some other strange form of Christianity.

The last passage woven in here is also taken from Isaiah, chapter 8, parts of verses 14–15. Those who reject the true cornerstone will find that it has become for them a stumbling stone, causing them to fall. If the cornerstone of the house is true, then the house of God is built. But some who seek to build a house reject the true stone and instead build on a faulty one, and they leave the true stone where they will stumble on it. So the true stone not chosen will cause them to fall. Yet the rejected stone has actually been chosen by God and will be used in the true church. Faulty foundations will never lead to the construction of the household of God. The famous hymn "The Church's One Foundation" makes the same point: Jesus Christ is the one, true foundation for the church. We cannot build on any other and still be the church.

The passage speaks not only of the foundation, but also of the stones that are to be built into the structure. In the mid-second century, Hermas, a Christian in Rome, wrote an account of his visions and other musings, a writing considered quite orthodox. In it he has a vision of Christians being built into God's house. He goes into some detail about the different kinds of stones, and the process necessary to make each stone fit. His writing reflects the process of the catechumenate (see pp. 21–25, "Further Reflections: The Catechumenate"). He sees some rough stones that need smoothing, others that need polishing, some that need a chipping away of the characteristics that would prevent a person from being used in the building. This does not mean that all Christians are to be alike; Paul's imagery of the body makes that clear. The stones in the building are of various shapes, but they all need to fit together to make the building.

Some stones refuse to undergo this process and are rejected by the builder. There were also white, round stones. When Hermas asked for an explanation of these, he was told:

> "These are those who have faith indeed, but they have also the riches of this world. When, therefore, tribulation comes, on account of their riches and business they deny the Lord." I answered and said to her, "When, then, will they be useful for the building, Lady?" "When the riches that now seduce them have been circumscribed, then will they be of use to God. For as a round stone cannot become square unless portions be cut off and cast away, so also those who are rich in this world cannot be useful to the Lord unless their riches be cut down."[2]

The conclusion of verse 8 speaks to the rejection of those who reject Christ. But what does it mean that those who are rejected were destined to be so? We need to remember that the whole thrust of this letter is to assure those scattered Christians in Asia that though they are nobodies in their cities, many of them not belonging to any household, they have been chosen—elected—by God to be part of God's own household. Their election is a theme that runs throughout the letter. If they have been elected, then there are others, probably members of other households, who have not been elected, others who have rejected the cornerstone. At the same time, Christians were inviting others to enter this new household, so there is not a clear-cut line between the elect and the rejected: some of the now apparently rejected may one day be part of the elect.

2:9–10
The Royal and Priestly People

The next two verses incorporate two more passages from the Old Testament, moving the argument in a new direction. The first of these is Exodus 19:6, where God tells Moses that, on the basis of the covenant, Israel shall be "a priestly kingdom and a holy nation." It is interesting that the previous verse in Exodus ends with the

---

2. Hermas, *Vision* 3.6 (*ANF* 2:15).

words: "Indeed, the whole earth is mine," and then goes into verse 6, "but you shall be for me a priestly kingdom and a holy nation." It is important to note that beginning: all the peoples of the earth are God's. God created all of them. The others do not belong to other gods, no matter what they themselves believe. All people are God's people in this sense. But God has chosen one people—in fact God has brought together in Israel, by means of the covenant, groups that could not be called "a people" before this. This elect people have a task, not simply an honor. They are to be priests, representing the king of the universe in the midst of a world that does not acknowledge its creator. It is for this reason that they can intercede on behalf of the rest of the world.

There is a long history of the power of this intercession: in Genesis 18:23–33 there is the extensive bargaining of Abraham with God concerning the destruction of Sodom, and from that bargaining came the tradition in Judaism that wherever ten faithful Jewish men gather in a city to praise God, the city will be saved. This is a priestly function—interceding before God for those who cannot pray for themselves because they do not know God. It also witnesses to the need for a *community* of prayer and intercession. Within the early church, the custom of anointing the newly baptized with oil followed the ancient pattern in Israel of anointing with oil the priests and the kings. This shows that the newly baptized now held this position—they are a royal priesthood. (See pp. 47–49, "Further Reflections: Early Baptismal Practices.")

> They are a royal priesthood because they are united to the body of Christ, the supreme king and true priest. As sovereign he grants them his kingdom, and as high priest he washes away their sins.
>
> **—Venerable Bede**
>
> Quoted in *The Liturgy of the Hours* (New York: Catholic Book Publishing, 1976), 2:704.

The second passage used here is an adaptation of Hosea 2:23, with the stress on the fact that these members of the church previously had not been "a people," that is, they had not belonged anywhere, they had no status in the community, or they had belonged to a variety of different households in the city. Yet now they are God's own people. Becoming part of God's people means that God has shown mercy upon them. This is the culmination of this section, telling them that they are a blessed people, called to a life of holiness, living as God's priestly people in the midst of a world that belongs to God but does not or does not yet believe that.

This describes the role that we also, as a local congregation, have in the midst of our world. It is complicated by the fact that, for most of us, in most communities, we would never say that our congregation is the only group that acknowledges God as the creator and Lord of the universe. Other Christian congregations also do so. How do we relate to them? Do we have a common witness in this community? Do we have a priestly role here? What about Jewish congregations that also acknowledge God as the

> In the Second Vatican Council of the Roman Catholic Church, the ancient place for the prayers of the people was restored:
>
> > The "common prayer" or "prayer of the faithful" is to be restored after the gospel and homily, especially on Sundays and holidays of obligation. By this prayer in which the people are to take part, intercession will be made for holy Church, for the civil authorities, for those oppressed by various needs, for all mankind, and for the salvation of the entire world.
> >
> > —"The Sacred Liturgy"
>
> In *Documents of Vatican II*, ed. Austin P. Flannery (Grand Rapids: Eerdmans, 1975), 18.

creator and Lord of the universe? How are we related to them? What are the situations in our own community that need our intercessory prayers? What about the wider nation and the whole world?

Often in our worship services the prayers of the people are limited to the sick in our own congregation, or to friends and family. If a natural disaster or some other dire situation has made it into the headlines, that probably will be included. But the week-by-week prayers often ignore the continuing problems that do not make headlines. The situations we know exist all of the time in our community—poverty, homelessness, unemployment, conflict between groups—are completely ignored.

If a congregation is involved in local social action, the members so involved might well ask the congregation to pray for the problems they see. If in their daily employment members are aware of difficulties that can be mentioned without betraying confidences, those too could be added. These prayers need not be simply for individuals, but for societal problems that are worldwide but seen also in their local manifestation. What matters is that the prayers of corporate worship are the training ground for the private prayers of church members. There needs to be clear teaching about the congregation's role as a priestly people and that same role for each member, who even when alone needs to understand her- or himself as part of the priestly people.

Verse 9 makes very clear that the election of the people of God is for a purpose. Not only does it have a priestly role, it also has the task of witnessing to God's mighty acts on its behalf. This was the same role Israel had. Granted, there is a difference in the "mighty acts"—for Christians it is the incarnation, the crucifixion, and the resurrection of Jesus that are central, even as the exodus, the giving of the covenant, and the promised land were central to Israel's witness. Israel often forgot that it has a task, and thought of its election simply as status given to it. The church has often had the same problem. We have been chosen by God to form a new people, and that election has been for a purpose: we are to be God's witnesses in the world, testifying that God is the Creator and Redeemer of the world; and we are to be a priestly people, interceding with God on behalf of that world.

The passage 2:2–10 is the Epistle lesson for the fifth Sunday of Easter in Year A in the lectionary. It makes clear that our new status as a royal priesthood is based on the resurrection, which has ushered in the new creation of which we are now a part. These verses help us understand what the role of the congregation is in the midst of God's world: it is a priestly people, called to witness to the rest of the world and to intercede for that world.

2:11–12
The Life Expected of God's Holy People in This World

Now that the identity of these Christians is clarified—they are God's priestly household—it follows that their lives must be lived in a new way. They are citizens of two worlds, the old one in which they were socialized before their baptism and the new one into which they were born through baptism. Their social situation in the old world has not changed. Those who were slaves remain slaves; those who were married, perhaps to a nonbeliever, remain married. The issue for them now is how to live a new life in those old relationships.

They are still aliens and exiles. Perhaps most of them were that before their baptism, but their alienation is increased by their membership in the church, a movement viewed with suspicion by many of their neighbors. For most of us, living in a society that has long considered itself Christian, these words may not seem to apply. If we grew up in the church, perhaps baptized as infants, we have no idea that the life before baptism was any different than after that event. After all, for generations, belonging to a church was a necessity for one to be considered a good citizen. Those running for office put their church membership as part of their credentials. That is changing, but the overtones still remain. So we would see no great difficulty in returning to our previous relationships with little change after our baptism. We can assume that a Christian view of the relationship of husbands and wives is what the society also supports. Granted it took a long time to deal with the issue of slaves and masters, but if we transpose that to the relationship of employer and employee, we would have little reason to think that baptism should change those relationships.

Yet we may be assuming too much. It is true that the gospel has had a great influence on our society, much of it won only after centuries of slow changes. Slavery and the social condition of women, particularly married women, have been altered dramatically. The protection of children and the handicapped also has grown greatly over the centuries. The church can rightly claim credit for much of this, although it also bears the burden of having moved entirely too slowly or actively opposed needed change.

At the same time, the church has also adapted itself sufficiently to the culture that its cutting edge is gone. Christians accept much as perfectly acceptable that those earlier Christians would have recognized very quickly as opposing the message of the gospel. The text says that Christians are to "abstain from the desires of the flesh that wage war against the soul." We could understand this to mean that Christians are to have a negative view of sex, and pride ourselves on how enlightened we have become in comparison to the Christians of the first century. But that is to read into the text much that is not there. There is no reason to believe that those early Christians opposed sex. It is clear that they opposed the easy sex, sex outside marriage, that was a great challenge in that culture. Our situation is different, but we cannot say that the easy sex of our culture is a good thing. We do have problems they did not face: a far longer period of time between physical maturity and readiness to support a family. We live in a sexually charged culture, and yet young people are expected to postpone marriage until after they have finished their education. Our life span is far longer than that of the ancient world, and a marriage contracted between sixteen-year-olds may not survive the maturity each partner reaches at thirty. Simple words of abstinence may not be sufficient. Premarital sex is a difficult issue for us and for our children. But the multiple partners, unprotected sex, sex as a recreational activity rather than as a serious human encounter, all are opposed to the gospel. Especially in our contemporary situation, we need to consider what are the "desires of the flesh" that run counter to the faith.

It is wrong to reduce "the desires of the flesh" to sex. The search for wealth and power are equally such desires. Ambition to get ahead in the world is now viewed as a very positive characteristic, but the gospel is much more concerned that we get ahead in love and humility than in financial success. Overlooking people we think are beneath us and seeking relationships with those who can help us in the future are accepted ways of living our lives. Yet such actions are totally opposed to the gospel. How do we reconcile these goals?

Often we view such directives as external laws that we have to obey in order to be saved. That is not the way they are presented in this letter. The behavior required of Christians is for the purpose of letting the soul, the heart of a person, remain free. The text assumes a warfare between "the desires of the flesh" and the soul. This does not mean a conflict between the material and the spiritual. It is a conflict between that which would drag people down, subject them to the powers of evil, and the power of the Holy Spirit that seeks to free the person from sin. The works of evil are not material only but spiritual as well. They are envy and greed, hatred and malice. The works of the

Holy Spirit are not only spiritual but also material: making sure the hungry are fed, seeking the welfare of abused children. To give in to the "desires of the flesh" denies us the freedom that Christ has given us. The way of the gospel is not a series of onerous commandments that limit us but rather the power to become the new, free persons that God intends.

The major way the church spread rapidly in its early years was by the new lives that Christians exhibited to their neighbors. These Christians were not marked by the burden of laws they had to live by but by the joy and freedom that made their neighbors wonder what had happened to them. Their lives witnessed to something they possessed, not things they had to give up. There was no evangelism committee in the local church. Rather, the lives of Christians engaged others.

> One trait of human nature seems to be that people watch strangers more closely. If Peter's original readers were in fact displaced people, they likely attracted more scrutiny from the indigenous population. Therefore, as Christians they must be especially mindful of how their behavior would be evaluated by the norms of that society. . . . A major concern of Peter is how the newly formed Christian religion will be perceived and evaluated by the norms and ideals of Greco-Roman society.
> —Karen H. Jobes
>
> *1 Peter*, BECNT (Grand Rapids: Baker Academic, 2005), 171.

At the same time, some of the actions of Christians did make their neighbors suspicious. Christians did not go into the temples of the local gods. They did not take part in civil celebrations that included worship of these gods. Some in society viewed such actions as treasonous. There also were rumors that Christians had "orgies" because they held "love feasts." They called one another brother and sister, so these might even be incestuous orgies! They spoke of eating bodies and drinking blood, and there were wild rumors as to what this meant. (These were frequent misunderstandings in the first century. By the second century, a group of writers known as apologists wrote to those outside the church to make clear that such charges were baseless.) Christians needed to show by their good behavior, by their acts of love toward all people, even the neighbors who were suspicious of them, that they were not a people to be feared. Even if they were falsely accused of something, their good behavior might make their enemies think again. How could people who lived such good lives, helping others, not trying to get ahead of them, not looking down on them, how could such people do the evil things they were accused of? The non-Christian neighbors might be witnesses to their good behavior and even testify to it when God judges the world.

2:13–17

The Relationship of Christians to Human Institutions

These verses make very clear that these new Christians, though they have begun to be part of the new creation, are still living in the old world. They are to live in the society as they find it. Human society is a gift of God. We are intended to live in community—even large communities. Creation may have begun in a garden, but if humans always were fruitful and multiplied, they would form such large groups that some sort of government would be necessary. Historically, however, there have been some differences of opinion on this matter. At the point of the Protestant Reformation, Luther and Calvin differed as to whether God always intended government or God instituted government only because of human sin. Luther believed that a sinless humanity would need no government, but love would allow humans to live without any political structure. The fall corrupted that picture, and God created human government in order to limit the power of sin. Calvin, on the other hand, agreed with Aristotle that human beings are by nature political, and governmental structures would be needed even if humanity were sinless. Large groups need some way to make decisions. Sin adds to the task of government, but even a perfect humanity would need decision-making bodies.

However we view the origin of government, Christians are to be part of the society in which they live. They are to respect the government, and to understand that one of its functions is to punish evildoers. Christians should behave in such a way that there is no cause for the government to do anything but exonerate them. The view of the Roman government seen here is very much like the one we find in Romans 13:1–3. It is very different than the view we see in the book of Revelation. There the Roman Empire is the enemy, persecuting the church and making life very difficult for Christians. In 1 Peter and Romans the government of the empire is more benign. There is no systematic persecution. Granted, there could be problems in local communities or within a household, but the empire itself is still not seen as the enemy. This is one reason for dating 1 Peter earlier in the first century rather than very late, when there was serious persecution.

We live in a somewhat similar situation. There is no governmental persecution of Christians. But we know there is such persecution in other areas of the world, and these Christians should be part of our prayers, for they are part of our family. At the same time, even in our own society, Christians who try to lead a more serious Christian life may run into difficulties within their own family or circle of friends who think they are acting in a foolish way. If the others are also Christians, then they may feel that these more dedicated Christians are judging them. It is a difficult path to walk.

Christ has made us free to do the good, free to be holy, free to be part of God's household. We are not free in order to harm others or do evil. What would a serious but joyful Christian, pursuing a life of holiness, look like in the midst of our congregation, or our family? This is the sort of situation 1 Peter is addressing, for which the author is giving counsel.

> Unlike Paul, who puts family relationships first in his list, Peter puts government authorities first. This shows his context of persecution; he will always assume that the person in question is non-Christian and very likely oppressive. The "king" is first, for he is indeed "the supreme authority" and perhaps the one Christians would find it hardest theologically to submit to because of his claims to divinity. The word "king" clearly means the Roman Emperor. . . . Governors deserve submission because even the worst of them preserve some semblance of conformity to pagan standards of good, and that is better than chaos.
>
> —Peter H. Davids
>
> *The First Epistle of Peter*, NICNT (Grand Rapids: Eerdmans, 1990), 99–100.

Finally, the letter encourages Christians to honor everyone. They are especially to love the household of God. Such honor cannot stop with the church. It has to be to those outside the church and not only within. Love cannot be turned off at the boundary of the congregation. Gregory the Great, the bishop of Rome around the year 600, lived in the midst of constant war and turmoil. The attacking groups were not part of the church that he headed. However, he always wrote to their kings as those who hopefully would be brothers in Christ sometime in the future. Eventually, whole tribes were converted. Gregory's honoring of the enemy as possible future brothers and sisters made it easier for them to become part of the church. It would have been more difficult if they had been viewed by the church as eternal enemies. Those outside the household of God should never be treated with disdain, but rather as those whom God may be calling through our witness and actions.

The household of God that must be loved means not only the local gathering of Christians but the whole church, other gatherings in our own community and the church worldwide. The Christian church in all its manifold forms is a worldwide network. We have the possibility of learning what is happening in all parts of the world through that network. Probably our own denomination has good communication with the worldwide church, but often at the local level we make little use of these resources. Rather, our view of the global situation is likely to be based on what we see on television, in the newspaper, or on the Internet, and many times we miss significant issues because they were not considered newsworthy. The situation of refugees, the plight of those in famine-stricken areas— often these are not in the headlines. If we are to love the household of God, we need to increase our connection and communication with the brothers and sisters in other areas of the world.

Christians are to honor the emperor—that is, recognize the legitimacy of the government, and that it is an institution God has given us, faulty as it may be. Two things need to be said about this honoring. First, it does not mean that there is no role for challenging the laws or actions of the government. There is a civil disobedience that opposes an unjust human law on the basis of God's law, and yet is willing to suffer the consequences of the act. From the early martyrs to Roger Williams to the modern civil rights movements, this has been understood. But in these cases it is a particular law and not the fact of government that is questioned. Second, we do not live in the Roman Empire, where the populace had no part in making the laws. We live in a democratic republic in which we are partly responsible for the government, and our duty is to make that government the best that a human government can be. We are not to resign ourselves to whatever is, but exercise our citizenship by electing those who do carry out justice, punish evildoers, and promote peace. This does not mean simply voting for those who are church members, but voting for those who best help government be what God created it to be.

We are to honor the emperor—just as we honor all others. But we are to fear God. It is clear we are not to fear the emperor or anyone else. Fearing God does not mean cringing in terror, but reverencing God, acknowledging that God alone is the head of the household to which we belong. God is God, and we are God's servants. God is not our servant. So much of popular theology loses sight of the reverence that is owed to God. "The Man Upstairs" is clearly not what is meant here.

This whole section helps us see what the task of the Christian life is: to grow in our ability to love others, to be God's priests in a world that does not acknowledge God's rule, to witness to the world about a new life that is free from the bondage to sin, and above all to be part of a community of faith that helps us grow and mature as God's people. Christians are not removed from the world because of their faith. They are not to establish separate,

> Christians ought to interest themselves, and collaborate with others, in the right ordering of social and economic affairs. . . . They should . . . share in the efforts of those people who, in fighting against famine, ignorance and disease, are striving to bring about better living conditions and bring about peace in the world. In this work the faithful, after due consideration, should be eager to collaborate in projects initiated by private, public, state, or international bodies, or by other Christian or even non-Christian communities.
> —"Decree on the Church's Missionary Activity"
>
> In *Documents of Vatican II*, ed. Austin P. Flannery (Grand Rapids: Eerdmans, 1975), 826.

parallel societies and reject the world around them. In the long history of the church there have been many attempts to withdraw from the society and build a "Christian" one instead. The ancient Montanists did this, and several groups at the time of the Protestant Reformation also tried to do so. But 1 Peter makes clear that Christians are called to live in the society, sinful as it is, and to live willingly under the conditions of that society. Yet they are not to give up the new, free life they have been given in Christ. They are to use that freedom to be part of the society and witness to the new world God has begun in Christ.

2:18–3:12

Living in the Old World in a New Way

One of the problems many Christians have in reading and applying Scripture is knowing what to do with elements of the texts that show life lived in very different ways than we now live. How are texts that deal with kings to be interpreted? Do we need to have monarchies, or are these passages simply irrelevant for us today? Often we make a simple division: some texts are timeless and therefore readily apply to us as well as to the people who originally heard them. Other texts, however, are not of eternal significance because they belong to an ancient culture and can be ignored now. Usually the "eternal" ones appear simply to be ethical or theological statements. This division, however, does not work for at least two reasons. First, every word of God, even the theological statements, was and is heard and interpreted within a specific culture. The ethical teachings are also related to issues and conditions in a particular society. If the words were not related to that culture they could not have been heard and understood by those who received the teaching. Second, there is no agreement as to which texts are "eternal" and which are temporally limited in importance.

The passage we deal with here is a clear example of that second problem. When slavery was a major issue in the United States, these words were used to show that it is quite legitimate for Christians to own slaves. The words here were understood to apply to all cultures at all times. Now that slavery has been abolished, we can ignore these words because they no longer have any application. For some, the word to wives is equally to be understood as telling wives of every age how they should behave. In the latter part of the twentieth century, as a reaction to a resurgence of the feminist movement, these words were used to show what some believed God intended for all times and places: wives are always to be subject to their husbands. As serious conflicts in the past two centuries have shown, there is often no agreement as to which passages are time bound and which are timeless. Obviously, in the case of both slaves and wives other readers believed that these words were signs of an ancient culture and should not be applied to our own time.

Many Christians, both women and the descendants of slaves, have heard these passages used to prevent their own movement toward liberation from oppressive conditions. From that perspective, it is almost impossible to do anything with these texts but simply to say they represent an unfortunate bowing to an unjust society by the church in the first centuries. They are not only time bound; they show the limited vision of the early church. In a sense, they are unredeemable texts for our society.

Some Christians will say that because the church expected the end of history shortly, and because Christians were few in number and had no power in the society to change the situation of slaves or wives, it is understandable that the church simply accepted the situation as it was.

There are other options, however, if we look closely at the passage within its own context. Though Christians had no power to change the surrounding society, did they expect the community of the

The Bible's status within the Christian community as an authoritative text whose content is seen as binding upon one's existence always has been a complicated matter. Its role for marginalized readers—especially those who read the Bible in order to get some idea of who they are in the presence of God or who they are in relation to other people—is even more complicated and problematic. Depending upon the social location of the reader, the history of African Americans exemplifies the ways in which the Bible can and has been used, in the name of its supposed authority, to sanction the subjugation and enslavement of people or to instigate insurrection and buttress liberation efforts of oppressed people.

—Renita J. Weems

"Reading *Her Way* through the Struggle: African American Women and the Bible," in *Stony the Road We Trod: African American Biblical Interpretation*, ed. Cain Hope Felder (Minneapolis: Fortress, 1991), 63.

church to live by different standards than those of the world around it? As we examine these verses, we need to look for the contrast between the society of the Roman Empire and the community of faith in regard to both slaves and wives. The church did have power within itself to offer a different vision of how human life is intended to be lived.

2:18–20

A Word to Slaves

Three times in the New Testament we find directions to various members of households. There were similar "household codes" in secular writings of the time. The most extensive code in the New Testament is in Ephesians 5:22–6:9. In that text there is advice to wives and husbands, children and fathers, slaves and masters. In Colossians 3:18–4:1 these six groups are again mentioned, although more briefly. Here in 1 Peter 2:18–3:7, there is nothing about fathers and children, and masters are not mentioned. Husbands receive very brief advice, whereas slaves and wives are discussed extensively. (First Timothy also includes words to both slaves and wives, but in a less formal fashion. See 1 Tim. 2:8ff. and 6:1ff.)

When we read the words to slaves, we may be tempted to ignore these passages since we no longer face the terrible reality of slavery. But, particularly in 1 Peter, it would be unwise to pass by these difficult words, because they lead directly into the model that Jesus has given all of his followers. The slaves mentioned here are household slaves. Although their situation could be terrible, depending on the character of their master, they did have a place in society. They were attached to a household, but their place in that household was difficult. The paterfamilias had absolute power over them, including the power of death. This, however, was also true of some blood members of the household. Slaves here are told to accept their situation, and do their best in it. Christians were in no position to end the institution of slavery, and if a slave before baptism had been halfhearted in his or her work, and now, because of the faith, the slave was a willing servant of the master, then the new faith would not be seen by the master as a problem but as a benefit. This would facilitate a slave's continued participation in the church, and some leniency might be shown for not being fully involved in whatever pagan rites in which the slave might be expected to participate.

Some of the rationale for the advice in this passage was to try to make it possible for a slave to find sufficient favor with the master so as to continue being part of the church. Christian house churches met at least daily for prayers and often for meals, and this could be very difficult for someone completely under another's control. How did slaves refuse to participate in the worship of household gods? How could they be active in the life of a congregation that met so often?

All that has been said so far can appear to be self-preservation without a serious matter of faith behind it. But there is more than that here. The author is using the example of slaves to show how all Christians should behave. One commentator points out that the word used here for "submit" means that Christians are not to withdraw from the situation in which they find themselves. They are to remain involved in the society in which they live.[1] (How they could possibly withdraw is another question. It may simply mean that they are to be engaged willingly.) Yet their new life as Christians means there will be a difference in the way they live. They will not be able to worship the gods of the household or the city. They cannot perform tasks that would harm others. If aside from specific acts that Christians cannot do, they carry out their role as slaves in the household, what reward should they expect? But if, when they have done nothing wrong in God's eyes, they are still punished, then, though this is unjust, it is exactly what Jesus experienced. He suffered though he was innocent—he suffered even to the point of death. He did what God required, yet he was counted by society as guilty, just as a slave who does that which God requires may face punishment because he or she is counted as guilty by that society. What is clear is that the behavior that is recommended here for slaves is also recommended for all Christians: they are to carry out whatever role they have in society as obediently as possible, but that implies not doing some

1. Joel B. Green, *1 Peter*, THNTC (Grand Rapids: Eerdmans, 2007), 79.

things that the master might require. They may be punished for this, but such suffering is what all Christians may expect when they live a new life in the midst of a fallen world. Just as Christ's suffering was redemptive for others, so their suffering may lead to the redemption of those who are converted through their obedience. Twice in this passage—2:21 and 3:9b—we are told that we are all called to such unjust suffering, just as Christ was called. This is a difficult saying: we have been called to suffer. Indeed, it is in such suffering that we are truly following in the steps of Jesus, and it is in such suffering that our faith is refined and found to be true.

The phrase in verse 21—that we are to follow "in his steps"—was used as the title of a famous novel by Charles Shelton published in 1896. It posed the question of what Jesus would do in various situations in contemporary society. Shelton was not so much concerned with private morality but what people in various occupations or social settings would do, especially how Christians should relate to the poor.

Our society is radically different from the ancient Greco-Roman world. We generally do not have to stay in the social situation into which we are born, and throughout our lives we have some possibilities of changing things—though for some, especially the very poor, it may be close to impossible to change their situation. But with that social mobility taken into account, whatever situation we find ourselves in, we are to do our best to fulfill that role while, at the same time, living according to the lifestyle the gospel requires. We do not generally have the problem of the worship of other gods within the household or the business establishment, so the question of idolatry is not as acute for us as it was for those early Christians. We may think that some people worship money or success, but this does

> Be sure to note carefully the extent to which Peter beholds glory even in the state of slavery, by saying that those who do well and are blameless but who are beaten by cruel and dishonest masters, are following in the footsteps of Christ, who suffered unjustly on our behalf. That is something to rejoice about!
> —**Venerable Bede**
>
> Quoted in *James, 1–2 Peter, 1–3 John, Jude*, ed. Gerald Bray, ACCSNT 11 (Downers Grove, IL: InterVarsity Press, 2000), 94.

not include specific ceremonies dedicated to a particular god—ceremonies that were part of family life within the home—nor does it involve going to the temple of a god to offer sacrifices. Such worship today is part of the wider problem of a Christian life in the modern world. We generally do not need to find a way to join the congregation every day. But the advice here remains for us. Often we have to find ways not to rock the boat for insignificant reasons while living according to our faith. In that ancient situation, slaves would hope not to be forced to choose between faithfulness and death, but that was a reality for them that we generally do not face. There are Christians around the globe, however, for whom that is a real choice, especially where Christians are a powerless minority. Those who face that choice have the awareness that they are following exactly the way Jesus followed, and that this is the calling of all Christians, slaves and masters alike. Christ had given them a new freedom, freedom from the bondage to sin and death. This freedom, however, did not alter their social situation in the Roman Empire. They were to use their new freedom to be engaged in the society while still living the new life that Christ had given them. Though they are freed in one sense, they have become slaves, servants of God, in another sense. Their obedience to God takes precedence over all human lordships, and this can lead their human masters to punish them.

There were many more slaves than masters in the early church. On occasion, however, there might be a slave whose master was also part of the church. We have one case of that in the New Testament: Onesimus and Philemon, recorded in Paul's Letter to Philemon. Philemon was a Christian converted by Paul. His slave, Onesimus, had run away, and while away had also been converted by Paul. Paul then sent him back with this letter, saying that Philemon owed his new life to Paul, and on that account he was to receive Onesimus back, not punish him for running away, but receive him as a brother in Christ. (In the United States, in the arguments leading up to the Civil War, those who supported slavery used this letter to show that God approved of slavery and runaway slaves should be returned to their masters just as Paul returned Onesimus.) The system of slavery had not ended, nor could Philemon simply free Onesimus. The law of Augustus at the beginning of the Christian era made manumission of slaves quite difficult.[2] But even within that system, Onesimus was now a brother of Philemon, though still a slave. They would have to work out what that meant, and Paul is calling upon Philemon to do that. Onesimus might even do some of the work of the church, perhaps being sent back to help Paul. But Paul assumed that Onesimus, who was not very useful to Philemon before, would be very useful to him now. At the same time, he is now related to his master as a fellow slave of their one Master, God. (In this country, the slave owners had a difficult time explaining what Paul meant that the slave and his Christian master were now brothers—and so they spoke of a "spiritual" relationship that had no effect on their roles as slave and master.)

In the year 107, Bishop Ignatius of Antioch, a prisoner on his way to Rome and martyrdom, wrote a letter to the church at Ephesus. He referred to their bishop, who had come to see him with many members of that church. The bishop is named Onesimus. There is a tradition that this is the same Onesimus who had been a slave of Philemon. If that is true, then clearly he had been given the freedom to work for the church, perhaps with Paul. We do not know if he had managed to become a freedman, although the law still required a freedman to relate to his former master as his patron. He may simply have been given the freedom to become an associate of Paul, living as a free person within the church regardless of his official status in the society. In the early church, such an event might well have been possible. It is interesting to note that in the mid-fifth century, Leo I, bishop of Rome, known as "Leo the Great," wrote a letter stating that the high office of the priesthood within the church should not be given to those of low birth, such as slaves. The social acceptance of the church at the time of Constantine meant that many of the attitudes of the old society now became normative within the life of the church.

When Christians had positions of power in the state, as became the case in the fourth century, they did have the possibility of ending slavery. It took entirely too long for the Christian consciences of various cultures to do this, but at least there was a possibility to

2. *Encyclopedia Britannica*, 11th ed., s.v. "Slavery."

end slavery that had not been there at the time of 1 Peter. The slavery of the Roman Empire and that which developed in the English colonies in the seventeenth century and beyond were quite different. In Rome, though slavery was considered a contemptible status, many slaves were captives from wars and may have been of high status in the conquered society; others had been enslaved because of debt. Many were highly educated, and taught their master's children. There was no "racial" character to such slavery. In the English colonies, slaves came from a different race that was considered inferior. There was little education for them, and they were thought to be incapable of much education.

It is interesting to note that some of the spread of Christianity into northern and eastern Europe happened because Christians who lived within the Roman Empire were captured and made slaves. Patrick, who had been a slave in Ireland and escaped, later returned to the land of his enslavement to evangelize his former captors. He had learned their language while a slave and now was called to return. He was very successful. In the east, Ulfilas was the child of Christians captured by the Goths, who asked him to go to Constantinople to be trained in the faith, of which they wished to hear more. He then returned to the Goths and taught them the Christian faith. He had grown up knowing both Gothic and Greek, and could be such a bridge. Later, many in the Nordic countries were converted by Christians they had captured from raids in Ireland and made slaves.

When the enslavement of Africans began in the modern period, it presented a different situation, both because those enslaved were considered "racially" inferior to those who enslaved them even before they became slaves, and because those who enslaved them were Christians. In other words, in the situation of 1 Peter, most slave masters were not Christian, and the whole structure of slavery was part of a non-Christian society. The usual pattern was a non-Christian master and a Christian slave. In the more recent form of slavery in the United States, the pattern at the beginning was a Christian master and non-Christian slaves. Slavery therefore had to be interpreted within the context of society, most of whose members professed Christianity—and it was then that the arguments mentioned above about Philemon's relationship to Onesimus became critical. The household passages were used to show that God did not disapprove of slavery. Some slave owners did not want slaves to be evangelized precisely because it raised the serious question of what relationship they should then have with their slaves. (There were some slaves who had already been converted in Africa because they lived in Portuguese colonies and were Roman Catholic.) But after some generations, the majority of slaves were Christians. At that time, there was a heated debate among white Christians about the validity of slavery. The abolitionists based their beliefs on the inherent equality of all persons and on the fact that the slaves were their brothers and sisters in Christ, whereas those who supported slavery believed the slaves were inferior by reason of their race, and were by nature slaves, and their relationship in Christ was "spiritual" and had no bearing on their daily lives as slaves and masters.

The issue we need to study, stated briefly, is this. In 1 Peter we see a setting in which Christians have to live in two worlds—the sinful world of the Roman Empire in the first century, and the redeemed world of the church, the new creation. In terms of the issue of slavery, they needed to live in Roman society in the old way, but within the community of believers there was an overcoming of the division between slave and master and other hierarchical structures of the old creation. But if the society becomes largely Christian, then should there be such a contrast? Ought Christians still feel that they are living in two different worlds? It would have been a great thing

---

Now Paul, who in verse 9 had claimed paternity to Onesimus, used the same term that he had applied to Philemon to describe Onesimus. He is no longer a slave; rather he is more than a slave—he is a beloved brother, just as Philemon is Paul's "brother" and is "beloved" by God. Onesimus thus stands on a par with Paul and his former master.

. . . What Paul does . . . is to make himself, in essence, the envoy of Onesimus. . . . Thus Paul has brought to light the implications of being his child and the child of God in a community where equal status under the gospel, as shown in Galatians, is a virtue. . . . He now leaves it to Philemon to decide what understanding of Onesimus within his household would best reflect this reality.

—Lloyd A. Lewis

"An African-American Appraisal of the Philemon-Paul-Onesimus Triangle," in *Stony the Road We Trod: African American Biblical Interpretation*, ed. Cain Hope Felder (Minneapolis: Fortress, 1991), 245–46.

if the society within the church—relating to one another as equals across all lines of status—had meant the abolition of all such divisions. We know from the Letters of Paul that the ideal was always a goal, and also that often the church continued practicing the sinful divisions of the society even within the church (see especially 1 Cor. 11 and 12). But the early Christians had enough experience of this different society within the church to feel that they were living in two worlds. Clearly, in this letter as in so many other places in the New Testament, the distinction between slave and free, male and female, Jew and Gentile, was not supposed to continue in the church. But when the church became the dominant religion, there were still two worlds. The pattern of Roman society continued with little change. After the wide conversion of the empire, Christians may have felt they lived only in one world; but in that case it was the world of the empire that had invaded the church itself.

Part of the reason is that the church went so quickly from being a persecuted minority within the empire to being the dominant religious institution, supported by the emperor. The worst persecution in the history of the church began in the first decade of the fourth century. It ended abruptly when Emperor Constantine declared toleration in 313. He also gave the Christian church many favors, such as free postal service, exemption of clergy from military service, and tax-free status. This meant that many people decided they wished to be part of the religion that the emperor favored, and there was an overwhelming application to the church for membership. By the end of the fourth century, Christianity became the only government-supported religion. Christianity—along with Judaism, which was tolerated, but received no official or social support— became the only permitted public worship. Almost all non-Jews within the Roman Empire were now Christians. Some still practiced the old Roman and Greek religions, but generally they were peasants out in the countryside, who had little effect on the policies of the state. That was an unbelievably rapid change. The church could not keep up with it in the sense that it could no longer devote the usual time—two or three years—to the preparation of candidates for baptism. (See pp. 47–49, "Further Reflections: Early Baptismal Practices.") Nor could it turn people away and say they would have to wait decades before there were enough teachers and mentors for all those who desired to be Christian. Many, and perhaps most, joined the church for social reasons and simply continued their earlier styles of life. There was little if any change in the lives of those who were part of this mass conversion. It was still the old society.

Therefore we can say that even when all the members of a society are part of the church, that society is still a fallen society, and the church still has the task of providing a model of the true life God intends for the world. In that sense, there is no such thing as a "Christian" society. Indeed, it may be harder for congregations really to exhibit that different life, that life of the new creation, when the whole or most of the society is considered Christian. In some ways, monasticism tried to be that alternative society as a witness to the rest of the church, but that has its own limitations, and often involves a withdrawal rather than an engagement with the wider society.

This does not mean that the church has had no impact on the society around it. It did take centuries, but the influence of the church can be seen in the increasing sensitivity of the society to those whose lives need care and protection. The end of slavery, the emancipation of women, the concern for the welfare of children, reforms in prisons, care for the sick and the mentally ill, and a whole host of other social situations needing attention have been signs of the church's influence, however long it has taken. Even now, the church has a role to continue pricking the conscience of the society around it.

We stand at the end of the period called "Constantinian," meaning a time in which the church had the wide support of the society. Even though in the United States we do not have an established state church, the general culture has supported Christianity, especially in its traditional Protestant forms. That support, however, is obviously lessening, and the society is becoming more secular. Whether we look at portrayals of Christians or clergy in popular media or find our children having to choose between soccer games or Sunday school on Sunday morning, society is clearly changing. There is no longer any great need for someone to be part of the church for social reasons. It may be easier, therefore, for the church to return to the pattern 1 Peter sees as the role of the church: living a new life, as a new society, in the midst of an old world.

2:21–25

Slaves as Suffering Servants

These are very important verses. They sound familiar—for good reason. They are an adaptation rather than a direct quotation of Isaiah 53, the famous Suffering Servant passage. The passage begins with the quotation of Isaiah 53:9b and then expands this to show that Jesus did not retaliate when he was mistreated but trusted God in the midst of his suffering. It was for our sins that he suffered. The author uses the imagery of Isaiah 53:9—that the Servant was innocent and yet spoke nothing deceitful—followed by the words of 53:6—that we are all sheep that have gone astray. Both of these images are expanded. Jesus trusted God throughout his suffering. He not only suffered without reviling those who mistreated him, but his suffering for the wandering sheep has led them back to God, their true shepherd.

This is a classic example of the use of typology in the New Testament. (See pp. 17–20, "Further Reflections: Typology.") Very often the discussion of Isaiah 53 is limited to the question the Ethiopian eunuch asked Philip: "About whom, may I ask you, does the prophet say this, about himself or about someone else?" (Acts 8:34). Many have assumed that if we understand the words of Isaiah 53 to be a prophecy about Jesus as the coming Suffering Servant, then it could not mean anything about someone at the time they were first spoken. It seems we have to choose: the words have to refer either to someone in ancient Israel or to Jesus. But typology sees things differently. It understands that the words did apply to someone at the time they were spoken—or perhaps to the whole people of Israel, suffering in exile in Babylon (assuming that ch. 53 is part of Second Isaiah, written

> [N]ote that the sequence of Peter's affirmations does not replicate the order of the source material in Isaiah 53. Instead, his order follows that of the passion accounts, moving from Jesus' trials (during which he remained silent while he was mocked and beaten) to the cross and its significance. Apparently, Peter found in Isaiah 53 a commentary on Jesus' passion which he then organized in relation to the events of Jesus' suffering and death.
>
> —Joel B. Green
>
> *1 Peter*, THNTC (Grand Rapids: Eerdmans, 2007), 85.

in the sixth century before Christ). At the same time, that ancient example of the Suffering Servant is a pattern that Jesus lived out in its supreme form. He is the fullness of the Suffering Servant. But typology also insists that the meaning of the pattern is not exhausted in Jesus but provides the model for the Christian life as well. The exiled, suffering people of Israel are told that they have suffered more than they deserved (Isa. 40:1–2). Their suffering can be redemptive for the wider world, and Isaiah 53 points to this. The words apply to Jesus above all, but then they become the model for our own lives. This is the culmination of the passage in 1 Peter about how slaves are to conduct themselves, but it is the model for all Christians who find themselves suffering unjustly.

The image of God as a shepherd is a frequent one in both the Old and the New Testaments. It is interesting that though most of us live in societies in which we know the work of a shepherd only from hearsay, we have little trouble transferring this imagery to our own situations. Here the author of 1 Peter takes a word spoken to an agricultural and sheepherding culture many centuries earlier and uses it to show an urban audience in a very different locale how it applies to them. From Psalm 23 to the prophets, the image is powerful. In Isaiah 53:6 the people are described as sheep that have gone astray. That image is picked up here, but added to it is the image of God as the shepherd. The second-century theologian Irenaeus frequently used the image of God as the shepherd of the whole creation, guiding it through history

> Though his discussion was about servants, yet this passage ought not to be confined to that subject. The apostle here reminds all the godly in common what the condition of Christianity is, as though he were saying that we are called by the Lord on condition that we patiently bear wrongs, and, as he says in another place, that we are appointed to this. In case this should seem grievous to us, he consoles us with the example of Christ. Nothing seems more unworthy, and therefore less tolerable, than undeservedly to suffer, but when we turn our eyes to the Son of God, this bitterness is mitigated, for who would refuse to follow Him as He goes before us?
>
> —John Calvin
>
> *The Epistle of Paul The Apostle to the Hebrews and the First and Second Epistles of St. Peter*, trans. William B. Johnston (Grand Rapids: Eerdmans, 1963), 275.

until it reaches the goals for which God created it. Here the work of Christ is to seek out and bring back to the fold those sheep who have gone astray. Though they are mostly Gentiles, they still belong to God's fold, since God is their creator. Christ is the Good Shepherd, and although the Isaiah 53 passage mentions only the sheep and not the shepherd, the addition here makes quite clear that Jesus is the one who brings back the wandering sheep. The Gospel of John uses this image also, but there it is based more on Ezekiel 34 than on Isaiah 53. In both cases, God, in the person of the incarnate Son, is seen as the true shepherd. In John 10:16 Jesus said that he had other sheep, not of this fold. If that meant other than the fold of Israel, then his work was to gather the sheep even among the Gentiles.

God is not only the shepherd. God is also "the guardian of our souls." Souls are not to be taken as something spiritual in contrast to the body. Souls are our inner reality, our minds, our identity, our egos. Our soul is the agent of sin as well as of faith. When we choose to sin, it is an act of the self. If we allow ourselves to let the desires of the body govern our actions, that too is an act of the self. If we turn to God in repentance, it is the self that does this. God is our creator, but God also guides our lives and guards us against going astray. That we once were astray shows our freedom. That we have been returned to the shepherd shows God's care and love for us. God guards us, so that we will not go astray again. Part of the way God guards us is by calling us into the community of faith, where our lives can be shaped by hearing again and again the word of the gospel. This section—1 Peter 2:19–25—is used as the Epistle passage for the fourth Sunday of Easter in Year A of the lectionary. Those who have new life because of the Suffering Servant are called to live as such servants themselves. Our suffering can be redemptive.

3:1–7

A Word to Wives and Husbands

The next group to receive instruction is wives. As we saw earlier, these passages have been used to keep wives in subjection, even as the earlier part of the passage was used to prevent the liberation of slaves. Though wives might have had far more comfortable lives than slaves, they often had similarly limited freedom of decision about their lives, even to the point of not being able to decide if a child born to them would live as part of the family or be put out in a public place to die or for someone else to pick up for whatever purpose. There were many wives who became Christians whose husbands did not. The church had less appeal to a husband, who might have to change his life and lose his freedom to have concubines, or who might have to change the way he treated his wife and his slaves. That the author spends far more time addressing wives in the congregation than husbands probably means there were far fewer husbands expected to be present, in the same way that nothing was said earlier to masters because there were probably few of them in the congregation.

As in the case of slaves, the advice to wives also may appear very conservative to us. The directions are clearly to women whose husbands are not Christians. These women will have some of the same difficulties faced by slaves: How can they arrange to meet with the church daily? How can they be excused from offering sacrifices to the household and city gods? The word to these wives is to try to show their husbands that by being Christians they have become better wives, more loving, less demanding for expensive clothing and jewelry. This involves obedience to the authority of their husbands—which was demanded by the culture—but with a willing spirit that would make them even more attractive to their husbands. The example of Sarah is used, since she accepted the authority of Abraham.

Passages such as this and the similar ones in Colossians and Ephesians need to be handled with care. Though there are no slaves in our culture today, there are of course wives, and it is possible to interpret these words in such a way that a wife must be obedient to her husband even in cases of abuse. We need to recognize that society has changed drastically since the first century, due in good measure to the power of the gospel. Our society does not require a woman to stay in a marriage that is abusive, nor is she under the authority of her husband in the way that was typical in other periods or in other parts of the world today that have not been influenced by the gospel over the centuries. In the nineteenth century when missionary couples were sent into parts of the world that had not been influenced by the gospel, it was assumed that the couple would be a witness to the true meaning of marriage, often at great odds with the understanding of marriage in the surrounding culture. Marriage in our culture today assumes mutual responsibility and mutual love. Rather than a corporation headed by the husband as CEO, marriage is understood as a cooperative, where husband and wife make decisions jointly, with mutual respect. A wife today is not necessarily economically dependent on her husband, nor does he have an automatic right to the children if there is a separation. The attempt by some Christians to enforce these ancient cultural forms in today's world is foreign to the gospel and is an attempt to undo the work of the Holy Spirit altering the world around us. It would make as much sense as trying to reinstate slavery because it is found in Scripture, without acknowledging the centuries of work of the Holy Spirit within and outside the church to eliminate slavery from God's creation.

At the same time, there is some good advice in this passage. The character of the Christian life, for men as well as for women, is one of simplicity, not showy ostentation; of modesty in dress and behavior. This may be difficult in a consumer-oriented society that prides itself on keeping up with the Joneses, or surpassing them. Cultural characteristics change and need to be kept in mind. For instance,

---

The critical evaluation of the household code trajectory and its scholarly interpretations has found that its patriarchal ethics was asserted in contrast to an "egalitarian" Christian ethos. Biblical and moral theologians have labeled this ethos as unrealistic enthusiasm, gnostic spiritualism, ascetic emigration, or antinomian behavior that did not take seriously the given patriarchal structures of the everyday life and the world. Early Christian women and slaves who took the gospel of freedom seriously are thereby disqualified and their experience of faith and praxis are rendered rationally or theologically suspect. This preference for the historical feasibility and theological orthodoxy of the biblical pattern of patriarchal submission in contrast to the "unworldliness" or "heresy" of the egalitarian ethos implies a historical-theological evaluation that is not derived from the New Testament itself.

—Elisabeth Schüssler Fiorenza

Bread Not Stone: The Challenge of Feminist Biblical Interpretation (Boston: Beacon, 1984), 87–88.

braided hair on a woman in that society was a sign of immodesty, whereas for us an older woman with braided hair is probably considered quite conservative. We are not to follow the exact descriptions here in regard to hairstyles, but in whatever culture, be modest in appearance, not drawing attention or being provocative.

There are far fewer directives aimed at husbands, probably because there were few of them in the church. It also appears from verse 7 that most of the husbands present were married to Christian women. Perhaps the behavior of their wives influenced them to become Christians. There is a mention of women as "the weaker sex." This may mean simply that physically and socially they were not as powerful as their husbands, or it may be a reference to the story of the fall, where Eve is the first deceived and therefore was considered more easily seduced by evil. We see elements of that interpretation in 1 Timothy 2:13–14, and it seems to have been fairly common in the early church. (John Milton also interprets the fall story in the same way in *Paradise Lost*.)

Husbands are to honor their wives. The idea is revolutionary that whatever their social relation as superior and inferior, they are joint heirs of salvation. In the gospel, and therefore in the church, husbands and wives have an equality as sons and daughters of God, as brothers and sisters of Jesus Christ, as equal heirs of the kingdom. The progress that women have achieved in the wider society over the centuries owes a great deal to this understanding of men and women as joint heirs. Where the church has been an influential part of society, the laws regarding marriage have gradually changed to show this equality. We may view the church as sometimes lagging in regard to liberal influences in society, but we need also to see that in many ways it has been on the cutting edge of changes. Where there is a strong sense of the church living now by the mores of the new creation, the church is a strong beacon in society to move forward toward the equality of all people, regardless of social condition. When the church loses its sense of the new creation, expecting it only after death, the church is more liable to settle down comfortably in the values of the present society, as happened in the fourth century. If culture holds women to be inferior to men, wives are not

likely to be thought of as equal to their husbands. Where there is
equality in the wider society, that equality will probably be there
within marriage as well. In the case of the early church, couples had
the difficult task of holding to equality within the marriage while living, outside the congregation, in a world that held a very different
view of the matter.

Karl Barth, whose *Church Dogmatics* dominated Protestant theology in much of the twentieth century, was the rare theologian who
really dealt theologically with the issue of the relation of man and
woman, and whose perspective was totally integrated into the rest
of his theology. We may not agree with all that Barth did with the
issue, but his theology takes gender seriously, unlike theologies that
deal with "the human" as though we were all alike. For Barth, that
God created humanity as male and female means that humanity is
always related humanity, always in community. The genders also
are a sign of a humanity in which there are differences that remain
generation after generation. For Barth, the man is the initiator and
woman the responder in order to create community. This parallels
the relationship of God and humanity, in which it is God who ini-
tiates and the human who responds. Barth's Christology stands at
the center of this model. Jesus, as fully human, is the model of the
human response to God's initiative, and therefore the model of the
female. Jesus, as fully God, is the model of the initiator, and there-

---

**Schleiermacher preached a sermon on Christian marriage in 1818. He was far
ahead of his time on the issue of the role of women, although still holding
many of the attitudes of his time:**

> We know that as our Rescuer, Christ redeemed us specifically from bondage,
> for it is to the freedom of the children of God that we are redeemed (Gal.
> 5:1). A husband should take this liberating love as his example; he should be
> the head of his wife in such a way that he liberates her more and more, both
> inwardly and outwardly, from every servitude to which this sex so easily gives
> in, and removes all restrictions from her, so that the power of the common life
> can rule in her unhindered. Then the inequality will be resolved into equality
> in this respect as well.

—**Friedrich Schleiermacher**

Servant of the Word: Selected Sermons of Friedrich Schleiermacher, trans. Dawn De Vries (Philadelphia:
Fortress, 1987), 193.

fore the model of the male.[3] (This parallels the biblical imagery of the church as the bride of Christ in Eph. 5, in which both male and female in the congregation are part of the bride.) Both male and female are fully human, but they are created to be together. The man is not fully a man unless he is in community, nor is the woman. This does not mean that everyone should be married, but it does point to the need for both men and women to be full sharers in all human communities. There are some problems with Barth's approach, but it is refreshing to have genders recognized theologically.

There is an unusual rationale here in verse 7 for husbands honoring their wives: if they do not, their prayers may be hindered! Why? Does this refer to both of them praying together? Does this mean an unhappy wife might interrupt his prayers? (There is a story about John Wesley's wife throwing a cat at him while he was praying, and there are indications that Wesley's own view of marriage was not very egalitarian!) Prayers are to be offered as heirs of this new life, as those living in the new creation. If the husband does not treat his wife in that fashion, then his prayers are being offered as one who is still in the old world, and his access to God is thus limited. He is not approaching God as a child, but as one still estranged from God in the old creation. That estrangement from God is a hindrance to the life of prayer.

It is taken for granted that Christian husbands should not abuse their wives; nor should Christian wives tolerate such abuse, and the church should make clear that abusive behavior is not tolerated. The church could do little about the Christian wife of an abusive non-Christian husband. It is clear that even today the church closes its eyes to abuse that may be going on within the families of the church. In some ways, the effect of the gospel on the wider society—passing laws that criminalize abuse—has sometimes been greater than within the church, where abuse is often ignored. The church needs to be proactive in regard to the abuse of wives, of children, and increasingly of the elderly.

The church needs to help families stay together, to avoid divorce

---

3. Karl Barth, *Church Dogmatics*, III/1, *Doctrine of Creation*, trans. J. W. Edwards, O. Bussey, and Harold Knight (Edinburgh: T. & T. Clark, 1958), 288–329.

with all of the consequences the ending of a marriage has, especially
on children. But these efforts cannot be at the expense of women
who are abused within that marriage. That too has lasting consequences on children, teaching them that abuse is an acceptable and
normal way of life. The church's task is to develop and support good
marriages. This can involve the support of an abused woman whose
husband refuses or is unable to change, as well as trying to prevent
such abuse from happening in the first place.

3:8-9

A Word to All

This passage culminates in words to the whole church: slaves, wives,
husbands, and others. The author has spoken of their lives outside
the church and now returns to the kind of life they are to lead within
the community of faith. Regardless of their social status, all are to
be united in sympathy, love, and humility. The previous directions
were largely about the relationship of Christians to those outside the
church—Christian slaves to non-Christian masters, Christian wives
to nonbelieving husbands. These closing words are about relationships within the congregation. How difficult would it be for a church
in the midst of a highly stratified culture to ignore all those social
expectations during the time they gather together? Could the high-
born person relate to a slave as an equal? Could the slave believe a
wealthy fellow Christian was really a brother or sister? Could men
and women believe they were equals in the Lord? Once they left the
church meeting, all of those social distinctions would still be there,
and believers would be forced to readjust their behavior. Yet this
experience of a new society in which all are equally children of God's
household was clearly the goal of the gospel.

It is even more difficult when the church has as members people
from ethnic groups that have been enemies for generations. Always
there is the remembrance of the evil deeds done by the other group.
Even if the enmity began centuries ago, the bitterness can still be
there. Think of the "ethnic cleansing" that occurred in the former
Yugoslavia once the dictatorship ended that had held the groups

together forcibly. The rationale for the enmity on all sides seemed to go back generations, even though neighbors had lived next door to one another in a peaceful manner until the old enmities were fanned into flames. Perhaps the churches that received this letter did have such possible ethnic enmity in their membership. The words here are clear: "Do not repay evil with evil or abuse for abuse." Instead they are to return blessings for abuse, and this is the life to which they are called. Again, this does not mean they are to tolerate abuse.

For the early church there was only one church in a community, and those who were Christians were part of that one church. In later centuries, especially after the Protestant Reformation, that there were many different churches—denominations—meant that it was possible to continue social distinctions within the Christian community. For instance, in India the "untouchables" could be in one denomination and the higher castes in another. Or in Yugoslavia, Croatians were Roman Catholic and Serbians were Orthodox. In such situations, one of the greatest witnesses of the gospel is compromised because the divisions of society are continued within the church. Churches in the United States are generally divided into denominations by race, by economic status, by national origin.

Friedrich Schleiermacher, the great Reformed theologian of the nineteenth century, dealt with this issue in a very clear way. He understood that hatred and enmity pass easily from one generation to another. Abuse also passes on, not only as teaching but as stunted personalities, so the child who is abused becomes an abuser. The daughter of an abused wife chooses an abusing man as a husband. If we learn to hate our enemies, we pass that on so that the next generation learns to hate members of the group we hated. Generation after generation the negative actions and attitudes persist, and appear to be perfectly reasonable responses to the situation in which we find ourselves. But if someone in that chain does not return evil for evil or abuse for abuse, but instead offers a blessing, the chain is broken. A new chain of positive actions and attitudes is begun. The person who blesses has taken the abuse and ended it. Such a person has, by the act of blessing, forgiven the abuser. This is the power of nonviolent confrontation. This is what Christians are called to do: to return blessing for evil, and thereby change the future by forgiving the past.

The future will no longer be determined by the evil actions committed for generations, but will be open to new possibilities. Indeed, when Christians do return blessing for abuse they overcome those broken generations that occurred up to that point. The old evil no longer has the power to continue.[4]

Each one of us stands at the nexus of the effects of sin going back centuries. Yet there is a possibility, by the grace of God, to redeem that past. By blessing the one out of that unhappy past who treats us negatively, we open the way for a new and blessed future for both the abuser and the abused. Blessing or cursing are the choice we each make in our response to countless hurts, small and large, that we face every day. Blessing may not be a human possibility, but, as part of the new creation, the grace is there to begin practicing a life of blessing.

Such blessing does not mean being a doormat, allowing others to walk all over us. Nor is it to be confused with a martyr complex that looks for such suffering and yet does not truly bless in response. Part of the blessing is the clear message that those who abuse or are hateful are wrong and they have the opportunity to change their lives. This is a costly forgiveness, and it is not always accepted readily. But when forgiveness is given and received, it alters the future and ends the terrible consequences of a warped past.

3:10–12

The Doorway to Prayer

This section closes with a quotation from Psalm 34:12–16. The translation found here differs slightly from the NRSV version of Psalm 34. Most notably, the word translated as "cry" in verse 15 of the psalm was translated as "prayer" in the version used by the author of the letter. The behavior praised in the psalm is the same that this passage in 1 Peter calls for, showing that the goal of the law and that of the gospel are the same. The good life for the individual and the good life for the world itself are possible only when people

---

4. Friedrich Schleiermacher, *The Christian Faith*, ed. H. R. Mackintosh and J. S. Stewart (Edinburgh: T. & T. Clark, 1928), 452–66.

do not speak evil of others and do not do hateful actions against others. We are to seek peace, to do what is good, and relate to others in a way that blesses them. If we live this kind of life, even as slaves or wives, then we are among the righteous to whom God listens when they pray. Those who continue to spread hate and abuse are cut off from God's hearing. This is similar to the advice given to husbands a few verses earlier, that if they did not treat their wives as joint heirs of salvation, their prayers would be hampered.

We have the same understanding in the Lord's Prayer: if we wish God to hear our plea for forgiveness, we must also forgive those who injure us. It also means that Christians, who do have the ear of God, are called upon to pray for those who, because they are estranged from God, are not able to pray.

We might assume that there is a difference between the behavior expected in the Old Testament and that of the New in regard to the forgiveness of enemies. We often think that only in the New Testament is there such forgiveness, whereas the Old Testament assumes "an eye for an eye." Yet the argument of 1 Peter puts such a contrast in a different light. The use of Isaiah, culminating in the Suffering Servant passages, especially Isaiah 53, points to the interpretation of suffering as redemptive for enemies. Beginning in Isaiah 40, the Israelites in exile are told that they have suffered more than they deserved. In fact, they have "received from the LORD's hand double for all [Israel's] sins" (Isa. 40:2b). By chapter 53, the argument is clear: Israel's unjust suffering is for the purpose of redeeming the nations that once despised Israel. These nations respond in great surprise, that Israel "was wounded for our transgressions" (Isa. 53:5), and "the righteous one, my servant, shall make many righteous, and he shall bear their iniquities" (Isa. 53:11b). In the case of the suffering of the exile, Israel, the servant of God, paid this price, although not directly willing to do so. The model, however, was there. In the case of Jesus, he willingly took on the sin of all humanity; and by his suffering forgiveness has come for all who accept it. Their sinful pasts are erased and their future is now a future that could not have been the outcome of their own lives. What 1 Peter points out is that when we live this form of life, taking on the sin of others by forgiving

them, we live out the model that was given Israel and willingly fulfilled by Jesus. We make real and possible to others the new life we
have found in him.

It would be an interesting exercise for a pastor or a congregation
to try to update this passage. If we analyze our own work situations,
families, or neighborhoods, what does this passage in 1 Peter help
us to see as our responsibilities in our own day? What should be
our responses when we are dealing with other Christians in these
relationships and when we are dealing with persons who are of other
faiths or totally secular? What is our witness to the new creation of
which we have a foretaste? Though our social situation is quite different from that of 1 Peter, this is still the Word of God for us just as
it was for those ancient Christians.

3:13–17

Why Do Christians Suffer?

These five verses weave together an understanding of why Christians suffer, their attitude and behavior in the midst of possible suffering, and the method of evangelism that stems from such behavior. The previous section called them to follow in the steps of the Suffering Servant, and now the writer spells out what this means for the Christians who received this letter. We need to remember that, though still a very small group when this letter was written, the church was growing rapidly. The church had no committees or programs of evangelization; and yet it grew. What was the reason for its growth, when it would appear more sensible for people to stay away from a group that the government viewed with enough suspicion that its members were haled before the courts and even killed? The connection between persecution and church growth is laid out here.

3:13–15a
When Christians Suffer for Doing What Is Right

The first verse is a rhetorical question: "Now who will harm you if you are eager to do what is good?" In a perfect world, the answer would be no one. However, as the rest of the section makes clear, and as we know from our own experience, we do not live in a perfect world. Those who seek to do what is good are often harmed by those whose interests lie in doing what is evil. The person who cuts corners in business does not wish to be shown up by someone who is more careful to do what is right. Greed often dominates life in a fallen world, and those who give generously without hope of return may find themselves without the friendship of those who see no reason to give when there is nothing to be gained. From minor name-calling—"goody two shoes"—to real violence, those who live their lives by skirting the law or breaking it, or who obey unjust human laws, have little tolerance for those who seek to live justly both by human laws and by God's law.

If many in the original audience were wives and slaves, the answer would have been even clearer. If the husband or master lived with the mores of a fallen society, then the good example of the Christian wife or slave was also a rebuke to the husband or master's lifestyle, no matter how silently such a witness was given. That may have been an intolerable affront. The hope, as we saw in 3:1–2, was that Christians' good behavior would make them even more acceptable to non-Christians who controlled their lives. But that would not always be the case. Instead, such behavior might anger the master or husband. Think of the story at the beginning of the book of Esther. The first wife, Vashti, was appropriately modest in her behavior, and the king wanted her to be immodest in the presence of his male guests. When she refused, he removed her from being queen, and replaced her with Esther (Esth. 1:10–20). Today, just as truly as in ancient times, modesty in dress and behavior does not help a woman whose husband wishes to show off her beauty to other men, and thus requires her to dress in an extravagant and revealing manner. Slaves were in an equally difficult position if required to do that which was against a Christian conscience. In both cases, however, the letter urges that they choose their battles carefully.

There are counterparts to such conflicts in almost every work setting today, although employers do not have such total power over employees as ancient slave masters had over their slaves. In a poor economy when jobs are scarce, however, there can be enormous pressure to conform to patterns in the work place that are in conflict with God's requirement of love and justice. The choices are not always easy, and there can be enormous consequences for the family dependent on the income of the person employed. The text recognizes that such battles will be there, and Christians may well have to suffer when they do what is right.

The first advice here is, "Do not fear what they fear." These were the same words God spoke to the prophet Isaiah (Isa. 8:12), and it is good advice to God's faithful in every generation. We all face situations that make us afraid. That is part of human life. Most of us are afraid of being held up to ridicule, or of being physically harmed. That is natural. The bullies of the world, whether in the school yard or the office, know this. The Christian, however, is not to be afraid of such things. Be afraid only of abandoning the Lord, who has given you a new life. How difficult that is, however. In 2:17, as shown above, Christians were called to fear God only, and God was loving as well as to be feared because God is our creator and savior. This fear is not the same as fear of some earthly bully.

The next word is, "do not be intimidated." These two pieces of advice are directly related to each other. The master or husband of the ancient world or the bully or employer in our own day knows what frightens people: pain, even to the point of death, being held up to ridicule and shame. But if the Christian does not fear what others fear, then the threats have lost their power to intimidate. This cannot, however, be a false bravado; it must be real faith on the part of the Christian. It must be true that one's greatest fear is turning away from Christ, abandoning the new life one has experienced and thereby returning to the old life that is now unsatisfying. If Queen Vashti's greatest fear had been the loss of her throne, then surely she would not have risked it. Esther herself would face the same dilemma later: whether to fear the king's wrath more than harm to her people—the fear of losing the opportunity God had given her to save them.

If we learn to change what we fear we have taken a great step toward faithfulness. If we are not afraid of public ridicule, then it is easier to do what is right when the social expectation is to do otherwise. For these early Christians, faith was based on the experienced new life and being part of a new community that lived by very different values than those of Roman society. Slaves and slave owners were equally valued in this new community. Women and men were also considered joint heirs in this new world. Greeks and barbarians, Jews and Gentiles, all were part of one community that, ideally, erased all the barriers that Roman culture erected between such groups. We can see from Paul's letters to the Corinthians that the ideal was not always met. Yet, for many, this experience was such a reality, so much better than the life they had lived in the midst of the old world, that they did not wish to abandon such a life. They feared losing that new life more than they feared the threats or ridicule they received from their masters. They believed that the new life already tasted in the church was the beginning, the down payment, of an eternal life they did not want to forfeit. It was not simply a promise of future happiness and joy, but an experienced reality of joy in a life now lived in the risen Christ and therefore a life guaranteed to go on even after death.

The nineteenth-century theologian Friedrich Schleiermacher described the old life, the life lived according to the values of a fallen world, as one in which our chief goals are seeking pleasure and avoiding pain. This is the nature of human life from infancy onward. What we fear is the threat of pain and the loss of pleasure, probably in that order. We know how difficult it is to teach children the value of delayed gratification, of losing immediate pleasure for the sake of greater pleasure later. It is equally difficult for adults not to seek to avoid pain at almost all costs, hiding that which would cause shame or punishment. In both cases, the motto of seek pleasure and avoid pain holds true.[1]

The Christian life shows a great change in values: now the greatest fear is not living according to the will of God. This is not a matter of delayed gratification. Even though such a life may decrease worldly pleasure and lead to pain, it provides a joy that surpasses such losses, and that joy has already been experienced within the community of faith. That joy is therefore not to be doubted. It is not only a promise. It is a promise already being fulfilled. Christ himself, facing the cross, is the great example of this. He endured the cross with all its pain because it was the will of God, and because of the joy that he knew this pain would bring. In the words of Hebrews: "Let us run with perseverance the race that is set before us, looking to Jesus the pioneer and perfecter of our faith, who for the sake of the joy

---

1. Friedrich Schleiermacher, *The Christian Faith*, ed. H. R. Mackintosh and J. S. Stewart (Edinburgh: T. & T. Clark, 1928), 18–26.

that was set before him endured the cross, disregarding its shame" (Heb. 12:1b–2a). Disregarding shame is what 1 Peter urges in saying Christians should not be intimidated or fear what others fear. Believers can do this because of the joy that is set before them. This change in values, in what we fear and what we desire, is exactly what this epistle is urging. At least, it is calling those who have already tasted this new life to remember that joy and hold it as their highest value. They are to remember this new life precisely at the moment that the world around them is threatening their lives.

Those who seek to control others by threats of pain or withdrawal of pleasure—and this is a frequent form of control—are at a loss when their threats do not bring the desired behavior. This can be very bad, when the usual threats of fines or prison fail to deter criminals. The drunk driver may be so entrenched in alcoholism that no threats that the state issues will change that behavior. However, the person who seeks to improve a community by ending water pollution that a company is causing may put the welfare of the town above the fear of retribution by the company. The person who seeks to do God's will, acting according to that imperative, may confuse those who seek to prevent such behavior when they discover that their threats are useless. The Roman Empire found that its threats against Christians often led to martyrdom of the Christians, and the witness that these Christians gave with their lives made many of the observers wish that they had the same fearlessness and joy that the martyrs demonstrated. Some of those observers sought out Christians to discover what was the secret of their strange strength and joy that made them unafraid of public humiliation and death.

Discipleship means allegiance to the suffering Christ, and it is therefore not surprising that Christians should be called upon to suffer. In fact, it is a joy and a privilege, and a token of His grace. The acts of the early Christian martyrs are full of evidence which shows how Christ glorifies His own in the hour of their mortal agony by granting them the unspeakable assurance of His presence. In the hour of the cruellest torture they bear for His sake, they are made partakers in the perfect joy and bliss of fellowship with him. To bear the cross proves to be the only way of triumphing over suffering.

—Dietrich Bonhoeffer

The Cost of Discipleship, trans. R. H. Fuller (New York: Macmillan, 1955), 75.

Nor was the Christian witness of fearlessness made only in the face of human threats. In times of plague, when all around them families were abandoning their sick, running away from the area, leaving their dead unburied, Christians responded in a very different fashion. Not only did they care for their own sick and bury their own dead; they also cared for those not of their faith who had been abandoned. They buried the dead for whom they had no responsibility. They were unafraid of the disease, unintimidated by the plague, and they continued to show mercy to its victims. This also impressed their neighbors. It even impressed a young Constantine, and when he became emperor and ended the persecution of Christians, he made the church tax-exempt, thinking this would make it possible for the church to be of even greater help in meeting the needs of the society.

John Calvin had the same emphasis on the reordered values of a Christian, but phrased it in a different way. For him, sinful human beings place at the center of their actions what will bring them glory, or at least, will benefit them in a way the world understands. However, that is in itself a warped form of human life. We were created to give God glory, to seek what God wishes, and not our own desires. When, through faith, we are transformed, we actually do seek what glorifies God and not ourselves, and in so doing, we become the creatures we were always intended to be. We become truly human beings. As a result, God glorifies us and brings us into God's own presence. The Reformed tradition, stemming from Calvin, has as a trademark the stress on glorifying God as the chief goal of human life.

In our society, where the church has been so much a part of the culture and most people in the church have been there since birth, there may be little awareness of a great newness of life that Christ has given us. Indeed, that is more likely the experience of those who

---

This central affirmation of what it means to be human is placed as the first question of the Westminster Shorter Catechism, though it uses archaic language:

What is the chief end of man? Man's chief end is to glorify God and to enjoy him forever.
—Presbyterian Church (U.S.A.)

Book of Confessions: Study Edition (Louisville: Geneva Press, 1999), 229.

once totally ignored the church and lived a life that was far outside the bounds of Christian values. Their life in the church began with a strong conversion experience, and that new life is something so surprising, so transforming, that these people can readily see the difference between the old life and the new. New converts cling to the community of faith and are eager to spend time within it since it reinforces the faith that has begun. This may seem strange to those who have been part of the church all of their lives, and see nothing revolutionary in their own lives.

One of the greatest challenges to the historic churches today in our society is to help longtime Christians understand and experience that newness of life when there has been no overwhelming conversion experience, and an hour a week is grudgingly given to the church. Often the church seems more in need of their help than they are of the church's. In our setting, the goal of preaching needs to be the gradual and constant conversion of Christians, making clear that even in a country long considered part of Christendom, it is still possible to enter into a profoundly new life. In many ways, it is easier to be an experiential Christian in a non-Christian area of the world than in one where the church has been a powerful part of society for generations.

How can the preacher do this? First, the preacher needs to help the congregation see that what passes for the Christian life may often be simply living by society's standards, which in many cases are a very watered-down version of true Christian life. We need to ask: What are the parallels today of that early church's experience? What are the divisions, the barriers to community that our society erects? Part of the problem we have is the divisions in the church itself. The most radical barriers between people in our culture are often still there on Sunday morning. Our congregations are usually limited to people of a narrow band of income, poor people in one denomination, well-to-do in another. We are often divided by race and culture as well. So our congregations do not give us the experience of the radical difference between the community within the church and that in the wider society.

In much of the history of the church, this was not the case. There was only one congregation in an area, and all of the Christian people were part of it. That is a true "parish" system: a church for all those in a particular geographical area. The parish system is clearest when there is a state church with a monopoly on Christian congregations. That system has some values, but it also has many drawbacks, not the least of which is the idea of an exclusive state church. In a country, however, with a plethora of denominations, we are readily divided by income, education, and culture. This means that a true experience of community that overcomes the divisions in the wider society will have to be interdenominational or at least consciously attempted. Preaching can articulate the problem and lead the congregation to find solutions in its own life.

Second, many congregations have never had to educate those who wish to join the church in the difference between the Christian life and the life of a good citizen in the world around them. In our more secularized world, congregations may need to reinvent a form of the ancient catechumenate (see pp. 21–25, "Further Reflections: The Catechumenate"). How would this congregation prepare some of its members to be sponsors for new members? How would they plan such a program? Can they articulate what the Christian life is? Preparing a congregation to accept new adult members who have had little or no training in what the church believes and teaches can lead to renewal within the congregation itself.

The end of the sentence that began in verse 14 points to the way in which Christians can learn not to fear what others fear or be intimidated by threats that could be expected to intimidate: they are to sanctify Christ as Lord in their hearts. "In your hearts" means at the center of their lives, not merely acknowledging him with their lips. Holding Christ as the Lord of our lives is not just a matter of repeating the Apostles' Creed; it is a matter of the heart, of living our lives on the basis that Christ is indeed Lord. If Christ is our Lord, then our obedience is to him above all. If the state or the employer is the lord of our lives, or if our goal of the good life based on a good salary is the lord of our lives, then we are much more in danger of being afraid of anything that would challenge those lords. We cannot be unafraid or unintimidated if Christ is not truly, in our hearts, the Lord.

3:15b–17

The Witness of Suffering Christians

If what Christians fear is very different from the things that others fear, surely their peculiar behavior—not being afraid of threats of physical violence or shame—will make onlookers wonder about their faith. They may well be asked why they are not afraid, or why they are not intimidated by threats. When questions come, Christians are to explain what Christ has done for them, and why they are more afraid of losing the joy and new life they have found in the church than they are afraid of the threats. This is the witness they are to give when the occasion arises. Their witness is to be given in a gentle and polite fashion, letting others in on the secret of their actions.

Often, in our own time, a Christian witness begins by trying to make others afraid—afraid of hell, of punishment, of judgment. However, such an approach is based on the same fear of physical harm or shame, now from God rather than from earthly masters, that early Christians did not employ. It is not an appropriate witness. The hope we have in Christ is not an avoidance of pain and an increase in pleasure but rather a new life, with joy and love at the center, a life whose beginning has been experienced here and now. An old hymn says:

> My God, I love Thee; not because I hope for heaven thereby,
> Nor yet because who love Thee not Must die eternally.[2]

It then goes on to give the true reason for loving God: because God first loved us. The church destroys its own witness if it uses the same means of fear and intimidation in order to convert people that the world uses in order to prevent such conversion. The ends do not justify the means. This passage in 1 Peter makes clear that the Christian witness is to be given "with gentleness and reverence."

Nor can we try to convert others by promising them all sorts of happiness, which again is an appeal to the pleasure principle that is typical of fallen human life. John Calvin wrote a reply to Cardinal

---

2. Trans. by Edward Caswall from a Spanish sonnet attributed to Francis Xavier, in *The Hymnal* (Philadelphia: Presbyterian Board of Christian Education, 1935), no. 313.

Sadolet, who had written to the citizens of Geneva urging them to return to the Catholic Church on the grounds that it was more likely to guarantee their salvation because it had been here longer than the new Protestant churches. In his reply Calvin stated that any religion whose main concern is our own salvation is by definition selfish and unworthy of the name of Christian. The function of religion is to let us know what God wishes us to do and for us to do it.[3] There is an old story about a Scottish seminarian who was being questioned by the presbytery. He was asked: "Would you be willing to be damned for the glory of God?" It is reported that the student replied that he was quite willing to have the entire presbytery damned for God's glory! Both the question and answer are a rather extreme way of stating the case, but in a culture where even salvation is urged on the basis of the pleasure it can give us now or later and the pain it can help us avoid, the story has a point.

In our own day some Christian preachers stress the increase in worldly pleasure and the avoidance of physical pain that faith can give. Various forms of a prosperity gospel or a gospel of success do this, and some forms of faith healing have the same basis. But whether we think of Paul's "thorn in the flesh" (2 Cor. 12:7–9) or the martyrdom of early Christians, it is clear that the biblical witness does not guarantee success in the world's terms or the lack of physical suffering.

The witness Christians give to the world is positive and gentle, and respects the other person. The gospel is good news, not a severe word that punishment awaits unless the other person believes what we say. The times may have changed from the first century, but the word about how we are to share the gospel with others remains the same. Scaring people into believing is using the methods of the fallen world, little different from the husband or master threatening abuse if the wife or slave is not obedient. The Inquisition of the Middle Ages supported torture on the grounds that such methods could bring about conversion and therefore the salvation of the victim. Offering converts an increase in pleasure or a decrease in pain in

---

3. John Calvin, "Reply to Sadolet," in *Calvin: Theological Treatises*, trans. J. K. S. Reid, LCC 22 (Philadelphia: Westminster Press, 1954), 228.

the world's terms is outside the bounds of legitimate mission. What faith can offer is a joy and happiness that sounds like foolishness in the world's terms (1 Cor. 1:23–24). To keep a clear conscience Christians are not to use the same methods for the gospel that others are using against them. Their good behavior, along with their clear testimony about the work of Christ in their lives, can put to shame those who are persecuting them.

Finally, those who have power over the lives of Christians may not wonder about their strange behavior and ask about it. Even if a Christian witness is given, the persecutors may not be moved by it. In spite of their excellent behavior, Christians may still suffer. They will have a clear conscience because they are suffering for doing good rather than being punished for doing evil. In their own eyes and in the eyes of God they are doing what is right. In the eyes of society, however, they may well be considered evildoers, since they are breaking the laws or the mores of the society.

It would appear that suffering for doing what is right is a thoroughly unjust thing. By the standards of the world, however, those who are living this new life are likely to be trampling on age-old customs and laws that are the hallmark of a fallen creation. Jesus is the highest example of one who was totally innocent, who did what was right, and yet suffered even to the point of death. He was tried and found guilty by Roman law. He has given us the model to follow. His suffering was redemptive and brought to Christians the new life they now enjoy. His suffering was the once and for all suffering that made salvation possible.

Human laws are not always just. Think of the laws of segregation or apartheid. The laws were enacted legitimately. They had been obeyed for generations, and at least on the part of the group that held power they were probably seen as good laws, necessary for the preservation of the society. Those who did not have power and were humiliated by these laws saw them differently. But to change such laws often requires that the unjust character of the law be laid bare. Civil disobedience is a powerful means by which people protest an unjust law by breaking it, peacefully, and then taking the consequences for their behavior. Christians see God's law as superior to human law, and God's law is the judge of human law.

However, for those who are brought up in a sinful society—and we all are—our consciences are at least partially formed by that society, and going against its standards can lead to a sense of guilt. The church in our culture has often failed to nurture a Christian conscience, to show in what ways what society upholds legally may be at odds with God's law. Often the church seems to say that in Christ our guilt is forgiven without saying clearly that some of the things we feel guilty about we should not feel guilty about, and some of the things we do not feel guilty about, we should. Prayers of confession cannot be too specific, but if a sermon tries to spell out such differences it would be possible to follow the sermon with a prayer that does deal with specific issues about which there is a difference between the wider society and the church.

Christians in the ancient world were at risk of being persecuted for their faith. In the midst of such suffering, they gave witness to the power of that faith. The same is true of Christians in some places in our world today. Their witness often led and is still leading to the conversion of others. But that is not usually our situation. There is no overt persecution in our society, even if there is a sense that Christians may be quite foolish and outdated to hold to what they believe. Should we wish to be persecuted in order that we might make such a witness? That hardly seems appropriate. Suffering and martyrdom are not to be sought out, even though Christians should be ready for them if they do come. If, then, we have little chance of real persecution, what can our witness be? What is it that Christians do in our culture today that makes them stand out enough that others ask what is the source of their strength and joy? We go to church on Sunday. Perhaps we bow our heads and say grace before a meal in public. But that hardly would bring a bystander to ask a question. Sometimes Christians are noted more for what they do not do—do not gamble, do not drink, do not dance, do not go to movies, and so on—but bystanders are more likely to think such behavior is odd rather than desirable. Are we to think, then, that in our day, in our society, nothing marks a Christian that is in any way different from a good, upstanding citizen? Is there, for us, a peace and joy that comes through our participation in the risen Christ that others can notice? How does it manifest itself in our daily life? Is there a difference between the community that exists within the congregation of which we are a part and the secular community within which we live our daily lives? Is our relationship to neighbors who are also Christians different from our relationship with other neighbors?

All of these are questions to which the early church would have had ready answers. But we probably have a much more difficult time discovering clear distinctions. That is a major problem with which the church in our own day must deal. Precisely because few bystanders are asking questions of Christians, we have moved to other forms of evangelism, with committees and programs. Yet if there is little difference between those in the church and those outside, what are we offering, except a promise of something later?

Christians need to rediscover the understanding that we live even now in the new creation. That is not something that begins only after death. It is a reality now. In some ways we live now on the other side of death, having a foretaste of the risen life. There are accounts of people of who have been clinically dead—dying on the operating table—and yet have been brought back to life. Many report that their lives have changed dramatically. They no longer fear death. Their priorities have changed. They are more concerned with relationships than with things. This is probably the closest parallel many of us have to the experience of early Christians.

The renewal of this understanding probably needs to begin within the life of the congregation, rather than with the individual Christian's life, and worship is a significant part of this renewal. At the same time, raising some of the questions listed above for discussion in small groups such as Sunday school classes, or the governing body of the congregation, could begin a process of renewal for the whole congregation.

3:18–22

The Cosmic Significance of Christ's Work

The next few verses may seem very strange—indeed, they are some of the strangest in the New Testament. Even so, these verses find a place in the lectionary as the Epistle reading for the sixth Sunday in Easter in Year A and for the first Sunday in Lent in Year B. They contain two images, neither of which has been common in the life of the church for generations. The first is the image of Christ going to the dead after his death. The second has to do with the story of the flood, when Noah and his family were saved from death through the ark. This second image is then connected to baptism. We have already discussed typology (see pp. 17–20, "Further Reflections: Typology"), a major form of biblical interpretation in the early church. Here we are given an extended example of how this method is employed. It connects events in the past with what is happening in our own day, making us part of the ongoing history of God's activity in the world. That is, the flood occurred in the past but baptism is an event in our own lives that connects us to the meaning of that ancient happening. (We may have questions about the historicity of the flood as recorded in Genesis, but ancient writers had no such questions.)

3:18

The Power of the Death of Christ

The message of the cross is that the death of Christ, the righteous one, opened the way for us to return to God. This is the message of the atonement, central to the gospel. There is, however, no clear doctrine of the atonement here in the sense that we are told in what way his death accomplished this. What we have here is the simple fact that, however we interpret it, the death of Christ was for the purpose of bringing us to God, and that it was once and for all. In the West, for centuries, most Christians, Protestant and Catholic, have understood the atonement to mean that, because of human sin, a debt was owed to God, and that debt could be paid only by Christ. He died in our place. The death of Christ is seen in the New Testament as a sacrifice for sin, which was indeed a payment of a debt. In the time of the temple, sacrifices were offered to pay for sin. But there is also a view, held strongly by the early church, that the human problem was not a debt owed to God, but that sin had allowed Satan, the powers of evil, to have dominion over us. The powers of sin, death, and evil are all bound together, and we are under that sway. At the cross, all of these powers tried to capture Jesus and, at least on Friday and Saturday, that seemed to have happened. Death and evil had won. In the resurrection on Easter morning it became clear that Christ has triumphed over all of these powers, and now those who believe in him are able to begin to live the new life free from the bondage to sin and death.

Furthermore, whereas we are unrighteous, he was righteous. He died for the unrighteous, and only those who know themselves to be unrighteous can benefit from his death. As Jesus said, those who are healthy have no need of a physician; he came to heal sinners (Matt. 9:12). Very often the church thinks of itself as the haven of the righteous, calling them out of the sinful world. This is only partly true, however. The church is always made up of unrighteous people who have been rescued from their unrighteousness by the death of Christ, the righteous one. And even though we are part of the new life, we are still unrighteous in the sense that we still are sinners. If we forget this, and assume that we are not sinners like those outside the church, we place ourselves outside the bounds of the work of Christ. It is in that world that we are to live and make our witness.

When the church has been a significant part of society for generations, and we are born into its membership, it may be difficult for us to think of ourselves as unrighteous. Yet that is the basic step needed in order to understand the work of Christ. Redemption in Christ means forgiveness and repentance. Those who think of themselves as righteous have difficulty thinking they need either. This image of the death of Christ and its significance harks back to the words of Isaiah 53:11b: "The righteous one, my servant, shall make many righteous, and he shall bear their iniquities." His death brings us to God, but only when we know ourselves to be part of the unrighteous for whom he died.

The "once-and-for-all" time character of Christ's death is essential. At the point of the Protestant Reformation, one of the issues was the medieval stress on the Mass as an unbloody resacrifice of Christ, which to the Reformers implied that his death at Calvary was not sufficient. It was not "once and for all." Protestants emphasized that in the cross Christ had accomplished all that needed to be done to overcome the separation of sinful humanity from its creator. Jesus is not sacrificed again and again on the altar. This still remains an issue, though some Catholic interpretations now have less emphasis on this aspect of the Mass.

But Protestants have some difficulty with another aspect of the once-and-for-all character of his death. As we saw earlier in this letter, Jesus' death is the model for our own lives if we are called upon to suffer for doing what is good (2:21–25). Just as his death led to our redemption when we were unrighteous, we too must follow in his steps. Writing to the Colossians, and speaking of his own suffering, Paul said: "I am now rejoicing in my sufferings for your sake, and in my flesh I am completing what is lacking in Christ's afflictions for the sake of his body, that is, the church" (Col. 1:24). These are strange words, but the suffering of Christ somehow continues in the suffering of his church, so that our own suffering can be redemptive for others, but only because we are part of the body of Christ. His death was once and for all, but his suffering may continue in his body, though he himself has passed beyond death. Many martyrs in the early church witnessed that in their suffering they experienced the risen Christ joining them, relieving them of the burden or sharing in their sufferings. Any completion of what was lacking in Christ's death takes place in his body, the church, and not in the sacrament of the Lord's Supper. His death was at a datable moment in history, and is not repeated in any way.

His death is "in order to bring you to God." This echoes the earlier words in this letter in 2:25, when the readers are described as the sheep who have gone astray, now returned to the shepherd. Irenaeus, a second-century bishop, had a Trinitarian understanding of God as the Shepherd. He said the Son and the Spirit were the two hands of God, through which God—the Trinity—created the world. In the creation of human beings, the Son was the model. He was the first Adam and the human creation was the second Adam (Rom. 5:14). The incarnation was therefore an easy matter for the Son, since he was the model of the human. He came in order to bring us back to God, acting as a shepherd leading us to God, our true shepherd.

It was "in the flesh" that Christ suffered, but he was raised "in the spirit." This is not a denial of the bodily resurrection. Often in Scripture the term "flesh" refers to this mortal life. The resurrection is in the realm of the spirit, but, as Paul says, "This perishable body must put on imperishability, and this mortal body must put on immortality" (1 Cor. 15:53). Christ is now in the realm of the spirit, but this also means that he has helped us to be in the realm of the spirit, with the sending of the Holy Spirit, which unites believers to him, even though he is on the other side of death, and we still face physical death.

This one verse is a brief statement of almost the whole gospel. Christ suffered for us, though he was righteous, in order to bring us to God. The verse includes part of a sentence, completed in the next verse. He suffered in the flesh but was raised in the spirit. That leads to the next section, with Christ's sojourn among the spirits in prison between the cross and the resurrection.

3:19–20

Jesus Preaches to the Dead

After his death but before his resurrection Christ went to the place where the spirits were held in prison. He went there because he himself was truly dead. There he proclaimed his victory over sin and death, and from there he rose from the dead. "Spirits in prison" may seem strange to us, but as we have seen, the earliest understandings of the cross saw Jesus freeing those whom Satan had held. They were prisoners of Satan because of the fall. Human beings, living and dead, were under the power of evil because they had sinned. Christ entered the place of the dead and freed those who were held in bondage. He freed them by proclaiming the gospel in the heart of Satan's dominion.

These images of proclaiming the gospel to the dead are part of the long history of theology, even if they have not been common in more recent generations. The Apostles' Creed now used by many churches includes the phrase "he descended into hell." It was not part of the earliest form of this creed, but was added in the early Middle Ages to counteract a belief that Jesus did not truly die. All churches agree with the meaning of the phrase, though some do not use it. It is a confusing phrase because the term "hell" means for us a place of condemnation, whereas that was not the meaning of the phrase originally. Some contemporary translations of the Creed use the words "the place of the dead" in order to make this clearer. In addition, more recent theology has assumed that a person at death goes to either heaven or hell, and the concept of a place that was neither, but where the dead awaited the final judgment, does not fit.

However, if redemption depends upon the work of Christ, what happened to those who died before the incarnation? Essentially, this epistle already signaled an understanding of Christ's work helping those who had gone before when, in 1:12, even the ancient faithful

---

Though the theology of recent centuries generally held to the view of Christ's death paying a debt to God, many hymns were retained from the earlier period that stressed the cross as the victory over the powers of evil, sin, and death. Two hymns by John of Damascus in the eighth century are still in many of our hymnbooks. "Come, Ye Faithful, Raise the Strain" considers the resurrection of Christ as "bursting his prison," and leading us to freedom in the same way that God led the Hebrew people from Pharaoh's oppression to freedom through the Red Sea. In the other hymn, "The Day of Resurrection," the resurrection is called the Passover of God, in that Christ has led us from death to life, and has become the victor.

—"Come, Ye Faithful, Raise the Strain" and "The Day of Resurrection!"

In *The Presbyterian Hymnal* (Louisville: Westminster/John Knox Press, 1990), nos. 114 and 118, respectively. These hymns can also be found in many other hymnals.

are seen as waiting until redemption was completed in Christ before they could receive the fruits. Medieval paintings often depict what in Old English was termed "the harrowing of hell." The risen Christ is pictured leading a host out from hell on Easter morning. There is an echo of this understanding in Ephesians 4:7–10, where Christ led captivity captive. The captivity of death, humanity held in bondage because of sin, was ended with the resurrection, so those who are in Christ rise with him, free from the bondage sin had imposed. (There are interesting reflections of this in Matt. 27:52–53, where the tombs of the faithful dead are opened at the death of Christ, and after his resurrection they appeared to many in Jerusalem.)

What of those who live after the incarnation and yet are not believers? Does this mean that there is a second chance, a time after death when the gospel can be embraced? That is not the issue that concerns the writer of 1 Peter. Rather, he is establishing the link between the salvation of Noah and his family and our own salvation represented by baptism. Other theologians have considered the possibility that those who have not heard the gospel, or those who have heard only a false view of the gospel, may encounter the risen Christ at death, and, with the truth of Christ revealed, be able to affirm it. One of the most important contemporary theologians who considered this was the Jesuit theologian Karl Rahner. In his little book *On the Theology of Death*, he writes:

> [T]his descent of Christ into hell is not simply based on a soteriological act on behalf of the saved who lived before Christ. . . . [W]e may suppose in general that when we think of man entering the lower world we at least implicitly think of him as establishing contact with the intrinsic, radically unified, ultimate and deepest level of the reality of the world. . . . Consequently, if the reality of Christ, as consummated through his death, in his death is built into this unity of the cosmos, thus becoming a feature and intrinsic principle of it, . . . [it] means that the world as a whole and as the scene of personal human actions has become different from what it would have been had Christ not died.[1]

1. Karl Rahner, *On the Theology of Death*, trans. C. H. Henkey (New York: Herder & Herder, 1965), 64–65.

Rahner goes on to say that in his death Christ was poured out into the whole cosmos. This implies that in any person's death, there can be an encounter with Christ in this pan-cosmic sense.

It is interesting that John Wesley also believed that the death of Christ changed all humanity, although for Wesley it was a matter that his death provided all humanity with prevenient grace so they could accept the gospel.

According to the text in 1 Peter, among those who heard this message were those who had ridiculed Noah when he built the ark. At this point the image shifts to the ark, the means of saving Noah and his family when the flood destroyed everything.

3:21–22
The Ark and Baptism

The flood described in Genesis 6 to 9 was a judgment upon a sinful creation. All of creation was wiped out, except for those who were saved in the ark built by Noah. The animals and the eight humans were survivors and the seeds of a new creation. Granted, this new creation was not totally new. There were changes, however. Whereas in the first creation human beings and animals lived together without fear, and both animals and humans were vegetarians (Gen. 1:29–30), now both animals and humans will eat meat, which means there will be fear among animals and between animals and humans (Gen. 9:2–5). This new creation is one fit for sinful humanity, and it was marked by violence even at its beginning. What is begun in Christ is a truly new creation, which is peaceful and loving, but the ark remains a symbol of safety in the midst of God's judgment.

This understanding that the flood led to a different created order than had been there at the beginning is very important. Darwin's understanding that we live in a world dominated by "the survival of the fittest"—that the weak are overcome by the strong, that both animals and humans live by killing and eating each other—is a far greater problem for Christians than how many days it took to create the world. How can God call creation "good" if violence is a natural part of it? The story of the flood describes a judgment of God upon a sinful humanity that has already put violence into the world. Now, after the flood, God has let us live in a world that does include violence—a fallen creation, not only a fallen humanity. The vision of "the peaceable kingdom" at the end of history continues this theme—a redemption of both the creation and its human inhabitants. The vision of a new earth is a vision glimpsed in Isaiah 11:1–9 and 65:17–25. In turn, there are overtones of this fall of creation in Romans 8:19–25 and in Revelation 21. Ultimately, the creation will be free of violence. Lions and lambs will be able to live together without violence, as was originally intended. The resurrection of Christ is the beginning of this redemption, although until its fulfillment, we cannot leave the lions with the lambs.

The ark prefigured baptism ("prefigured" means it was a type of baptism), since it saves us through water just as the ark saved Noah and his family. Baptism implies dying to the old life and rising to the new life in Christ. For believers, baptism is like the flood that destroyed the sinful creation and at the same time lifts us out of the flood into the ark that begins a new life. Our old life is drowned in the flood. Our new life is in the ark.

Judgment is part of the meaning of baptism. To be baptized is to be judged in the sense that the old life is condemned even as the new begins. None of us totally ends the old life until we die. Even if the new life has begun and grows stronger, the old is not completely overcome. This is what Luther meant when he insisted that we are justified sinners: justified by grace but still sinners in need of forgiveness. If the Christian life develops as it should, the old life grows weaker daily and the new creation in us grows stronger. But Christians are still sinners, and our need for God's forgiveness does not end with baptism. Indeed, one might say that baptism implies a willingness to be judged, to have our lives open to the scrutiny of God through the work of the Holy Spirit, so that we can root out sin. We can be open to judgment because we know through the work of Christ that God loves us and forgives us, wants us to be perfect, and is willing to guide us in that direction.

The ark was a major icon in the early church, already appearing on a baptistry in the third century. The ark is the symbol of the church,

Martin Luther had a "Flood Prayer" in the baptismal service. In its modern form it includes these words:

> By the waters of the flood you condemned the wicked and saved those whom you had chosen, Noah and his family. You led Israel by the pillar of cloud and fire through the sea, out of slavery into the freedom of the promised land.

Lutheran Book of Worship (Minneapolis: Augsburg, 1978), 122.

the ark of salvation, into which we are rescued from the flood. The water of baptism symbolizes this, bringing us from the old life of sin into the new one of grace. Water in this instance is not bathing the body, but washing the soul, the inner person, who now, because of forgiveness, is able to stand in the presence of God with a clear conscience. All of this is based on the work of Christ—his sinless life, his sacrificial death on the cross, and the victory over sin and death that we see in the resurrection. For most Christian traditions, baptism is the sign of inclusion in the church. It is the rescue from the world that is condemned into the ark, the safe haven God has provided.

Christ's victory is sealed by his ascension to be "at the right hand of God," showing that he came from God and has returned to God now that his work is complete. This whole section has strong echoes of the early creed: Jesus "was crucified, dead, and buried. He descended into hell and rose again. He ascended into heaven and is seated at the right hand of God." He now shares in the power of the Most High, with all of creation subject to him, both in heaven and on earth. The text is clear that Christ has authority over the "angels, authorities, and powers." This victory is the counterpart of the descent into the place of the dead. If humanity was under the power of evil, traditionally understood as the power of fallen angels, Christ's resurrection shows his victory over all of these powers. Neither Christianity nor Judaism could imagine a power of evil that was independent of God. God is the creator of all things, and there is nothing that was not created by God. Everything God created was good. However, if angels that were created by God and were good turned away from God and did that which was evil, then there would be superhuman powers of evil that were originally part of God's good creation. This has been the understanding of the source of evil powers in the world for both Judaism and Christianity. Not all of the "angels, authorities, and powers" are evil, but Jesus has authority over all of them. He gained victory over the evil ones in his resurrection, and the good ones recognized his authority as the Son of God.

Another passage in this epistle refers to Christ's preaching to the dead: 4:6. The question is whether these are two different groups of the dead. In the present case, where it is specifically those who mocked Noah, there may be overtones of an understanding that was frequent in Judaism in the first century. The offspring of the mating of angels or "the sons of God" with human women are mentioned in Genesis 6:1–4. This passage, and its explication in *1 Enoch*, were commonly cited in the first century. (*First Enoch* is a Jewish writing used by many early Christian writers.) We will run into them again in 2 Peter and in Jude. These offspring were often blamed for the wickedness that led to the flood. If it is to these spirits that Jesus proclaims a message, it is not clear whether it is a redemptive word or the announcement of his victory over them. In any case, Jesus' authority over all such powers is part of his victory that ends the oppression of sin and death in the life of humanity.

Christ has won the victory. Those who are part of Christ's body, the church, also share in his victory now, in this life, in brief and hidden ways, but fully in the life to come. The goal of our salvation is to join Christ. In Hebrews 2:5–9 we are reminded that human beings were intended to stand over all creation (the passage uses Gen. 1:27–28 and Ps. 8), and yet, at the present time, we do not see that dominion. In fact, rather than having dominion over all things, human beings are now in bondage to sin and death. But Jesus, who is one of us, has attained that position. He now sits at God's right hand, and has

> Peter wishes to connect the sins of angelic beings in the ancient past, the victorious proclamation of the risen Christ, and the lives of Christian believers "now." He uses the flood as a type of God's catastrophic judgment, which happened only after God's restrained patience, and he poses the survival of Noah from that divine judgment as a type of Christian salvation, which involves the tamed waters of baptism.
>
> —Karen H. Jobes
>
> *1 Peter*, BECNT (Grand Rapids: Baker Academic, 2005), 247.

conquered all that keeps us from the role God intended for human beings in creation. He is the guarantee that we who are part of his body will also finally be what we were created to be. We have a foretaste now, so that we can be assured of that which is to come. Christians are those who by faith live now with the knowledge of a future in which God's intentions for creation will be fulfilled.

Many say that the current exploitation of the earth and its resources can be blamed on the Bible, since it says human beings are to have dominion and therefore humanity is responsible for all the destruction. But as we have seen, for the early church, human beings did not really have such dominion now because they were under the power of evil. It is that evil that has been detrimental to the earth. It is only when humanity is freed from such bondage that it will be able to exercise the dominion it is intended to have. Those who have tried to exercise responsible dominion understand that their role is to safeguard creation, not to exploit it. A better understanding of the power of evil in our world as well as the question of what is, biblically, the proper role for human beings in regard to the rest of creation, would be a great help in creating a theological view of ecology and environmental issues.

4:1–19

The Approaching Judgment

After elaborating the work of Christ, from his suffering to his victory, the author now turns to the readers, with the recognition that they need to prepare themselves for the possibility that they will have to suffer unjustly. The judgment of the whole world is at hand. Christ is their model. Their suffering can be redemptive. They too will be victorious. They are to live now so that if they are called upon to suffer they will be ready. They must die now to sin—that is what their baptism means—so that they will not be afraid of the martyrdom that may come. Their new life in Christ will flourish to the degree that they die to their old life.

[T]radition from earliest times attributed to martyrdom the same power of justification as to baptism. Martyrdom possesses this power not merely because as an act of believing love it justifies even before the reception of the sacrament like any other act of charity. . . . Martyrdom cannot be called a sacrament in the common sense of the word because it does not belong to the daily and normal order of the holy signs instituted by Christ; such a death is always something extraordinary. Another reason is that, in martyrdom, what had previously been signified and made present through the sacramental sign of baptism is here simply fulfilled, namely dying and being baptized into the death of Christ.

—Karl Rahner

On the Theology of Death, translated by C. H. Henkey and revised by W. J. O'Hara, 2nd ed. (New York: Herder & Herder, 1965), 102–3.

4:1–4

Living the New Life

Living life in the flesh in this context is similar to the words in 3:18—that Christ was put to death in the flesh—that is, in this earthly life. How are we to live this new life now? For the author of 1 Peter it means dying to our own desires and living according to the will of God. Those who no longer seek to gain pleasure and avoid pain will be able to deal with suffering when it is God's will far better than those whose lives are geared to avoiding pain. What does it mean that "whoever has suffered in the flesh has finished with sin"? The suffering here may refer to suffering endured because of the faith, or it might mean suffering more broadly. But, as we saw earlier, using the categories of Schleiermacher, if the sinful life is characterized by avoiding pain and increasing pleasure, and if because of one's faith one has endured pain, then clearly a choice has been made that there are values higher than avoiding pain, and remaining faithful to Christ is chief among them. That in itself shows that the sinful life has been left behind, and one is now living life in the spirit that is characterized by seeking the will of God rather than seeking plea-sure or avoiding personal pain. At the same time, the early church was very clear that martyrdom was never to be sought. If there were prudent steps that could be taken to avoid persecution, one was to take them. Leaving town for a while or hiding out at a neighbor's were considered prudent steps. Never was a Christian to run after the persecutors and ask to be taken to be a martyr. Only God could choose who would be a martyr, and those who offered themselves were viewed as either mentally disturbed or seeking vainglory.

Even physical pain brought on by illness or injury rather than by persecution can be endured faithfully, rather than giving in to the pain and simply being miserable. There is, therefore, truth in the words that those who suffer physically may well have begun a life that is not dominated by sin but rather by grace, the grace that causes us to seek God's will rather than our own. This does not mean that such persons are sinless, but rather that their lives are now domi-nated by grace rather than by sin. In traditional language, they are on the path of sanctification, becoming holier and therefore less sinful.

They have made a definitive turning away from the old life and they have begun a new life that is daily growing stronger.

Baptism is the sign that we have died to that old life with its values and have been raised to a new life, a foretaste of the life to come, in which doing the will of God is our chief pleasure. This is a repetition of the major themes of chapter 3.

Verse 3 is another clue that most of the members of the congregations receiving this letter were Gentiles. The Gentile lifestyle of the Greco-Roman world would, by Jewish standards, be licentious and idolatrous, that is, pleasure-seeking and pain-avoiding. Even the idols were seen as gods who could help relieve pain and make pleasure possible. The idols were not sought out in order to find out what they wanted but rather to aid in achieving the worshiper's goals. That was why the church required the period of the catechumenate (see pp. 21–25, "Further Reflections: The Catechumenate") before baptizing such Gentile converts, because these converts should not approach the true God with the same attitude that they had toward the old gods—trying to have the gods fulfill the petitioners' desires. We should approach the true God with a desire to do God's will rather than our own. These Gentile converts have been through the long process leading to baptism. Their lives have changed. However, their friends do not understand why they no longer join in their old activities.

4:5–6

More Preaching to the Dead

Their old companions' judgment will come. In 3:15 the faithful were told to be ready to give an account to the unbelievers of the hope that they, the Christians, had. Here the Gentiles will have to give an account for the sins that they have committed. The argument stresses the universality of judgment: both the living and the dead will be judged; both Christian and non-Christian will be judged. It is not stated who the divine judge will be, the risen Christ or God the Father. What is clear is that Christ proclaimed the gospel to the dead because judgment is coming. Whether these are the same ones mentioned in 3:19 we do not know, but here clearly it is all those who died before the coming of Christ. Perhaps those who mocked Noah are among them, but that is not mentioned. Everyone will be judged. Those who have died have already been judged according to what they did during their earthly lives. The question is what the work of Christ can do for those judged and found wanting. His work of redemption was carried out at a specific moment in time: the first century of the present era. Yet his redemption has cosmic significance. Surely it has a significance for those who died before his earthly life, as well as for those born long after.

These verses about preaching to the dead raise many questions but do not answer them. The author, both in the earlier chapter and here, is dealing with specific issues. Before, the author was leading into the typology of the ark. Here the issue is the approaching judgment. The writing is not dealing with issues we might have in mind, even though the comments might raise them. For instance, what happens to people who never heard the gospel, either because they lived before Christ or because they lived in areas where they did not hear it? What happens to those who rejected the gospel in this life— is there another chance after death? What if their rejection of the gospel was because it was presented to them in a poor, unchristian manner? These brief verses do not answer such questions, but they remain intriguing hints on issues that we often think about. There is some hope in the end of verse 6, that those who had been judged and condemned at the end of their earthly lives might be given the ability to live in the spirit just as God lives. We have already been told that Christ now lives in the spirit, and that is the goal God has for everyone. The former companions of these converts have been judged on the basis of their earthly life, but there is hope that they will be able to live a new life, just as these Gentile converts have begun to do.

In the history of the church, one name stands out for championing the idea that everyone will be saved, even Satan, who was understood to be a fallen angel. That name is Origen, a theologian at the end of the second century and the beginning of the third. He was faithful in his witness, and was arrested and tortured for his faith during a persecution. He later died because of this ill-treatment.

However, valuable as many of his writings are, he was condemned for this opinion, and ever since it has been voiced cautiously as a remote possibility, but never to be taught. Karl Barth spoke of "universal election in Christ," but also warned that such a doctrine could never be stated absolutely. The Scripture itself has many words about eternal damnation of some, but also a few words that point in a different direction, most particularly Romans 5:18: "Therefore just as one man's trespass led to condemnation for all, so one man's act of righteousness leads to justification and life for all." Judgment must be taken seriously. The possibility of condemnation can never be removed. At the same time, Christians ought never to underestimate the mercy and love of God toward the creation.

4:7–11

Training for Judgment

Judgment is near for the whole world. This judgment is connected with growing persecution that these Christians will have to endure. The nearness of the final judgment, the end of history, the dawning of the full kingdom of God with the return of Christ, all of this seems to be clearly anticipated in this letter, which is one of the reasons for assuming a date in the first century for its composition. Because the end is near, it is necessary to be prepared, knowing that God may call one to be a martyr.

Dame Julian, an anchoress in the fifteenth century, saw the Lord in a vision, and he said that, in the end, all things would be well. She then asked:

One article of our faith is that many creatures will be damned, such as the angels who fell out of heaven because of pride, who now are devils, and many men upon earth who die out of the faith of Holy Church, that is to say those who are pagans and many who have received baptism and who live unchristian lives and so die out of God's love. All these will be eternally condemned to hell, as Holy Church teaches me to believe.

In response to this, Jesus answered: "What is impossible to you is not impossible to me. I shall preserve my word in everything, and I shall make everything well."

—Julian of Norwich

Showings, trans. Edmund Colledge and James Walsh (New York: Paulist Press, 1978), 233.

The epistle assumes that persecution is likely. There were sporadic, local persecutions in the first century. We know of the one in Rome during the time of Nero. The writer may well have seen the handwriting on the wall, that greater, more systematic persecution was on the horizon. Perhaps there had been some serious incidents in the area of the churches to which the letter is addressed. What is clear is that persecution of the church by the Roman Empire did increase because the church was seen as a major cause for the empire's decline. That awareness took almost two centuries. But this writer sees that as the future, as does the writer of Revelation as few years later.

The preparation of a Christian is different but no less strenuous than that of an athlete. An athlete may need to run a certain number of miles each day, or lift weights, or whatever is helpful for the particular sport. The Christian's preparation involves learning to seek the will of God rather than his or her own desires. This practice, however, requires prayer. This is the second time in this brief letter that something has been urged for the sake of the Christian's prayers. The first time was in 3:7, where husbands were urged to have consideration for their wives so that their prayers would not be hindered. The will of God for the Christian's own life can be learned, in general, from the church. But these general guidelines, along with what may well be specific to the particular Christian's life, can only be discerned through prayer. So the discipline required is for the sake of a deep prayer life. It may include fasting, studying Scripture, or using different forms of prayer, but the function of all of these is allowing the will of God for the particular person to become clearer and more readily lived.

Though the preparation for the possible coming persecution so far seems directed at the individual, verse 8 makes clear that the congregation is deeply involved. A strong congregation that in its own corporate life seeks to fulfill the will of God is able to nourish and sustain individual members who are called upon to suffer for their faith. The congregation prepares by practicing mutual love. No program of congregational development, of renewal that will strengthen congregations, will take the place of love, constant and growing love for one another within the congregation.

But what does it mean that "love covers a multitude of sins"? Is it my love for another that puts their sins in the background? Or is it the love of others for me that makes my sins less important? Or is it the forgiving love of God for all of us that we reflect in our love for one another? Probably it works all of these ways. Love is so important to a Christian congregation, so absolutely essential, that if there is little love, all the sins of the congregation will appear very great. But if within a congregation there is love, sincere and constantly growing love for one another, almost all of its sins will fade into the background because love is the most important character both of the individual Christian life and of the life of a congregation. It is difficult to imagine Christian love in a single individual, since a loving character involves the recipient of such love. Within the congregation, love is given and received and it therefore shapes the whole congregation. A very loving congregation cannot be a weak one, since the love that is shared makes it strong. Love does cover a multitude of sins.

This love is clearly for fellow Christians within the church. But love cannot stop at the border of the community. It flows over that fellowship and becomes love of enemies, even the persecutors. Such love was the hallmark of early Christians, and is called for in every generation. This love also covers a multitude of sins. It may even be a way of forgiving the sins of the enemies. The power of love over sin was shown by Jesus himself when he forgave the sins of the woman who washed his feet with her tears. When questioned why

---

If among Christians mutuality should become a defining practice, if Christians should embrace the ideal of other-oriented service without reference to status honor, and if Christians should exercise among themselves unwavering love, then this cannot help but score a blow against a world distinguished by status-based distribution of power and privilege. That Peter counsels a relational ethic focused on the mutuality of "one another" statements while at the same time celebrating Christ (and not one's social betters) as the rightful recipient of "glory" .... is thus an intensely political statement....

[I]t is difficult to avoid the conclusion that Peter's household ethic is purposely dissident, dramatically so.

—Joel B. Green

1 Peter, THNTC (Grand Rapids: Eerdmans, 2007), 140–41.

he allowed such a woman to touch him, he replied: "Her sins, which were many, have been forgiven; hence she has shown great love. But the one to whom little is forgiven, loves little" (Luke 7:47). A congregation that is aware of its own sinfulness, and is also aware that through Christ all of these sins have been forgiven, is in a position to be a very loving congregation. As mentioned earlier, a congregation that thinks of itself as composed of the most respectable people in the community, with the real sinners outside, is unlikely to be a very loving congregation. It is also unlikely to be very loving to those outside, which will make it quite unattractive. There will be little love to cover its multitude of sins, especially the sins of which it is unaware because it thinks of itself as righteous.

One of the major ways of showing love to one another in the early church was through hospitality. Paul makes this plea in Romans 12:9–21. Hospitality was not simply inviting friends to dinner. It meant sharing food and lodging with Christians who were strangers in the city, or making sure the poor within the congregation had food, even when it meant inviting them into your home. This was not the usual hospitality that fully expected to be returned. One is reminded of the words of Jesus to the Pharisee who had invited him to dinner: "When you give a luncheon or a dinner, do not invite your friends or your brothers or your relatives or rich neighbors, in case they may invite you in return, and you would be repaid. But when you give a banquet, invite the poor" (Luke 14:12–14). Within the early house churches, those who had more money were always on the giving end, since many of the members were poor and could hardly entertain anyone in their quarters. Often Christians met twice a day, or at least tried to gather as frequently as possible, commonly before the work day began and then at dusk when it ended. A meal was usually part of this gathering, and the Christians who had houses large enough to include the community of faith needed to be hospitable. That the text adds the words, "without complaining," shows that often it would be quite human for there to have been complaints!

Many Christians in that early period were small tradesmen, going on a circuit from town to town, plying their trade. If they found other Christians there, they might well be invited to stay with them, or at least join them for common meals. Again, hospitality would be an important virtue and a sign of Christian love extended to these brothers and sisters in Christ who might well be complete strangers.

The chapter continues with other ways in which Christians are to show their love. They have all received gifts from God, given by God in order to be shared with the community. Those who have sizable houses and plenty of food have received this gift in order to show hospitality to others. Their hospitality is the good stewardship of the gifts that they have been given. Others have been given the ability to preach or to pray. This gift was also shared at the communal gatherings in homes. The speech of those so gifted is to be truly God's word and not simply their own. This text is one that every preacher should hear.

In our own day, when authority is only grudgingly given to any person or office, we often forget that the Reformers of the sixteenth century had a very powerful understanding of the role of the preacher. For them, the words on the page of the Bible are the potential word of God. That is, they are truly the word of God spoken to an ancient people. But it is quite easy to look at these words, agree completely that they were indeed the word of God, accurate and to the point. But what they mean to us, other than accurate history, remains to be seen. We can agree completely on what God did when ancient kings were disobedient. We can agree completely on Isaiah's words to them and that the words the prophet spoke were indeed God's word. But it is not until those ancient words are preached to the gathered community now, showing how they apply to us, that they become the living word of God, able to convict us of sin and show us the promise of God's love and forgiveness. Those who are given the gift of speaking God's word need to be faithful in their task, studying diligently both the ancient word and the present state of affairs, and prayerfully and with fear and trembling, speak that word to God's people now. This ability is a gift that God has given for the health of the whole community.

The letter then returns to those who have been given gifts of service, which probably includes again hospitality. God gives them not only the goods and talents in order to serve, but gives them also the strength they will need to do so without complaining. In all things in the church, all are to use their gifts for the glory of God. That means that the gifts are not to be used to enhance the individual's own glory—or even the congregation's own glory. In our day, most congregations gather in church buildings, and they do not expect to meet in one another's homes for meals morning and evening. Moreover, few Christians travel from one town to another and expect to be taken care of by Christians in the new town. At the same time, the practice of hospitality is still a cardinal virtue within the church. What does it mean for us in our situation?

We who live in areas that for centuries have been considered Christian, where almost all the population was assumed to be Christian even if they rarely were involved in the life of the church, have a difficult time imagining caring for all of those considered Christian who are poor, homeless, or otherwise destitute. Thinking of them as brothers and sisters in the faith is hard. It is much easier to imagine an area of the world today where Christians are an extreme minority, perhaps persecuted for their faith. In that case, even a stranger visiting our town might well be recognized as part of our family of faith. Such a stranger would obviously be an active Christian, for what would be the purpose of willingly acknowledging membership in a group that others despised if such membership meant little or nothing to you?

Here, then, is the sovereign power with which the pastors of the church, by whatever name they be called, ought to be endowed. That is that they may dare boldly to do all things by God's Word; may compel all worldly power, glory, wisdom, and exaltation to yield to and obey his majesty; supported by his power, may command all from the highest even to the last; may build up Christ's household and cast down Satan's; may feed the sheep and drive away the wolves; may instruct and exhort the teachable; may accuse, rebuke, and subdue the rebellious and stubborn; may bind and loose; finally, if need be, may launch thunderbolts and lightnings; but do all things in God's Word.

—John Calvin

Institutes of the Christian Religion 4.8.9; ed. John T. McNeill, trans. Ford Lewis Battles, LCC 20–21 (Philadelphia: Westminster, 1960), 2:1156–57.

We obviously must be concerned for the poor and homeless regardless of their religious affiliation. That is not the question. But if we discover people in our own congregation who have lost their job, lost their house, and are in danger of actually being part of the homeless population of the city, do we have any sense of responsibility as a congregation to find them shelter, even in our homes? It may well be that they would disappear from the congregation without letting anyone know what had happened, since they might be ashamed of their situation even if it had happened through no fault of their own. What does hospitality mean in our day? That is a serious question that congregations should wrestle with. Christian families also need to think about it. We do live in somewhat dangerous times, and one cannot invite into one's home total strangers without some sense of who they are, of whether they can be trusted with our children. Yet hospitality remains a major part of Christian love, and it cannot simply be put aside as impractical. It was probably viewed as equally impractical in the first century.

Many churches practice hospitality now in terms of shelters for the homeless or soup kitchens. This is very helpful. At the same time, often those Christians who serve in these places could not imagine having the recipients of their services as part of the same congregation. Nor are we clear that some of those on the receiving end of such services are part of the same body of Christ as we are. Should it make a difference that they are Christians? Should we treat them any differently than we treat others who are in such unfortunate situations?

Returning to the text, we may think how mistaken these people were, believing that the end of history was at hand. Clearly the end was not to come in their near future. Even almost two thousand years later the end has still not come. At the same time, for each one of us, as well as for each generation in the church, our participation in this history does have a very limited time. Judgment on the life we have lived individually and as the church is always near. We may not have persecution to make us aware of the possibility of turning away from Christ and basing our lives on very different values, but we have other temptations that we may be less able to discover and avoid. We may have a difficult time discerning what are Christian values that differ from the values of the world around us. Yet that is clearly our task.

This section concludes with a doxology. It is not clear if the "him" refers to Christ, through whom we have access to the Father, or if it is God who is to receive the glory. In any case, the strength to do what is right comes from God. It is God's power that strengthens us, and without it we could not carry out God's will. The Spirit is not mentioned in this verse, but when we look back to the Trinitarian description in 1:2 it is clear that the divine power comes to us through the Holy Spirit in order to help us be obedient. Because of the work of Christ, made available to us through the Spirit, we are strengthened for holiness, and in this we give God glory. The work of the Spirit will be picked up a few verses later in this chapter.

Why a doxology at this point? The letter is going to continue. It is as though the writer was so caught up in the thought that Christians are actually able to form these loving, forgiving communities, with all the members using the gifts God had given them for the good of the whole, that it was simply impossible to go on without uttering such praise. We may think that the gifts God has given us for the sake of the whole church are quite minor. Many of us think that the talents we have, on which we draw in the secular world, are simply to be baptized within the church. So the banker who has a gift for finance is made head of the committee in the church that does the same thing, and the good cooks are made part of the committee that serves church dinners, and the musicians now perform in church, and the good speakers become preachers. But this should not necessarily be the case. Whatever secular talents we have may or may not correspond to what is needed in the church. The banker may have very different ideas about prudent financial policies than the church needs. Indeed, the way the church may faithfully spend its money could seem profligate to the banker. What if it is spent on true hospitality rather than on building maintenance? Church dinners might be for the homeless rather than just the congregation. The musicians may help the whole congregation learn new ways to praise God as a whole community, rather than being performers themselves. The preacher is not simply a good speaker. The talents used in secular occupations and pastimes do not include many gifts that God gives to people for the sake of the church. Among them are people powerful in prayer, able to teach others and pray for others. There are those who can discern in Scripture what God is saying to us today, even if they themselves are not the best speakers. Even Paul quotes some who challenged his ministry saying: "His letters are weighty and strong, but . . . his speech contemptible" (2 Cor. 10:10). Paul's response was: "I may be untrained in speech, but not in knowledge" (2 Cor. 11:6). The knowledge of what Scripture means in our setting is a gift to be used for the whole church, and it may or may not be accompanied by a great ability to speak.

Some church members are blessed with the ability to see the needs of the world around them and discern how the church can help. Some can show how faith leads to strength in difficult times, and minister to those who now face such times. If the church is satisfied with bringing into the church talents already exhibited in the wider world, it may miss out on the real gifts God has given to the congregation.

We are all to be good stewards of the manifold grace that God has showered upon us. We may not even know what gifts we have, but the congregation is there to help us all discern them. And gifts may be in unlikely persons. We often have an image of what a leader should be like, and immediately gravitate to such an individual for leadership in the church. But if the gifts are manifold, then some people who exhibit little leadership in the wider world may be the ones who are powerful in prayer, and need to learn to share that gift with others. If a congregation asks the question: Who among us is most faithful in the midst of difficult times? Who in our midst is known to have a powerful prayer life? Who in this congregation uses the money he or she has in a way that shows love and charity to others? Who is most hospitable when others are in need? If these are the questions asked when naming people to leadership in the church, the congregation might be very different than if it chooses those whose talents in the secular world are readily translated into roles in the life of the congregation.

While Christians await the end of history, whether as a cosmic event portending the coming of the reign of God in all its fullness, or the natural demise of our own generation's part in this long history, they are to prepare themselves at all times to be so thankful for God's love for us that they will respond in love for one another and, indeed, for the whole creation.

4:12

Readiness for Persecution

The "fiery ordeal" is near to them, and will possibly involve them. Does this refer to the form of martyrdom some Christians have already suffered? Perhaps. We know that in the persecution in Rome under Nero many Christians were burned alive as torches for the emperor's parties. What is interesting here is the word that they should not be surprised. It is not strange for Christians to be perse-cuted. As we mentioned before, this does not mean that Christians should seek persecution. But it does mean that when it comes, if it comes because Christians have behaved as Christians, then they should remember that this is an expected part of the Christian life. The values Christians live by are always a challenge to a sinful soci-ety, and we should not be surprised if the society reacts negatively. Persecution is not a strange thing. At the time of the Protestant Reformation, the radical wing of Protestants, groups such as the Mennonites, believed that Christians would always be persecuted. Indeed, if there were no persecution, then Christians had probably become too adapted to the evil world around them. Such groups were persecuted by both Roman Catholics and Protestants.

You see, my worthy brethren, if you conduct yourselves after this manner in your oppression and trials, if you drink with patience the cup of the Lord, give testimony to Christ Jesus and His holy Word in word and deed, if you allow yourselves as meek lambs for the testimony of Christ to be led with perfect constancy to the slaughter, then in you the name of God will be praised and made holy and glorious, the name of the saints will be revealed, the kingdom of heaven extended, the Word of God made known, and your poor weak brethren in the Lord will be strengthened and taught by your courage.

—Menno Simons

"The Cross of the Saints," in *The Complete Writings of Menno Simons*, trans. Leonard Verduin (Scottdale, PA: Herald, 1956), 620.

Persecution should indeed be a strange thing to Christians who believe that their faith is supposed to save them from unpleasantness and grant them a good life in the world's terms. That is never what was promised. That is a false gospel. Faith does not protect us from danger, but it does guarantee the strength and power to endure victoriously if we are called to such dangers by God. Persecution is in this sense a test, given by God, to see if these Christians are truly faithful, and have really understood what the gospel is about. As we have seen earlier in this epistle, testing the faith of believers is not the only purpose of persecution. It also serves as a witness to the world that the gospel is a source of power and victory, fearlessness in the face of death, love and joy that are beyond the usual human life. Such a witness also points out the falsity and weakness of the kind of life this sinful world provides. It is not that God wills persecution, but rather that it is the natural result of the conflict between the values of the present world and the values that Christians live by when they are faithful. It is that conflict that can, at times, erupt into overt persecution.

4:13–14

Sharing in Christ's Sufferings

Here we find again themes that have appeared throughout this letter, and yet something more is said. Not only is Christ our model in the midst of undeserved suffering, we also share in his sufferings. That is, his body on earth, the church, still suffers; and he is part of that body, although he is its victorious head. Since the end of history was expected quite soon, along with the full revelation of Christ in all of his glory, these Christians could be sure that if they shared in his sufferings now they would also share in his glory when it is revealed. To share in Christ's suffering implies that he shares in ours. We will not be alone when the fiery ordeal is upon us.

For Christians then and now, it may not be full-blown persecution that they suffer, but simply neighbors looking at them as dangerous, or stupid, or worthless, precisely because they are Christians. Many in our increasingly secular society think Christians are out of touch with the modern world. They find religious people in general and Christians in particular quaint, almost medieval, and perhaps dangerous in positions of power or influence or education. Christians are to view such negative attitudes that others hold about them as something positive, because the world also reviled Christ in the same way. What such reviling reveals is that they, the Christians, are blessed, because this proves that God's Spirit is resting upon them. As we saw in the doxology in 4:11, God's power and glory, made possible for us because of the work of Jesus Christ, are given to us by the Holy Spirit. Power and glory go together throughout the epistle. If we trust in our own strength and seek our own glory, then we will not be able to come through the fiery ordeal. But if the power we have is God's, and the glory we seek is God's, then our faithfulness will indeed lead to victory. We must remember that victory, in this case, may well look to the world like loss. The death of a martyr may prove to the world that the victim lost to the power of the state. However, the Roman Empire probably felt that way about the death of Jesus. It did appear that the empire had won. Yet in a few short centuries, the empire itself would acknowledge that the victim held the victory. The Lamb who was slain is now the one whom the whole of creation will say is worthy to receive "blessing and honor and glory and might" (Rev. 5:13).

We need to be clear about the opposition Christians receive. There seem always to be some Christians who take great pride in being treated negatively. They may be very quick to point out the errors of others or to refuse association with those they consider sinful. They may take pleasure in the sins of others because it makes them seem all the better. The hostility they engender may appear to them to be God's approval of their lives, whereas it is really their own judgmental attitude that causes others to reject them. We are not always the best judges of our own actions. It is the community itself that may help such people to see themselves more truly. The opposition they face is not because of the gospel but because of their own unloving actions and attitudes.

There are also Christians who oppose the gospel to science, and refuse to accept anything that does not agree with Scripture in terms of the dating of creation. We need to be clear that the opposition discussed in this letter is not of such a nature. It is helpful if the wisdom of the whole church is included in such matters, rather than dividing the church between those who hold to science and those who hold to an inerrant Bible. The opposition described in this letter is different: it comes because Christians are faithful to the lordship of Christ in a society that does not agree to that lordship.

4:15–16

Christians as Citizens

The theme we saw in 2:20 is picked up here: there is no value if your suffering is caused by your own evil actions. There is no glory in being punished for being a thief or a murderer! In that case, the state has every reason to punish. In fact, it is part of the duty of the state. It is interesting that among the civil crimes one should not commit is listed being "a mischief maker." That term covers a multitude of possibilities. At least it is clear that Christians are not to be troublemakers simply in order to upset the civil community. As far as possible, they are to be good citizens. They are to help the state by praying for it, and doing all that is possible to live peaceably with their neighbors (Rom. 12:14–13:7). But if they suffer for the name of Christ, having done nothing wrong, then that suffering is blessed. It is quite natural that someone who is held up to public ridicule would feel disgraced. Yet they are to feel blessed rather than disgraced. They are blessed because God has chosen them to join in Christ's suffering, and they therefore know that they will be glorified with him. In addition to what was counseled in 3:14, that Christians were not to fear what others feared or to be intimidated by what intimidates others, here they are told not to feel disgraced by what others understand to be disgrace. Those who have been called to suffer for the sake of Christ should feel honored. God has called them to this task. God will not leave them alone. God's power and glory will be with them in the time of suffering, and therefore they will have the strength to endure.

4:17–18

Judgment Has Begun

The time of judgment has actually begun. That is what the increasing persecution means. Judgment therefore is beginning with God's own household. These are very important words. Christians are not immune to judgment. Often, Christians seem to feel that because they have faith there is no judgment for them. Christ has taken on himself all of our judgment, and therefore we have nothing to fear.

True, Christians do not need to fear judgment; nonetheless, times of testing may occur, and this testing may find them wanting. It is indeed a judgment. Peter, the purported author of this epistle, was one of Jesus' closest companions; yet when there was the possibility of suffering because of that closeness, he betrayed Christ, denying that he even knew him (Luke 22:54–62). That moment in the courtyard was a time of judgment. It did not mean that Peter was no longer part of the household of God, but it was clearly a moment of judgment. Indeed, in the closing days of Christ's life, we can see much of what this letter is saying in the actual experience of Peter. He did fear what others feared. He was intimidated by both the Jewish and the Roman authorities. He did not wish to be disgraced by acknowledging his friendship with Jesus. All of this is true, and Peter discovered later, after the resurrection, that he was not only forgiven, but that his new life would be lived on the basis that is now advocated in this epistle. As a leader of the church, he did not fear what others feared. He could not be intimidated by the council and refused to obey it when ordered not to preach about Jesus. He even told them he would not obey their command (Acts 4:1–21). He was arrested and imprisoned, but had no fear. In fact, he witnessed the power of God that freed him from prison (Acts 12:6–11). The tradition is that he suffered the death of a martyr in Rome, during the persecution under Nero.

The household of God is not immune to judgment. The time of judgment has come. We often look at biblical passages that point to the expectation of the end of history coming very soon and simply pass them by as a wrong opinion held by the early church. We saw such a passage in 4:7. But in another way, the early church was quite right. We need to remember that the Pharisees did believe there was a resurrection of the dead. It would come at the end of history. When Jesus rose from the dead, the Pharisees could not imagine that a resurrection could occur and the end of history not be here also. The resurrection of Jesus was the inbreaking of the kingdom, the end time in the midst of history, the new creation in the midst of the old. There is a real sense in which the end of history did begin with the resurrection, and Christians now live with a foot in each of two worlds, born into the old creation and born again into the new.

The early church had another way of expressing this, as we saw earlier. For Pharisaic Judaism, the creation continued its weekly cycle, the seventh day was the Sabbath, followed by the first day of the week. But the belief was that one Sabbath would not be followed by the first day of the week but rather by the eternal Sabbath, the dawning of the kingdom of God, the Eighth Day. To Jewish Christians, which all the first Christians were, that Jesus rose on the first day of the week meant that the kingdom had dawned, though the old world continued. It was the continuation of the old world that was completely unexpected. Some early baptistries, especially in the fourth century when the church could have public buildings, were octagonal in shape, because through baptism we live in the eighth day, even though we still live also in the world with its continuing cycle of weeks.

The sense that Christians were already living in the new age was very strong in the early church. From the beginning they gathered on the Lord's Day—the first day of the week—to meet at the Lord's Table with their risen Lord. Sunday could never be a time of fasting, precisely because it was a foretaste of the final banquet. Any other day of the week Christians bowed their heads in prayer, and often knelt. Sunday, however, they never did this, because on the Lord's Day they were as children of the king who were visiting their father. The rest of the week Christians experienced life in the old creation much more, and on those days they behaved more as subjects of a king. It is very interesting that when Constantine began supporting the church, Sunday gradually became like any other day in this respect. It may be that the earthly king did not care for exceptions to bowing and kneeling! The Council of Nicaea in 325 required that all churches maintain the tradition of standing for prayer on the Lord's Day and from Easter to Pentecost.[1]

What is very clear is that early in the Middle Ages the sense that we already lived, at least a little bit, in the new age was generally lost. The Lord's Day was kept, but increasingly the Communion service was less like a mini-Easter and more like a mini–Good Friday. The end of history was now far off, and Christians lived all the time in this old creation, leaving the new creation to be discovered only after death. Baptism also lost the character of joining us to Christ's death and resurrection and became the means of wiping away the guilt of original sin. To state it more technically, by the Middle Ages the church lost almost all sense of eschatological reality in its present life.

The rediscovery of eschatology in the twentieth century occurred in formal theological writing, with Teilhard de Chardin as an early figure. This recovery of eschatology is also to be found in Karl Barth and many others, both Catholic and Protestant. The liturgical renewal movement also rediscovered eschatology, based in part on the recovery of early liturgies, and that has been a major way of helping Christians see again the inbreaking of the new creation in the midst of the old.

For the early church, as well as for the renewed liturgies of our own day, baptism means that we are living in the end times as well as in continuing history. The end times imply judgment. Judgment begins with the household of God because that household has already come to the end time. We are being judged now; we can avoid the rush of the end that is the complete terminus of the old creation when all will be judged. Our judgment comes in the midst of our faith that we know the judge, and the judge loves us. Yet still there is judgment. There is no growth without judgment showing us what is deficient in our lives. There is no sanctification unless we know what is unholy in our lives. The household of God agrees to be judged. It is willing to open its life to the Judge. That, in itself, is the attitude of faith. The faithless will be dragged kicking and screaming to judgment, trying to rationalize all that they did, showing that it was really quite acceptable. The Christian does not act this way, but

1. *The Seven Ecumenical Councils of the Undivided Church*, NPNF 14:42.

rather willingly lets the Judge inspect his or her life, as well as the life of the congregation, knowing that the judgment is carried out in love, and that sins are forgiven.

This attitude of accepting God's judgment willingly is not easy. Yet what will it be like for those who do not know God, or who are fearful? If it is such a difficult process even for believers, what will it be like for the ungodly? Believers should be glad that they are already being judged, and do not have to fear the end. This section closes with a quote from Proverbs 11:31. If one turns to the NRSV to look at this verse, the translation does not correspond, and the point of the quotation is somewhat lost, since the Septuagint version, which is generally quoted here in 1 Peter, deals with a future that may well be after death, whereas the text in the NRSV, translated from the Hebrew, clearly states an earthly reward for the faithful and punishment of the sinners. It reads: "If the righteous are repaid on earth, how much more the wicked and the sinner." For those whose suffering may well end in death, the Hebrew version is not particularly comforting. What Peter quotes speaks of salvation that is difficult even for the righteous, and therefore much harder for sinners.

4:19

In Summary

The whole section ends with a summary. There is only one thing for Christians who are suffering to do. If it is God's will that they suffer, they are to trust God and endure the suffering, knowing that God is faithful and will be with them. God is our creator and our redeemer. Suffering is no reason to cease to trust God. Some Christians, however, have been taught that if they are faithful God will save them from suffering. Therefore, when suffering comes, they not only find suffering difficult in itself, but they also lose their trust in God, since suffering was not supposed to be part of the bargain. This is a false teaching, however, and this epistle makes absolutely clear that Christians are not exempt from suffering, indeed, they should not be surprised at it. Nor is suffering any excuse to cease to trust God's love and protection. Indeed, suffering may prove that God has chosen a person for a particular blessing, even if that blessing is martyrdom.

A second teaching here should not be overlooked. Those Christians who are suffering should not only continue to trust God, but also continue to do what is good and right and holy. Suffering is also no excuse for not loving others, for seeking one's own good. Suffering is not an excuse for being self-centered, demanding, short-tempered, or impatient. Those who suffer must still do what is good and right and holy. One should not waste such an opportunity to learn what such suffering can teach. It should be a time of increased holiness, rather than an excuse to be less holy. At the same time, those who suffer should not turn away those who would help them or comfort them. The sufferers remain members of the one body of Christ, and others have a ministry that may be to them. There is a fine line between demanding or even expecting help and being open to receive it when it is offered.

Trusting oneself to a faithful Creator is not easy, and yet it is the test of one's faith. It shows that one's highest value is following the will of God. In this there is great blessing. The emphasis is on God's faithfulness, proven in the midst of suffering. God's faithfulness is far greater than our own. When our weak, human faithfulness reaches out to God, God's great faithfulness leads us farther on the path of holiness than we ever thought possible.

5:1–13

Final Words to All Members

As we might expect, the closing of the epistle is more personal, and echoes the major themes found in the body of the letter. The personal aspect further identifies the author as Peter. The theme is the anticipated persecution and suffering, along with the strength for the trials that can be expected from God. Suffering is something for which Christians can train, just as an athlete trains for a race. It is spiritual training, and includes the awareness of God's faithfulness to us in all circumstances.

5:1–4

Duties of Church Leaders

The author describes himself as an elder, a presbyter, one who has authority in a congregation. If this is Peter writing, or even one writing in the name of Peter, it is interesting that no greater title is used. He could have called himself an apostle, as he did in 1:1; or even the chief of the apostles, if he were laying claim to that; or bishop, although the early dating might make the use of that term unlikely. Instead, he claims no greater authority here than the elders in the churches to which he is writing. This may be a sign of humility, which is the great virtue to be extolled in the verses that follow. It may be a way of saying that the writer knows well the tasks and the difficulties that elders face, because he is one of them.

The term "elder" is the translation of the Greek term *presbyteros*, and it represents an office in the church. (It is confusing in English because the Greek term "presbyter" is contracted to the word "priest," and we often use the terms "elder," "priest," and "presbyter" to mean different offices in different denominations.) How structured the church was at this point in the first century is open to debate, but at least there were offices, leaders within congregations who had pastoral responsibility for house churches. Some may have had responsibility for more than one gathering. The early church developed as small gatherings, in homes when possible, out of doors in some cases. The church was largely an urban phenomenon, and as it grew there might be several small gatherings in any city. At this point the church had two choices. It could assume that each gathering was a separate church, independent of the others, or it could assume that all were part of one church. It chose this second option: it considered all of the gatherings in a city to be one church. Though each separate gathering might meet together daily or even twice daily, on Sunday, the Lord's Day, it was essential that they gather as one body to partake of the one bread, showing their unity. In fact, one of the favorite passages of Scripture in the early church was 1 Corinthians 10:16–17: "The cup of blessing that we bless, is it not a sharing in the blood of Christ? The bread that we break, is it not a sharing in the body of Christ? Because there is one bread [loaf], we who are many are one body, for we all partake of the one bread." In the fourth century Augustine used this text in a sermon to the newly baptized:

> As you have been made members of Christ, his body, take and eat the body of Christ. Take and drink the blood of Christ. So as not to be separated among yourselves, eat of the bond of our union. Do not underestimate your own value; drink of the price that was paid for you. Just as what you eat or drink turns into you, so do you, by living in obedience and piety, become the body of Christ. . . . Thus, you are beginning to receive what you have begun to be.[1]

At some point, depending on the growth of the church in any particular city, the unity of these several gatherings was shown by either a group of presbyters governing the whole, or one presbyter becoming the leader of all and the sign of their unity. By the end of the first

1. Augustine, Sermon 228B. 3–5 (au. trans.).

century this person was called the overseer or bishop. Although it is not clear how early the office of bishop developed in some cities, by early in the second century it was strongly developed throughout the empire.

What is of interest to us in our own day is how essential Christians believed it was for the church in a city to be unified, to recognize one another as brothers and sisters, and to acknowledge that they were all part of the one body of Christ that was rapidly encircling the whole Mediterranean world and beyond. The bishop in each city provided the link to the church in other cities. The writer of this epistle is showing that these churches in various cities in Asia Minor are not abandoned but are part of the great church. This was mentioned in the beginning of this study, in reference to 1:1. There Peter does claim the title of apostle; but here he claims only that of elder, as he prepares to speak to the elders in these distant places.

> I exhort you to study to do all things with a divine harmony, while your bishop presides in the place of God, and your presbyters in the place of the assembly of the apostles, along with your deacons, who are most dear to me, and are entrusted with the ministry of Jesus Christ, who was with the Father before the beginning of time.
>
> —Ignatius
>
> "Epistle to the Magnesians" (shorter version) 6 (*ANF* 1:61).

The claims of Peter are not only that he is an apostle (1:1) or that he is an elder, but that he was a witness to the sufferings of Christ. That is an interesting claim. In a tradition clearly stated by Irenaeus in the second century, Mark's Gospel contains the memories of Peter. But in that Gospel, Peter is nowhere to be found at the cross, the point of the great sufferings of Christ. After his denial he seems to disappear until after the resurrection, and the other three Gospels agree. We do not know when he again entered the story. Perhaps he was at the burial, but was not mentioned. In spite of that, it is clear that Peter was with Jesus throughout his ministry and was a witness to the risen Christ. In this context, however, where so much of the epistle is devoted to how Christians should face suffering, and the model of Jesus is used constantly in the letter, it is no wonder that the author points to having seen, personally, how Jesus reacted to his own suffering. That he can mention witnessing the suffering without any further comment about not witnessing the cross may indicate that once he had encountered the risen Christ and knew that he was forgiven, he no longer needed to dwell on that past act of betrayal.

Peter not only points to the suffering of Christ, but even more important in this context is the glory of the risen and victorious Jesus, in which glory Peter counts himself as one who shares. He is thus reminding these Christians that their suffering also will let them share in the glory of Christ. It is on this basis that he exhorts first the elders in these congregations, and then all the rest of the members. The sharing in glory is not simply to occur in a distant future. That sharing is now in a hidden fashion, and the full glory will be revealed only later.

The elders are to "tend the flock" that has been given to them. It is God's flock, not theirs. The imagery of the shepherd is used in various places in this epistle, as we have seen. God is the Shepherd. But these elders are also shepherds, pastors of that portion of God's flock for which they have been given responsibility. Two parallel phrases indicate how this work is to be carried out: "not under compulsion but willingly, . . . not for sordid gain but eagerly." One wonders why there might have been compulsion. Had the congregation or the wider church insisted someone become the pastor even though he did not want to be? The history of the church includes several such instances. Perhaps the most famous is Ambrose, the bishop of Milan in the fourth century. He was a catechumen, not yet baptized, the civil governor of the area of Milan under the Roman emperor. The church in Milan elected him its bishop by acclamation. Even though he hid, trying to avoid this appointment, he finally had to agree. He was baptized, ordained, and made bishop within a few days. But when he found himself in that position, he undertook it willingly, and with enthusiasm carried out his duties. Augustine, who was baptized by Bishop Ambrose, faced a similar but less dramatic entrance into the office of bishop, as did Gregory the Great, who became bishop of Rome in the late sixth century.

Often we stress the calling of the individual into the ministry; but there is also the calling of the church that sometimes surprises the individual. Most denominations, through the process leading to ordination, have ways in which the church can indicate that though some believe themselves called to ministry, the church itself does not agree that this is so. However, the church does not always take the initiative to indicate it believes someone might be called. When the church tells someone they really should consider the ministry—or some other role of leadership in the congregation—this call should be taken seriously by the member. In the contemporary church we do not permit kidnapping people, keeping them imprisoned until they agree to be ordained (which is about what happened to Ambrose), but at the same time we often so stress the individual's sense of call that we deny the duty of the church to point out to individuals that they may well be called by God and are not listening! In Acts 13:1–3 we have an instance of the Holy Spirit telling the church whom to set apart for specific work. The Holy Spirit still works through the church, helping it discern who is being called to various ministries, both by testing the call individuals experience and by urging others to be aware of a call that God may be giving them.

No matter whether pastors have been given the charge of the particular congregation because they were assigned by a bishop or elected by the congregation, they are to carry out this task willingly. They are to assume it is God who has given them this responsibility. Regardless of the salary, they are to be eager in their ministry. The text says that elders are not to be leaders in order to make money— "sordid gain." Within the first century, and clearly beyond, there was debate as to the payment of pastors. In fact, of the whole chapter 10 of the Gospel of Luke, which includes such famous passages as the parable of the Good Samaritan and the account of Jesus at the home of Mary and Martha, the most quoted verse in the writings we have up until the year 325 is verse 7: "The laborer deserves to be paid." Once the church grew to sufficient size in an area, there was need for full-time leaders. Often that meant losing the income from their previous jobs. There was a tendency to have wealthier members become leaders, and they might not need to be paid. Leadership in the church, even from the earliest days, required that one could read, since the Scriptures were essential for the life of the church. At first this was the Hebrew Scriptures, but eventually it included the writings of Christian leaders as well. The ability to read and write was not common among poorer people, and probably quite limited among the population in general.[2] By the third century, it was common that if a well-to-do person was elected bishop, he was expected to give to the poor all the assets he controlled, and to live simply. This would mean living on some income from the church.

Gregory the Great, bishop of Rome in the late sixth century, made a specific rule for how the income of the church was to be used. The income was under the supervision of the bishop for a fairly wide geographical area, and was to be divided into four parts. One-fourth was to be used for pastoral salaries; one-fourth for the upkeep of buildings; one-fourth for direct assistance to the poor; and the last fourth for the use of the bishop, including the hospitality he exercised for the refugees who came from outside his jurisdiction.[3] In the case of Gregory himself, the refugees included many who had to move because of war.

In our own day, the whole issue of pastoral salaries is very difficult. We look askance at the lifestyle of some televangelists, and yet most denominations assume that one's income should grow every year, if not by the growth of the congregation then by moving to a larger church. Most denominations treat the mission field very differently, with all salaries paid from a central office, and differentiation made only for family circumstances, the cost of living in an area, and length of service. Equalized salaries are the norm. If we ever really believed that the United States is now mission territory, the whole issue of ministerial salaries would likely be revised. It is difficult for a pastor to know whether seeking a larger church is a call from God or the desire to have a larger salary. If the pay were the same for pastors of smaller and larger churches, the whole picture of the church in this country might change quite radically. There might be fewer huge churches and more middle-size and smaller congregations. At the same time, the early church was quite right in believing that those whose responsibility is full-time work in the church do have a claim to support by the church.

Elders—pastors—are not to stress their authority in a dictatorial fashion, but to use the example of their lives as the major form

2. A very helpful discussion of literacy in the time of the early church is to be found in William V. Harris, *Ancient Literacy* (Cambridge: Harvard University Press, 1989). See especially ch. 7.
3. John Calvin, *Institutes of the Christian Religion* 4.5.7; ed. John T. McNeill, trans. Ford Lewis Battles, LCC 20–21 (Philadelphia: Westminster Press, 1960), 2:1074–75.

of leadership. This is a difficult teaching. How does a pastor show such leadership? Is it only in the life within the church, in worship, in meetings, in pastoral visits? Is it in family life, though the thought that the minister's family is constantly on display makes such a life very difficult? Is the way the pastor lives to be seen in his or her involvement in the community, in the style of life? These are questions every pastor must think about. The Chief Shepherd of the sheep is the one who will reward the faithful elders. They will share in unending glory. Although in 5:2 God is seen as the shepherd whose flock we are to tend, here in 5:4 it is clearly Jesus Christ who is the Chief Shepherd, since it is he whose appearance is expected.

The model for what a shepherd should be is given by God in guiding the whole of creation, as well as by Jesus Christ in his seeking out the lost sheep: God the Father sent the Son to seek the lost. If elders are to be models to their congregations by their behavior and not only by their words, they have the model of Christ, and they also have the model of how God has dealt with humanity from the beginning of creation. It is also clear that the great reward for a faithful elder is not money, but unending glory. That should be the reward sought. It is far easier for celibate clergy to decide that the salary is unimportant, since they do not have a family to consider. Married clergy need to consider the necessary support of children, their education, and in our own day, the occupation of a spouse. There is no answer to these questions that is easy or that is appropriate for all pastors. But the question must be faced by all churches and by all pastors: How does the life of a church leader show forth the gospel, and does it match the gospel that is proclaimed in words?

5:5

A Word to the Younger Members

There is a brief word to the younger members before the writer deals again with the whole church. If the elders are actual officers in the congregations—and they obviously are if the issue of payment for their work is raised—then the younger ones may well be not simply those who are younger in age, but those who are under the leadership of the elders. The elders may not always be older than the rest. They may be older in the faith, but younger in age, than newer converts. The call to these members is to be humble and accept the leadership of the elders. That is really the only word to them. The leaders are to lead in a graceful way, as the shepherd of the flock, and the flock is to follow the leadership of the pastor.

In every generation, leadership is exercised only if there is a genuine following. Office alone will not guarantee that others will follow. A person may think that he or she is a natural leader, and yet, if no one follows, that perception is faulty. Leadership always has to be earned, even if it is technically given by office. In our own day, however, many in our culture have a serious problem accepting the leadership of another. From the 1960s on, our society has questioned authority so completely that very few wish to follow anyone. Or, following may be quite temporary, constantly changing from one authority to another, which basically means that we are each our own authority. We accept what we like from many sources, and discard what we do not like. This will pose a serious problem for those leaders who seek to help others become part of a tradition. Obviously, the early catechetical process was precisely to bring new members into the tradition. Our own culture makes such a process very difficult. The character of our culture will be an important factor as we look at the next verses in this epistle.

This section closes with a quotation from Proverbs 3:34, which corresponds generally to the translation in the NRSV. The point is that God prefers the humble and is opposed to the proud. It is not a matter that leaders can be proud whereas followers should be humble. Leaders are to be humble, aware that the true leader in the church is Christ, and the best earthly leaders are those who follow Christ most closely.

5:6–11

Humility in Suffering

The model of humility for those under authority as well as for those in authority is seen ultimately in the relation of both the elders and the rest of the congregation to God in the midst of suffering. God is the one both elders and others are to follow, and the great test of our following—our discipleship—is in the midst of suffering. Many Christians are faithful as long as their lives benefit from their participation in the church. But suffering may turn them away because there seems to be no benefit to their involvement. Some Christians who have been assured that if they have faith their illness will end discover that their suffering does not end, and they therefore decide that faithfulness is a useless enterprise. In its various forms the gospel of prosperity or success has the same problems: it does not prepare the adherent for suffering, and those who do not find success lose both their hope and their faith.

What these Christians are counseled to do in the epistle is to submit to God's authority in the midst of suffering; to assume that God is indeed in charge of the world, even though evil or pain seem to have the upper hand at the present time. Humility toward earthly authority is paralleled in submission to God's authority. The elders are also to be humble, and are not exempt from suffering. During the first three centuries, what the Roman Empire feared was the increasing influence of the church, united through its bishops into a network all over the empire itself. It sought to prevent further growth and hoped to end the church's influence. Often during the persecutions of the church, the more visible leaders were the first to suffer. If they could be persuaded to turn against the faith, it would make it easier for members to abandon the church also. Therefore, those who were known to be Christian were offered the chance to recant and leave the church, so suffering could be readily avoided. The writer of the epistle needs to show those who remained firm that their faithfulness was what God was asking of them even in the midst of suffering.

The authority of God is depicted as "God's mighty hand." It might seem that the Roman Empire is the ultimate force in their world, but that is not true. God is mightier than any empire or any emperor. The future is safe in God's hands—much safer than in the hands of the empire. God is able to exalt, to glorify, those who remain faithful. This exaltation will happen in due time, that is, when God deems it appropriate.

Not only can God be trusted with the future, but even in the midst of suffering we can let God take care of our anxieties. There is no shame in being anxious when we are facing persecution. We may be worried about ourselves, how we will react, but we may also be anxious about our loved ones, especially if they depend upon us for their welfare. Anxiety is a totally human response in times of turmoil and danger. The reason we can trust God with our anxieties is that God cares for us. It would be easy to assume that if God really loved us, God would prevent the suffering that may come. How is love shown if God lets us suffer? That is the age-old question the faithful have always had to face. In the case of human parents, one would expect them to protect their children from danger. Letting them suffer when the parents could prevent it seems cruel. Yet parents know that they are not always able to prevent suffering, whether it is the result of illness or the consequence of the child's own actions. Parents have to let their children learn some things for themselves, and cannot always prevent harm. Parents who try to make all of the child's decisions even when the child is an adult will hardly promote the growth and independence of their offspring. Though there are parallels between human parents and children and our relationship to God, that parallel cannot be pushed too far. Human parents do not have the power of life and death in the sense that they cannot give life after death. Nor can they view the whole of human history, guiding the entire creation toward a goal in the future. God's perspective is very different from our more limited one.

At the same time, as we see in the incarnation itself, God is not removed from suffering, but God's care for us—and for the world—is seen in the cross. God is not asking of the faithful anything that God

> The mother may sometimes suffer the child to fall and to be distressed in various ways, for its own benefit, but she can never suffer any kind of peril to come to her child, because of her love. And though our earthly mother may suffer her child to perish, our heavenly Mother Jesus may never suffer us who are his children to perish, for he is almighty, all wisdom and all love, and so is none but he, blessed may he be.
>
> —Julian of Norwich
>
> *Showings*, trans. Edmund Colledge and James Walsh (New York: Paulist Press, 1978), 300–301.

the Son has not already done. That is why, throughout this letter, the model of how Jesus faced suffering is the model for the faithful. Jesus is more that just a model: he is the guarantee to the faithful that God can be trusted with our anxieties, and that God does care for us.

The incarnation is the intersection of God's activity toward us and the true human response to God. In Jesus Christ we see God the Chief Shepherd entering into our human history, seeking the lost sheep, bringing them back to God's fold. This is an act of humility on God's part, as we are told by Paul in the great hymn of Philippians 2:5–11, that Jesus humbled himself, even to the point of death on the cross. At the same time, in Jesus Christ we see the perfect human response to God, truly humbling himself under God's powerful hand. On both the human and the divine side, humility is a key virtue in the person of Jesus. Therefore it is not surprising that both elders and members are urged to be humble in their relationship with one another as well as with God.

It would appear that the persecution, although expected, has not yet arrived for these churches. The time now is to be used for training so that when persecution does come, Christians will be prepared. The means for doing this is discipline. In 1 Peter 4:7 there was the same call for discipline, saying it was necessary for the sake of Christians' prayers. Here discipline is needed so that Christians will be able to stand firm in the face of persecution. There may not be a great distinction between these two verses. Prayer will be one of the great resources for Christians. If they can keep their relationship with God strong—and prayer is a major vehicle for this—then they will be strengthened for the trials that lie ahead.

"Discipline" is an interesting word. It is related to "disciple"—one who practices a discipline in following a person or a tradition. We speak of a discipline in physical training, a plan of strengthening or exercise. We speak of disciplines of prayer, certain practices or times, a plan to develop and strengthen the life of prayer. Monasteries had a life of prayer that included several times of worship a day, a certain schedule, along with a schedule of psalms to be used in these times. But it is precisely at the point of discipline that the contemporary culture seems averse to such a life of faith. Discipline in matters of faith seems to go against the highly personal character most people associate with spiritual matters. Discipline may require practicing something even when it does not seem to be working, or requires long practice before we see the benefits.

Saint Teresa of Avila, the great sixteenth-century Spanish mystic, once wrote about the life of prayer, describing her various experiences and comparing them to the gardener's search for water. Often we go to the well, drop the bucket down, and discover that the well is dry. Yet we must go back day after day, lowering the bucket, only to find the well still empty. The going to the well and dropping the bucket down is discipline, the habit we must cultivate. There are other ways to try to deliver water to the garden—getting out the hose or building an irrigation system—but all involve discipline. Yet there are times when we do nothing, and God sends the rain. No work on our part is required. God is the one from whom we must seek the water of prayer. We cannot simply sit by, waiting for the rain. We must develop the habit of prayer, the going to the well, where sometimes we will find water. The discipline of prayer does give us the water of life, the connection with God, that we need. It is through this connection that we will recognize the grace of the rain when it comes without any effort on our part.

There is a connection between discipline and humility. Discipline assumes that we follow the directions, the authority, of one who has discovered the means by which we can develop a life of prayer. We must give authority to this tradition or person who has learned what we should do in order to cultivate a life of prayer. Giving authority to someone or to some tradition involves being humble—understanding that that person or tradition has something to teach us, that we need to learn something from that person or tradition. Yet precisely that humility, that assumption that we need to follow the directions of another, is what much of our modern culture opposes. We are the losers in two ways: first, we dislike giving any person or tradition authority over us; and second, we expect quick results, and if a discipline of prayer does not "work" immediately, we decide it is a fraud. But disciplines in the spiritual life are not learned quickly. They are sometimes like the dry well to which we must return again and again, waiting for the grace of God. We are a culture of instant gratification, and if something does not work quickly we are likely to give it up and try something else. Yet it is very interesting to see some of the developments in our own society. Protestants are redis-covering the usefulness of the discipline of the monastic prayer life. Courses on spirituality are popular, although sometimes they feed into the highly individualistic forms that avoid discipline. There are no shortcuts to discipline, no quick ways to become adept in the relationship with God.

The form of discipline needed for these Christians is to stay alert. They do not know when the danger will come. If they are not alert, they may slip into conformity to the surrounding culture and not be prepared for the persecution when it comes. It is discipline that will keep them alert. If they persevere in a life of prayer, even when they do not feel like it or it seems not to be working, they will be alert and ready to remain firm when the time of their testing comes.

Christians were told to be alert, ready for suffering if it does come, and at the same time they also prayed daily the words Jesus gave them, asking that they not be led into the time of testing or, in the more familiar translations, "lead us not into temptation." The words of the Lord's Prayer meant that, though Christians should be ready to be tested in persecution, they still should pray that such a test-ing not come upon them. It may seem that the two ideas conflict: do not let me be tested but let me be ready to be tested. Yet that is precisely what Christians need to do. Just as the person who asked to be persecuted was never thought to be a true martyr, even so no Christian should seek or even try to be persecuted. At the same time, all Christians should be prepared to endure suffering if that is God's choice for them. This attitude of not seeking and yet being prepared is also an act of humility. The person who believes that he or she could endure persecution and is anxious to show this is hardly hum-ble. They are proud of their ability to suffer! But if God leads us into such a time of trial, then we need to be ready to trust God's strength and not our own.

The image of a "roaring lion, looking for someone to devour," is another instance of using a phrase that represents one form of per-secution: putting Christians into the arena with wild animals for the entertainment of the crowd. In 4:12 there was the image of a fiery ordeal, which would bring to mind the burning alive of some

Christians in Rome. Part of this section has had a long history of being used in the monastic *Divine Office* during the time of prayer just before bedtime, an office called "Compline" or "Night Office." The words used are: "Stay alert. Like a roaring lion your adversary the devil prowls around, looking for someone to devour. Resist him, steadfast in your faith." This was the daily reading until the reforms of Vatican II, and continues to be used one day a week in the new form. Why is such a verse useful in an office just before going to sleep? In a brief dialogue essay, the Jesuit theologian Karl Rahner asked the same question. In an evening discussion with a devout Catholic psychologist who also knew the Night Office, they concluded that the verse brings to mind the danger of sleep, when we cannot control our thoughts, and the dangers and fears of the day may intrude as terrible nightmares or prevent sleep from coming at all. This verse reminds Christians of the dangers that sleep poses. In the newer form, this verse is followed by Jesus' words from the cross: "Into your hands, Lord, I commend my spirit." Then there are prayers that God will accompany us while we sleep. In other words, this verse from 1 Peter, followed by prayers, arm the sleeper with the name of Christ so that, if there are dangers and anxieties, Christ can deal with them and let us sleep. We can sleep because Christ is alert. We can be alert during our waking hours, but we can sleep peacefully, knowing that we can arise ready to continue to be alert. The final antiphon in the Night Office is this: "Protect us, Lord, as we stay awake; watch over us as we sleep, that awake, we may keep watch with Christ, and asleep, rest in his peace." This brief verse from 1 Peter is very useful in this disciplined time of prayer.[4]

Whether it is the Roman Empire or some other source of danger for Christians, in the view of the New Testament it is ultimately the devil, the power of evil, that is the enemy. Evil takes on many faces, but it is the same evil in all of its guises. This is also the view we find in the book of Revelation, where the various political entities, including the Roman Empire itself, are considered various faces of the one evil, the great centralized network of evil that dominates our world.

4. Karl Rahner, "A Spiritual Dialogue at Evening: On Sleep, Prayer, and Other Subjects," in *Theological Investigations*, vol. 3: *The Theology of the Spiritual Life*, trans. Karl -H. and Boniface Kruger (Baltimore: Helicon, 1967), 220–36.

We may think that we have moved far beyond a primitive view of the devil. We may think we are totally free to decide for good or evil, and that the power of evil is not as strong as our desire to do what is good. If we begin to tackle one evil in our society, however, we may well discover another has taken its place. It is rather like passing laws to outlaw the latest disasters caused by greed, only to discover greed has found new ways to carry out its desires. We can attack sins one by one, but Sin, with a capital letter, remains active in human life. We may not like the term "the devil," but it may also point to a reality of evil that our rationalist society does not understand.

The persecution that these Christians may have to face is not theirs alone, but is something Christians all around the empire will experience. Indeed, some may have already faced terrible suffering. If this letter is written from Rome, where the persecutions under Nero have already happened, that would strengthen its message. The writer is not asking of these Christians in a distant area anything that the church in Rome has not already had to face. The persecution may or may not kill them. What is promised is that God will strengthen them, whether in the midst of suffering, after the persecution has passed, or after death. Their suffering will be "for a little while," whereas the glory to which they are called will last forever.

There are overtones in this passage of the Trinitarian theology we saw earlier in the letter. It rounds out the letter by using words similar to the opening. God has called them; Christ will receive them in glory; and, though not named, it is the Spirit who will bring them the strength and grace of God in the midst of their ordeal. The power of God is mentioned, since the issue is God's power that is stronger than the power of evil, now seen in the empire that is persecuting them.

5:12–14

Closing Words

The writer closes with greetings from the circle around him. Silvanus is named as the one who is probably expected to carry this letter to the distant churches. We have to remember that letters such as this could not be sent by any postal service. They had to be hand carried by a trusted person who was probably expected to explain and add to the letter. It also means this is not a letter to one person, but a public letter to be read to the various congregations. It makes a difference to hear the content of this epistle in the company of others rather than reading it alone. As mentioned earlier, in English we no longer differentiate between the second person singular and the plural form, so when the text speaks to "you," we, reading alone, can see this as directed to us individually. But the text in Greek constantly uses the plural "you," which means the words are directed at least partially to the whole congregation and its corporate behavior. We live in such an individualistic culture that words directed to the corporate life of the congregation often go by without having any effect. It is the whole congregation that needs to supply the discipline for Christians so that they will be prepared for the persecution that may come.

The letter is evidently sent from one church to another—assuming the sister mentioned is the church in Rome. Babylon is a frequent code name for Rome, as we see in Revelation. Mark is also mentioned, whom early church history tells us was in Rome with Peter. The final statement about greeting one another with a kiss of love probably means exactly what the church also called the kiss of peace. It occurred at the beginning of the eucharistic service after the preaching service, and may mark the point in the service where it was expected this letter would be read. The words of peace to all would be an appropriate conclusion, leading directly into the Communion service. These words are similar to the conclusions of many other epistles in the New Testament, as well as the book of Revelation. Reading letters such as this in the midst of the congregation as part of its eucharistic service helps to show the unity of the churches across the distances, reinforcing the idea of the one body of Christ throughout the world. The church meets its Lord at the one Lord's Table, and it is part of the one body that may be suffering.

The awareness of the unity of the church is a strength for those who are suffering. In our own congregations, we need to think about the worldwide church. Many Christians today are suffering persecution. We need to lift them up in prayer in our own worship and, from them, learn to be more alert in our own setting. They may not be of our own denomination, but they are part of the one body of Christ for whom we are to pray, for their strengthening as well as for our own.

The conclusion of the letter emphasizes the themes that have been there throughout. It is a letter of encouragement, sent to Christians who may soon be suffering persecution. The "true grace" of God is seen by those who remain firm, who "stand fast." There are false understandings of grace that probably were circulating at the time, grace that let one avoid suffering, grace that made life easier for Christians than their unbelieving neighbors. But these false understandings are not part of the true gospel.

In our own day, there are many such false understandings. We need to hear again and again the message of this letter: the words about suffering, about staying alert, about the virtues and disciplines that will prepare us for the Christian life that is not the easy way, but is the narrow path. We need not only to pray for those Christians who today walk that narrow way faithfully, but we need to pray for ourselves, both that we are not led into such a time of trial, into the temptation to abandon our faith, and that we remain alert, able to see the evil around us and reject it.

Final Thoughts

This is not the first time I have read this brief epistle very closely. Yet this reading, looking specifically for theological insights, has given me a very different perspective. Four new understandings about the letter have emerged from this present work.

First, there is a highly Trinitarian view that lies behind the whole letter, from the first verse to the last. God the Father has called us and is the ultimate Shepherd of creation. The Father has sent the Son. Through his death and resurrection Jesus Christ has redeemed us and brought us back to God. The Holy Spirit leads us to holiness and gives us the strength of God for the difficulties we face. This Trinitarian theme is basic to the whole letter. For many generations, though the doctrine of the Trinity has been affirmed, it has functioned more as a matter for professional theologians. The rest of the church affirms the doctrine, but it has little significance in the life of faith. Indeed, many church members would be hard pressed to give a clear statement of what the doctrine means and its significance. In recent years, however, there has been a renewed interest in the meaning of the Trinity in the daily lives of Christians. How do we recognize the work of the Holy Spirit in our lives? What does it mean to follow in the steps of Jesus? How does the Holy Spirit help us in our discipleship? How do we understand God's work in Christ? Is God concerned about the whole world or only about the church? What is the role of the church in God's wider concerns? The answers to all of these questions depend upon an understanding of the Trinity, and this epistle leads us to this understanding.

The second learning: though I knew that Isaiah 53, the Suffering

Servant passage, was quoted and used in this letter, a closer study shows that the imagery from this passage also underlies all of the writing. Perhaps stemming from the use of Isaiah, images of sheep and shepherds appear throughout the letter, picking up other biblical uses of these images. Isaiah shows the Servant as the redeeming victim, whereas 1 Peter also sees God as a shepherd, and shows the pastoral character of elders. Simply going through the book showing all of the references to Isaiah 53, direct and oblique, leads to an astonishing number of instances. For example, 1:19 pictures Christ as the lamb without blemish, a reference to the Passover sacrifice but also to the lamb mentioned in Isaiah 53; 2:21–25 uses passages directly from Isaiah 53; and 3:18 has overtones of the Suffering Servant. It is as though the author began with Isaiah 53 and then, throughout the letter, used the imagery of the flock of God, the lamb that was sacrificed, the sheep that had strayed, the shepherd as God, as Jesus, as leaders in the church—all these images woven together.

Third, although in the introduction I found fault with Friedrich Schleiermacher's understanding of the church, in the body of the letter I found his understanding of the nature of the Christian life very helpful. In particular, Schleiermacher describes a self-centered life, based on seeking to avoid pain and to gain pleasure, as the condition of sin into which we are all born. Whether an infant who cries when there is pain or an adult who seeks to increase the pleasures of life and decrease its pain, human life lived on this basis shows the effects of sin. The infant cannot avoid this, but many human beings never outgrow such an orientation. On the other hand, Schleiermacher describes life in the state of grace as a life in which the chief goal is to follow the will of God, regardless of the pain it may lead to and the worldly pleasure it may eliminate. This grace-filled life is brought about by redemption in Christ. Schleiermacher has great emphasis on the growth in grace—sanctification—that follows when we know that our sins, our actions according to the pain/pleasure principle, have been forgiven, and we increasingly are able to live according to the will of God. Because 1 Peter is dealing precisely with the possibility of persecution that will cause pain, Schleiermacher's categories are very useful.

The fourth learning is about discipline. Throughout the letter there is a sense that the life we need to live is based on practice, on strengthening our ability to see temptation, to remain alert to the possibility of persecution, to develop a life of prayer that will keep us in touch with the will of God, to strengthen the life of the congregation so there will be a supportive community if we are called upon to suffer. Thus 1:13 tells us to discipline our minds; 1:22 calls us to learn to love one another more deeply; 2:11–25 spell out different areas of life in which we need to practice doing what is good, rather than what comes naturally to us; 4:7 tells us to be disciplined about our prayer life; and 5:8 calls us to discipline ourselves so that we will be able to endure suffering.

Throughout the letter, discipline, shepherding, pain and pleasure, and the Trinity are constant themes that hold the whole letter together. It was a beautiful and encouraging letter to those Christians who received it in the first century. It has words that we need to hear as the church in our own day.

PART 2
2 PETER

Introduction:
Why 2 Peter? Why Now?

One is tempted to respond to the question: Why 2 Peter? the way mountain climbers respond to: Why climb that mountain? Because it is there! Obviously, this epistle is in the NT canon, and that means it should be taken seriously by today's Christians. Historically, 2 Peter has elicited little interest in the life of the church. Both it and Jude are largely ignored. We find only one passage used in the lectionary, although we also find verses here and there that have been used much more frequently in the life of the church, and it is helpful to see them in their original context. At the same time, it is worthwhile to rediscover this letter. It deals with some issues that we also face, and it has much to teach us if we look at it deeply.

First, 2 Peter is quite concerned about authority. Who has authority in the church? Who decides if something is foreign to the gospel or can be part of it? These are contemporary issues in today's church, although we often decide that each Christian is the authority in his or her own life. We may assume that the Bible is our authority, but when we look at this letter, written before the New Testament was compiled, we see that the early church had its own problems with the Bible. The Old Testament was their Scripture, but there were also various Gospels and letters circulating. Paul presented problems because his letters seemed to give some people the idea that the law was no longer significant.

Second, the church in the time of this letter needed to train new members, those who had been very much a part of the pagan culture in which they lived. Who should teach them? What behavior is expected of new Christians and how does it differ from their earlier lives? Increasingly, in our churches, we are finding that some who wish to join the church have had almost no contact with the gospel before, and they do need to be trained. But can the congregation agree on what constitutes specifically Christian behavior? Do we live in a culture that can be called Christian? The issues raised in 2 Peter are similar to those our churches are beginning to raise, questions that the church has not been asking for generations in our society.

Second Peter and Jude are often considered together, and with good reason. Though almost half of Jude is to be found in 2 Peter, there is much of 2 Peter that is not in Jude. Their respective lengths would show that. Jude is only twenty-five verses—not enough to be divided into chapters. Second Peter, however, is sixty-one verses divided into three chapters. It is interesting to see what verses in Jude are not included in 2 Peter. The selection is purposeful, both in what is borrowed and in what is omitted.

Some Necessary Background

Second Peter is generally dated in the late first or early second century. A few scholars place it even later in the second century. Clearly it is well after 1 Peter, and the issues dealt with are quite different. As we saw, 1 Peter was directed to particular churches at a great distance from Rome, giving them support and encouragement to stand fast in the midst of persecution. In this second letter the danger to the unnamed churches is not from outsiders in persecution but from Christians who are preaching a gospel different from the one these congregations originally received—preaching a new gospel that is viewed as heretical.

Who are these churches to whom the letter is directed? We do not know, except that the author mentions he has written to them before. Most scholars, however, do not believe that the same author wrote both letters attributed to Peter, although after Peter's death both may have come from a circle that had formed around Peter in Rome. We may be expected to assume that 2 Peter is written to the same churches as 1 Peter. Both are written to churches largely composed of Gentile Christians, more at home in a Greek culture than a Jewish one. Within the letter, the author states that he expects to die soon, and for that reason is writing almost a farewell letter to help his addressees avoid the dangers he sees they are facing. Some of these dangers are already present, while others are in the future. He assumes the readers know Paul's letters, although he does not mention any specific letter. Indeed, the false teachers who are bringing a different gospel may be using Paul in an extreme fashion, and this letter is trying to reclaim Paul for orthodox Christianity against those who misuse him.

There is little connection between 1 and 2 Peter in terms of content. First Peter urges readers to maintain their love and humility toward one another. It assumes they know they are part of a new creation as well as living in the old, and their problems result from the conflict between these two cultures. Second Peter seems to be dealing with Christians who are in great danger of losing the sense that they are to lead new lives. Both letters are concerned with behavior, but the second letter focuses more on individual morality, whereas in the first love and humility that hold the community together are the great virtues. Judgment is stressed in both, as well as the reward God gives faithfulness, and yet 1 Peter is more concerned with the church as a body, whereas 2 Peter is directed more to individuals within the church.

It is interesting to look at the issue of authority in both letters. First Peter urges the readers to submit to the authority of God in the midst of suffering, following Jesus, the highest example of the Suffering Servant. But he also urges them to submit to the human authorities under whom they live: husbands, masters, the state. Within the congregation, all are to recognize the authority of the elders. Second Peter is also very concerned with authority, especially authority within the church, both at the local level and authority beyond: apostles such as Peter, the writings of Paul properly interpreted, the gospel originally proclaimed to them. These have authority, while the false teachers in their midst do not.

Our language may now be different: we do not speak of false teachers or false gospels quite as readily as this letter does. The church today, like the church then, has to deal with the basic issues of authority for what the church teaches and of the need to bear witness to one's faith in the way one lives.

As you read this letter, think about the situation of your own congregation. Are there dangers to the church coming from within or from without? Are there conflicts about what constitutes Christian behavior? Is there agreement as to what constitutes the authority that the congregation recognizes as to the meaning of the gospel for our lives? How does the author of 2 Peter answer these questions?

1:1–21

Preparing the Groundwork for Debate

By the late first and early second centuries, there were serious conflicts within some of the churches. New interpretations of the gospel had arisen in some areas, and these had to be challenged in order to keep the faith in the gospel originally proclaimed. How was this to be done? First of all, the congregations in which these new teachings were gaining ground must be shown that these teachings are in conflict with Scripture, which means the Old Testament, and with the gospel as it was given to the first disciples of Jesus. Those susceptible to these new interpretations are recent converts, who find that the gospel divides them from families and friends who do not understand their new behavior. The first generation of teachers had died, those who had actually been with Jesus and were grounded in Hebrew Scriptures. There are serious questions of authority that must be asked and answered in order to show how to judge what is authentic Christian teaching. This letter is written to such churches.

1:1–2

Our Common Faith

The author of this letter states that he is Peter the apostle, and yet he is but a slave or servant of Jesus Christ. He has apostolic authority within the churches; but in regard to Christ, he is equal to all other Christians, a servant or slave of the one Master. If the letter was written from Rome, which most scholars believe, there is a clear attempt here to show both the authority of Peter and that there is no question about the faith of the congregations receiving the letter. They have the same faith. They are equal to the church in Rome. But the author understands that either at the present time or in the near future their faith will be challenged by teachers who preach a different gospel. They are being warned at the same time as they are being praised for the true faith they now possess. The letter may well have originated in a circle of followers of Peter, just as 1 Peter most likely did. If so, we again have a letter from the center of the empire to churches outside that center. Rome gained authority quite early, partly because Peter and Paul were both assumed to have been there and to have died there. In addition, it was a church less subject to Greek influences because of its location, and it had a strong Jewish Christian background, which helped it maintain the gospel as proclaimed by the earliest Christians in the face of Gentile Christian influences that were stronger in other parts of the empire, especially in the Greek-speaking area of the eastern part.

There is a certain implied authority, therefore, in this letter. At the same time the author makes clear that the faith of these Christians to whom the letter is written is the same faith as that of the church in Rome. It is a common faith, linking them together as one church. Their faith, and that of the church of Rome, and the faith that we have today, all come to us through Jesus Christ. At the same time, there are serious challenges in some of these churches, challenges that would alter the common faith that now binds them together.

It is important for churches to recognize that other churches have the same faith. In fact, this is the basis for the ecumenical movement. There are different traditions, each with its nuances, its particular emphases, and yet there is a common faith that holds them all together. John Calvin, in the midst of the Protestant Reformation, said that Christians should never separate from a congregation unless there were serious matters of doctrine that forced them to separate. Then he listed such matters:

> [S]ome fault may creep into the administration of either doctrine or sacraments, but this ought not to estrange us from communion with the church. For not all the articles of true doctrine are of the same sort. Some are so necessary to know

that they should be certain and unquestioned by all men as the proper principles of religion. Such are: God is one, Christ is God and the Son of God; our salvation rests in God's mercy; and the like.[1]

Clearly, Calvin is not listing all the doctrines he considers essential, but it is obvious that there is a wide latitude in the differences there can be between Christians without damaging the fundamental unity they have in Christ.

There is an overtone of 1 Peter in the words about "a faith as precious as ours." First Peter 1:7 speaks of a faith "more precious than gold." It is "our faith," not ours versus yours. This faith is precious because it is a gift from God through Christ. We did not earn this faith or merit it in any way. We received this faith. This is a point that always has to be made clear.

Faith is a gift. We do not decide to have faith; it is not a matter of the will. So often we hear evangelists telling us to choose Christ, to accept Christ, as though we could make a decision to have faith. But that is not what is meant here. Christians are those to whom the gift of faith has been given. They have heard the gospel and found themselves attracted to it. Others heard the gospel proclaimed and found it strange or repellent. Why the difference? Christians believed that God had made it possible for them to believe by an act of grace. They could not explain it. Faith simply happens. It is an experience, however gradual or sudden. We find we have faith whereas earlier we did not. Acts of the will are involved. For instance, if, as unbelievers, we begin to find the lives of some Christians intriguing or a little positive, it may well be an act of the will to ask them about their faith, or to decide to go to a church to hear more about it. Or, on the contrary, we may decide not to do such investigation. Denominations are divided by their emphasis on free will or on the grace of God in regard to acquiring faith. The reality, however, is a mystery. We know that we cannot simply will ourselves to have faith. It must be an experience and not simply an intellectual decision. God's grace is involved. The work of the Holy Spirit is necessary. At the same

1. John Calvin, *Institutes of the Christian Religion* 4.1.11; ed. John T. McNeill, trans. Ford Lewis Battles, LCC 20–21 (Philadelphia: Westminster Press, 1960), 2:1025–26.

time, faith often develops slowly, through a long process in which we know we could have turned away any number of times along the way. We probably interpret our experience of faith according to the theological tradition in which we stand.

It is Jesus Christ who has brought to us all the righteousness of God. If we are accounted righteous, then obviously our sins are forgiven. All of this comes to us through Jesus Christ, here called God and our Savior. Does this refer to two persons—God and Jesus Christ—or is it applying two terms to the one Jesus Christ—our God and Savior? The latter is more likely. The early church had not yet tried to figure out how Jesus could be God as well as the God of Israel who sent him, though Christians were monotheists. They believed there was only one God and yet that God was in Christ in a unique way, and we could say that Jesus was the Son of God. We see that in the early form of the Apostles' Creed, in the early second century. It was the baptismal statement of faith of the church of Rome. Those to be baptized were asked if they believed in God the Father almighty, in Jesus Christ his Son, and in the Holy Spirit. In no way, however, did these Christians believe in three gods. It was not until the fourth century that the issue came to a head and the church made explicit its understanding of the Trinity at the councils of Nicaea and Constantinople. However we read it, the early church believed that Jesus was God incarnate and therefore the Savior.

The introduction to the letter ends with a prayer that grace and peace would be upon the recipients. This is a standard prayer in Christian epistles. Grace and peace go together. The peace that God gives to the faithful is because of God's grace, which we receive through the work of Jesus Christ. If we have no knowledge of God and Christ, then there is no way we can have the peace that God gives. Think of the famous words in John 14:27, that the peace Jesus gives is not the same as the peace the world gives. The peace the world gives is the result of circumstances that let us not worry, the good times when all is going our way. The problem is that the world cannot keep things that way, so peace is transient, dependent upon circumstances that cannot be controlled. The peace that God gives us through Christ is a peace that does not depend on outward realities. We can have peace even in the midst of terrible situations, a peace that the world cannot end. We may be sorrowful with good reason. We may face great difficulties, but even so, there can be peace at the center of our lives, even while we deal with the circumstances that we face. It is this sort of peace that the author prayed the churches would receive and live in. When we read the epistle as a letter to us as well as to those ancient Christians, the prayer is asking for the same peace to come to us because we also have the same faith.

There is a stress here on the knowledge that we have. Throughout this letter there is an emphasis on knowledge because the danger these churches face is new, different, and heretical teachings. If grace and peace come to us through the knowledge we have, then that grace and peace are both challenged by strange teachings. The gospel these churches had received gave them the knowledge that led to grace and peace. It was God's gift to them, along with faith. Now, if they accept the strange teachings that these new teachers proclaim, they will be in danger of losing their faith as well as the grace and peace that come with it because of the righteousness of God.

1:3–11

Participants in the Divine Nature

As in 1 Peter, great stress is laid on the fact that these church members have been called by God in Christ to be part of the church. It was not their own initiative that led them to the community of faith, but rather they were chosen and called to this life. The emphasis is on the gifts that God has given to them as part of their calling. They need nothing more than what they have been given in Christ. They have the knowledge they need, so these new teachers are not necessary. What they have been given is promises, promises that they will become participants in the divine nature, promises that they will share in the divine glory and goodness. At the end of the letter there is also the promise that they will inherit the new heaven and the new earth that God will bring. These promises come to us through God's grace, and are to lead us to godliness.

The connection between faith and promises is very important. Many of us think of faith as a set of doctrines to be believed. With the stress on knowledge that we find in this letter we might expect that faith would be acceptance of a series of doctrines. Doctrines are important, but faith, especially in the early church, was living life on the basis of the promises of God that Christians had been given. Belief in these promises is not only an intellectual activity. Granted, there has to be knowledge of the promises, and that is important. But even more essential is living our lives on the basis of these promises. This means bearing the fruits of faith, showing by our lives that we truly believe that God will bring about the future which we are promised, regardless of what we see around us. Great promises about sharing in the divine nature and in God's glory certainly would be astonishing to people who really were nobodies in their society. In the midst of the questions and even taunts of their families and neighbors, it might be difficult to believe.

This understanding of faith as believing in God's promises was a major issue in the Protestant Reformation. What Luther meant by "salvation by grace through faith" was holding to the promises of God, especially the promise that our sins have been forgiven. These promises are given to us by name in our baptism. Therefore, after baptism, when we turn to God in repentance, we hold to the promise of forgiveness already given us in baptism. In the late Middle Ages, faith had come to be the intellectual assent to what the church taught. Past sins were forgiven by baptism, but sins after that needed to be confessed to a priest and forgiven in order to restore one to baptismal purity.

The line is not easily drawn between Protestants and Catholics on this issue. All churches are tempted to substitute a list of doctrinal teachings for living on the basis of the promises of God. It is an easy thing to do, especially if there is a conflict about teachings, if heresies are suspected. It is easier to accept teachings and then not worry about how our lives are lived but only about what is intellectually accepted. Yet there is also a danger of emphasizing how we live our lives to the point that we fall into salvation by works, assuming that our salvation depends upon our own actions. There is a very delicate balance between grace and works, and between faith and intellectual belief. We may think of baptism more as our promise to God than as God's promises to us. Here, however, it is stated that everything we need has been given to us, especially the promises of God.

One of the promises is that we shall "become participants of the divine nature." This may sound strange to us. What does it mean to share in the divine nature? Does it mean we will become God? There is a strand of early theology that speaks of deification, and it is done in a very orthodox fashion. If we are baptized into Christ we are made part of his body, which is the church. Taken more literally than we usually do, this means that we

> For all who are led by the Spirit of God are children of God. For you did not receive a spirit of slavery to fall back into fear, but you have received a spirit of adoption. When we cry, "Abba! Father!" it is that very Spirit bearing witness with our spirit that we are children of God, and if children, then heirs, heirs of God and joint heirs with Christ—if, in fact, we suffer with him so that we may also be glorified with him.
> —Romans 8:14–17

are part of the body of the second person of the Trinity incarnate. We are part of the life of the Trinity, which makes us part of the divine nature. Another way of understanding this is to say, as many in the early church did, that we are by adoption what Jesus is by nature, children of God. We can speak of God as our Father because we are part of the Son or we are siblings of the Son. This does not mean that we are divine in ourselves, but that we are "participants of the divine nature."

The term "Father" is used in Christian tradition in regard to God in two different ways. (For the moment we will set aside the issue of gender-specific language.) First, we speak of God as our Father and we mean that the whole Trinity is called Father. Second, we use the Trinitarian terminology: we call the first person of the Trinity the Father, whereas the second person is the Son and the third person is the Holy Spirit. When we say the Lord's Prayer and pray to "Our Father," are we praying to God the Trinity or are we thinking of ourselves as part of the second person of the Trinity praying to the first person, the Father, through the power of the third person, who is the Holy Spirit, through whose action we have been engrafted into the body through baptism? This second understanding sounds very complicated, but it is part of a long tradition within the church. In other words, there are ways of thinking of ourselves as becoming

> Just as God stepped out of his nature to become a partaker of our humanity, so we are called to step out of our nature to become partakers of his divinity.
>
> —Hilary of Arles
>
> Quoted in *James, 1–2 Peter, 1–3 John, Jude*, ed. Gerald Bray, ACCSNT 11 (Downers Grove, IL: InterVarsity Press, 2000), 133.

more and more part of the life of God, never the equal of God, but increasingly part of the inner life of God as we grow in godliness. We have been grafted into the body of Christ, and he is part of the Trinity. Therefore, when we act as part of that body, we are involved in the inner life of God.

There are good reasons to find ways of speaking of God that do not depend on the traditional gender-specific language. The difficulty is trying to find terms that are personal and show the relationship of the three persons. "Parent" and "child" do this; "source" and "offspring" also can show this. We need to understand what the doctrine of the Trinity is safeguarding so that it remains safe when we make changes. The work of creation and redemption are works of the whole Trinity, and assigning them to one of the persons can present problems.

The church, historically, has been very careful to rule out any ideas that we cease to be creatures. We are not absorbed into God, losing our nature as creatures, which is what some Eastern philosophies taught. Even some forms of mysticism in the church have bordered on this understanding, and therefore have been highly questionable. We remain creatures with no possibility of life except that given to us by the Creator. Yet our Creator has wished us to be part of the divine life, through the action of the Son. His glory and goodness have made it possible for us, who know Christ Jesus, to lead godly lives, and increasingly to become participants in the divine nature.

The process of becoming godly involves loosening the ties to a fallen world in which sin dominates. This is not to say the world is not God's good creation, but sin has cast a pall over that world, and redemption involves being freed from the corruption that sin has placed in that creation. In this context, the work of Christ is to free us from the bondage to sin and corruption and to open to us the way to freedom and peace, life with God rather than life separated from God by sin.

The text speaks of lust as the principal form of corruption. This could easily be taken to mean that the primary sins are sexual, and godliness means avoiding sexual sins or even avoiding sexuality altogether. But lust has a far greater meaning than simply sexual desire. It covers desires for power, covetousness, anything that turns a person away from living a life of obedience to God's commands. There is a long tradition in the Western church of viewing lust—called concupiscence—as the root of all sin. It means a self-centeredness, a self-protectiveness, that may manifest itself in obvious pride or may be a shyness that does not wish to be viewed by the world. For Augustine such concupiscence was the character of original sin, and the basis of all actual sins. Baptism wiped away the guilt of original sin, but not its consequences, so that all children are born with concupiscence, even though they are too young to commit any actual sins until they reach the age of accountability—which for him began quite early. There is considerable correspondence between this view of sin as lust and what was discussed above about Schleiermacher's understanding of sin as the search for increased pleasure and decreased pain. If our circumstances are such that life is fairly easy, we may desire increased pleasure. If our lives are miserable, then decreasing the pain probably takes first place. In either case, we may be shy and retiring or prideful and aggressive in our search for what we desire.

If Christ has freed us from such corruption and given us everything we need to lead morally upright lives, then we should spend every effort to live such a life. This does not mean that we can, at once, lead perfect, sinless lives. Becoming freed from the corruption of a world held hostage by sin is not an instantaneous transformation. Rather it is a process, begun in baptism or the conversion that leads to

> The heart of Christian faith is the encounter with the God of Jesus Christ who makes possible both our union with God and communion with each other. In this encounter God invites people to share in divine life and grace through Jesus Christ by the power of the Holy Spirit; at the same time, we are called to live in new relationship with one [an]other, as we are gathered together by the Spirit into the body of Christ. The personal and communal dimensions of Christian faith are inseparable.
> —Catherine Mowry LaCugna
>
> "The Practical Trinity," in *Exploring Christian Spirituality: An Ecumenical Reader*, ed. Kenneth J. Collins (Grand Rapids: Baker, 2000), 274.

baptism, and continued throughout life, always with the need for the forgiveness of sins. But habits can be formed that make it more likely we will choose to do what God wants. We become more able to understand what is good, and we have more ability to go against our natural inclinations and choose to do what is good. We become more adept at seeing temptation early and not yielding to it. This takes a life of prayer, and learning through the church, through Scripture, what really is God's will, God's plans for the world, what human beings were created to be rather than what sin has caused us to be.

That brings us to the list of virtues in verses 5–7. They seem to follow a developmental path, although that may not be what is intended. The growth of virtue in a Christian ultimately leads to love, the highest virtue, although one assumes that one does not wait until the end to love. It may be that all of these virtues work to strengthen the ability to love. Faith must lead to goodness. Faith alone is not enough if it is simply in the mind and never leads to actions. This sentiment parallels that of James 2:14–26, that faith without works is a dead faith. Faith is the beginning of the Christian life, a gift of God, and it includes the knowledge of Christ and the promises of God. Because we are now recipients of the glory and goodness of Christ we must begin to grow in goodness ourselves. Goodness will lead to greater knowledge both of ourselves and of God's work in us. The knowledge of ourselves includes the awareness of the sinfulness of our lives, in particular and not just in general. This knowledge should increase our self-control because when we know we are prone to a particular sin we can begin to guard against it. We know what are the situations in which we commit this sin, and we can either avoid such situations or we can be on the lookout for the temptation to act in our usual way. A growth in self-control lessens the power of lust in all respects, and therefore increases the goodness in our lives. Faith gives us the beginning, showing us that Christ has freed us from the bonds of sin. We should not waste such freedom, but use it to strengthen our ability to do what is good. If we are able to practice self-control, our strength to resist sin will increase, leading to endurance on the path of goodness. This endurance increases our godliness, our participation in the divine nature, for which participation Christ died and was raised.

Godliness is love, above all. It leads to the love for one another that is the hallmark of the church, the redeemed life of believers. It is love for God who has given us all of these things and who has made it possible for us to live the life for which we were created. The list of virtues seems like a spiral that we are to go through all of our lives, increasing in faith in order to increase in all the rest. A little faith leads to a little self-awareness, a little self-control, a little love. Greater faith leads to greater capacity for goodness and love.

These virtues lead to the actions appropriate to those who know Christ. We are to be fruitful, our actions in the world showing that our faith is real. Those who acknowledge Christ and yet bear no such fruit have forgotten that their sins have been forgiven and that they have been freed from the power of sin. They are blind to the work of Christ, even if they are members of the church and profess to have faith. Theirs is a faith that is only in the mind, not in the heart and life. They do not really believe the promises of God and they show their lack of belief by basing their lives on self-preservation rather than on trust that God will actually fulfill what has been promised.

Our election is shown by our actions. At the same time, were we to assume that those who have been called are changed immediately into sinless creatures who are never tempted, who never sin, we would be in a hopeless situation, since we know all too well that such total transformation has not happened to us. With each stumble we would be sure we had been cast out forever. But the list of virtues given above, and the stress on increasing in these virtues, show that there is always room for improvement. We become more godly, but we still need the help of God and the community of faith to continue on our way.

Though the term "election" has been used throughout this passage, it is probably not a good idea to read a full doctrine of predestination into it. What does it mean to confirm our call and election? Those who are baptized have the sign of God's election. They can be assured that God has called them. The promises of God are given to them. To say that others are not elect, that our election means that we can never fall from grace, are additions to the understanding of election that may not be warranted by this passage. Indeed, there seem to be warnings here that those who have been called may fall away. If they do not use what they have been given, if they do not develop self-control and endurance, then perhaps, though elect in the sense of having been called into the church by God, they will not remain part of that blessed company. This section closes with words of assurance that those who manifest the kind of life called for here will be a part of the eternal kingdom Christ has established.

FURTHER REFLECTIONS
Predestination

Augustine was the first to develop a full system of theology that incorporated what we call predestination. This has also been called election, and therefore it is easy to read it into passages such as 2 Peter 1:10. There were words about election in 1 Peter as well (1 Pet. 1:1–2), although there the terms were "chosen" and "destined."

There is a certain election involved in simply being in an area of the world where the gospel is preached. If one had been born in Outer Mongolia in the fourth century, it would have been very unlikely that one would have heard the gospel, and therefore there was no way to respond to it. If one were born in a Muslim country at the present time, there might be so much antagonism to anything Christian because of political, social, or economic forces, that even if the gospel were preached, or read about, there would be little chance of really understanding. There is, therefore, a certain historical and geographical "election" that must be kept in mind.

But what election has meant, theologically, has more to do with the power of God to let us hear the gospel and, with the gift of faith, actually to believe it. It is with this election that Augustine was concerned. For him, when sin entered the world in the fall, as Genesis 3 describes it, the alteration that occurred in humanity was such that there was an actual physical change. Augustine believed that in the original creation it was expected that human beings would live in this world, in the garden of Eden, for a certain length of time, but not forever. He assumed they would have children, with approximately the same method of conception as now, but with momentous differences. Originally, Adam and Eve would have decided, rationally, that it was time to have a child. They would have engaged in sexual intercourse. Their bodies would have fully cooperated. He would have been potent and she would have been fertile. There would have been no passion involved, only a physical act governed by the mind. Nine months later, without pain, a child would have been born. Adam and Eve would have had however many children they deemed appropriate. They would have seen their grandchildren, but at whatever time God had deemed right, they would have completed their earthly life, and have been taken to the next life. There would have been no fear of death, no sad good-byes. They had completed fully their lives here and it was time to enter the next.

No children were conceived before the fall, however. The effect of sin was to disrupt this plan for everyone. Death entered, and there was fear, not knowing what lay on the other side. Death arrived at different times, when life was not really completed. And sexual life was dramatically changed. Passion was necessary for the sex act, at least on the part of the man. All children were therefore conceived in the midst of passion. Men were not always potent, and sex occurred when women were not fertile. There was desire for sex when there was no desire for children. There was desire for children when the sex act could not be completed, or it was complete but still there were no children. Human beings were corrupted with original sin, and could no longer see what God really wanted. They pursued what they wanted instead.

However, God chose some people to whom to give grace that, to some degree, overcame this concupiscence. Such people could begin to glimpse what God really wanted, what was really good. No one could choose this grace, because they could not understand it. Sin had corrupted every human faculty—human beings were totally depraved. Total depravity does not mean that every human being was completely sinful, but that every aspect of a human being has been tainted by sin, so what we think, what we feel, has all been corrupted to some degree. We may choose to do what is good, but only because it benefits us. We rationalize our actions, so that what is sinful appears the best choice available. Only what is called "irresistible grace" can overcome such depravity. Grace comes to us, we do not choose it. We see what grace allows us to see, and we cannot avoid seeing it.

Since grace came to us without our choice, we also cannot refuse it. Therefore, those who are elect will ultimately be saved. They will ultimately choose what God wants, even if they resist for a long time. Grace will have its way. Therefore, there is what Augustine called "the perseverance of the saints."

Augustine's writings set the stage for later theological understandings that used his thought. This includes Calvin in particular. The early Puritans were Calvinists and they had a strong doctrine of predestination. They could readily have interpreted 2 Peter 1:10–11 to show the accuracy of their doctrine. They have often been accused of constantly trying to be sure they were among the elect by looking at their actions. They were sure that if they were indeed among the elect they could not fall from grace and their ultimate salvation was assured. There are two problems with this. First, it is all too easy to fall back into a salvation by works—that we earn our salvation by what we do. That opinion totally undoes the Protestant Reformation. We are saved by God's grace. Our faith was itself a gift of God, nothing that we had earned. Second, this can easily become warped into deciding that those who are successful in this life, judged by the world's standard of success, are therefore definitely among the elect. Their works made them successful and their success shows their election. This is a caricature of Puritanism that at least points to the dangers inherent in some understandings of predestination. There is something egocentric about constantly worrying about our election. Our election is to free us from such worry and let us go about the task of becoming more holy, more able to follow God's will. At the same time, thinking that all we need to do is make a statement of faith with no amendment of life is equally strange, and a perversion of the understanding of salvation by grace alone.

This passage can be summarized by saying that Christians must remember that God has called them—elected them—to be part of the body of Christ. Everything they need in order to grow in this life, becoming more godly, has been given to them in Christ. They are to use what they have been given, especially the freedom from bondage to sin and the help of the church, in order to become more holy. This will ensure their inclusion in Christ's kingdom. But there is in this passage no assurance that those who are elect may not fall from grace and the passage does not provide a solid foundation for the entire system that Augustine created.

1:12–15

Personal Comments

These verses return to the more personal comments in which the author, understood as Peter, points to his death that is to take place soon. Because the end of his life is near, he is writing to the churches in order to warn them of dangers he sees coming and to urge them to faithfulness. Tradition holds that Peter died in Rome during Nero's persecution. If he were imprisoned in Rome, and knew that the date of his execution was near, it is understandable that he would take the time to write to the churches—not necessarily specific ones—a letter that would set forth his understanding of what was happening to them at the time, and how to guard against the dangers he sees. The specific dangers have not yet been set forth, but the stage is set by showing that the moral life of Christians is absolutely essential. They are called to holiness and godliness, and this should never be forgotten. A letter is the best way to give these warnings, giving the churches after his death a record of what he has said. Even though the majority of scholars do not believe that the apostle Peter wrote this letter, the form of a farewell letter in his name is a strong device employed later in the first or in the second century for showing the dangers Christians faced, using the authority of Peter to ensure a hearing.

1:16–21

The Charge

On first reading it is not clear whether the author is charging some with creating "cleverly devised myths" or refuting the charge that others have made against him. In the context, most scholars believe that it is the apostles who are accused of making up stories about

Christ. Here Peter is depicted as saying that he has firsthand knowledge, because he was an eyewitness to the transfiguration. He saw for himself Christ's glorification by the Father. In verses 16–18 the author reminds the readers that he, Peter, was among the few who were witnesses to this event on the mountain. They saw his majesty. They heard the voice that proclaimed him God's Son. (These verses are in the lectionary to be read at the Feast of the Transfiguration.) The words are here to reinforce the authority of the writer, and to show that he knows from personal experience the truth that Jesus Christ is God's Son and our Savior. We do not yet know what strange thing is being taught, but evidently there is a denial of what the apostles taught, and the early teachings are being called "cleverly devised myths." Peter defends against this change by stating his own experience of Christ.

The transfiguration is mentioned in all three of the Synoptic Gospels. Obviously, it is known to the writer of 2 Peter and to his readers. The writer could have chosen many different parts of the narrative of the life of Jesus in order to show that he was directly and personally a witness to who Jesus was. The choice of the transfiguration, however, is directly related to the charges others were making against the original gospel preached to the receiving church. The questionable teachers may have been denying that Jesus was to return in judgment. If so, the vision of the transfiguration would have refuted that. The vision of the transfiguration shows that Jesus is God's Son, and it gives a glimpse of the majesty that belongs to him. He is the one by whom all will be judged, and therefore any sense that Christians do not need to be concerned about how they live is false.

Verse 19 is a poetic way of stating that Scripture—in this case, the Old Testament—can be for them a bright light in the midst of darkness, until their faith is secure in this knowledge. This does not mean that at some point in their Christian lives they will be able to do without Scripture, since there is no perfect knowledge in this life. They are not to be confused by other teachings, but to listen only to what the Holy Spirit confirms. Prophecy is the work of God. It is the Holy Spirit that caused men and women in the past to prophesy truly about what God planned to do. It is the Holy Spirit also who will confirm in their hearts the truth of the message. No personal interpretation but only the Holy Spirit can give us the truth that is contained in Scripture. It is the church, through its apostolic witness, that has the true interpretation, so they should not believe others who come with their own understandings.

There has often been a conflict between two different understandings about how we read Scripture. On one side are those who hold that Scripture is clear in its meaning and those who read it with an open mind will be able to discern its truth. On the other side are those who believe that an understanding of Scripture requires the work of the Holy Spirit in the mind and

> Second Peter has distinguished the divine revelation found in scripture, both the prophets and the gospel, from competing forms of religious and philosophical propaganda. As long as believers hold fast to the apostolic tradition, the gospel, and the prophets, they can anticipate a vision of divine glory that carries with it participation in God. Who would want to turn aside from such a promise?
> —**Pheme Perkins**
>
> *First and Second Peter, James, and Jude*, Interpretation (Louisville: John Knox Press, 1995), 177.

heart of the reader. What we find here is an understanding that the apostolic preaching, the gospel originally delivered to these Christians, is the true interpretation of Scripture. Those who are part of the true church have this guidance and should not be swayed from their belief by teachers who say something very different. Within the church Scripture functions as a light in the midst of darkness.

The words "no prophecy of scripture is a matter of one's own interpretation" deserve to be considered more fully. Many Protestants believe that the great difference between Protestants and Roman Catholics is that Protestants read the Bible for themselves whereas Catholics have to believe what the church teaches. This is far too simplistic, and has more to do with the more recent centuries than with the Protestant reformers themselves. Both the Lutheran and the Reformed tradition created confessions of faith that were quite lengthy and were held to be the official interpretation of Scripture to which all pastors were bound.

At the same time, no Protestant would ever give these written confessions of faith equal standing with Scripture itself, which meant that the confessions were always subject to reinterpretation, and in the case of the Reformed tradition, the creation of new confessions. The Roman Catholic Church, for its part, has discovered that many Catholics agree with the church in many respects but still feel free to discard teachings they do not find congenial.

Both Catholics and Protestants today have to consider what it means that there is no private interpretation of Scripture. There is something wrong with expecting people to believe by an act of their wills what their minds neither understand nor agree with. Blind acceptance of authority has little place in the modern world. On the other hand, individually created beliefs that have no connection to what the church teaches would mean there is really no community of faith, only individual "faiths." Somewhere between these extremes is the understanding that the church does teach with authority, and that the Holy Spirit helps the community of faith discern the meaning of Scripture in its life. Christianity is a faith based on historical events, and those events individual believers cannot create for themselves. The church teaches the gospel it has received, and the implications of that gospel for the Christian life. But the church is not an impersonal authority. It is made up of people who hold a common faith, and who are able to discuss and confirm what these ancient teachings mean for Christians today. We can never be cut off from our historical roots without creating "cleverly devised myths" that have no rootage in the gospel. Our interpretation of Scripture is to be conducted within the church, learning from other Christians, past and present. Both Catholic and Protestant churches today are dealing with exactly what it means to have a common faith, based on Scripture, rooted in the gospel first proclaimed some twenty centuries ago. That gospel was the fulfillment of Scriptures from centuries before that. Now the proclamation of the gospel is still capable of transforming lives through the power of the Holy Spirit in today's world. Who has the authority to teach what is the true gospel? Who has the authority to say someone is preaching a false gospel? These are questions of Christians today. As we continue the study of 2 Peter, we will see that the early church struggled with many of the same issues.

2:1–22

The Challenge

The author is clear that the Christians to whom this letter is written are dealing with false teachers who have begun to preach a different gospel than the one preached by the apostles. Of course, those who listen to these people are not convinced the teachings are false. It is the task of the writer to show that the new versions go against the true gospel. In addition, the readers should remember that God does not deal lightly with those who proclaim false things in God's name. There was a reminder at the end of the last chapter that true prophecy is always the work of God through the Holy Spirit and not the creation of human beings. There was also the reminder that whenever there is true prophecy, false teachers or false prophets will arise.

2:1–3

False Teachers

It would seem that every time God raises up true prophets false ones arise as well. That happened in the Old Testament, so it will happen now, when false teachers arise against the gospel. Why would that be true? It may be because some people find the true gospel too difficult, and wish an easier, more comfortable one. Or these false teachers may wish to have power within the life of the church and try to gain a following by their words. If the purpose of prophecy is to show us what God wishes, what God thinks about what is happening in our lives, what God plans to do to "shepherd" creation toward the goal God has for it, then prophecy will naturally run counter to what a sinful humanity thinks. This does not mean that true prophecy always is negative. Granted, if prophets speak truly for God and say that what we are doing is wrong and will bring dire consequences, that will be negative from our point of view. But many prophecies in the Old Testament are quite positive: that God will bring the people home, that God will let them dwell happily in their own homes and not let anyone make them afraid. In the New Testament there are also promises. In 2 Peter 1:4 the readers have been reminded that God has given them great promises. But sinful people have as much trouble believing good news from God as they do believing warnings of destruction. A sense of guilt may make it seem that we will never deserve good things, that God will always be against us, and so forth. We may also be sufficiently satisfied with our lives as they are that we do not wish to change them very much—and the true gospel will definitely cause great changes.

Tertullian had to deal with a whole variety of false teachers who arose in the church in the second century:

> The Lord teaches us that many "ravening wolves shall come in sheep's clothing." Now, what are these sheep's clothings, but the external surface of the Christian profession? Who are the ravening wolves but those deceitful senses and spirits which are lurking within to waste the flock of Christ? Who are the false prophets but deceptive predictors of the future? . . . [P]ersecution makes even martyrs, (but) heresy only apostates.

—Tertullian

"The Prescription against Heretics" 4 (*ANF* 3:245).

These false teachers in 2 Peter were "bought" by Jesus—which points to the redemption they gained through the work of Christ. They had been freed from bondage, should be no longer slaves to sin. Yet they have turned against the one who gained them this freedom. So these false teachers are Christians, part of the church, not outsiders. Their view of the faith denies in some significant ways the earlier teachings. The author puts this in the future, seeing this as happening sometime after his death. The readers can therefore assume that the time of which Peter spoke has now come or is about to come. Perhaps the author saw such things happening in a few churches and is warning others.

The text says that these false teachers are secretly teaching "destructive opinions." They may have been church teachers, those who were supposed to be teaching the new converts the true doctrines, and yet they used the opportunity to give them their own false opinions. As we saw above (see pp. 21–25, "Further Reflections: The Catechumenate"), by the early second century, at least in areas where most of the converts were Gentiles unacquainted with Judaism, the church developed programs of teaching these converts for two or three years before they were baptized. In some areas this may well have been the practice in the late first century. At first this was quite informal, and many teachers set up their own classes. It took awhile before the church officially took control of this teaching. Having false teachers instruct catechumens would be particularly damaging. These catechumens were people who had little knowledge of what should be taught and therefore could be swayed easily. This would be especially true if the false teachers were presenting an easier way to be Christians with less conflict with the surrounding society.

We have some of the same problems today. For centuries in the United States the church could assume that everyone in the society knew what the gospel was. They had a basic acquaintance with the Bible. It was read in the public schools, and most literate people had a fairly good awareness of what the church taught. Whether people believed it or wished to be part of the church was a different issue. Revivals urged them to repent and join the faithful, but the revivals did not have to teach them what was to be believed. That is no longer the case. Many in our society have grown up completely outside the church, and when they wish to become part of it, there is a great educational task to be undertaken. Yet few churches have clear programs for this or well-trained teachers. Even the established Sunday schools often have difficulty in finding sufficient teachers, and that means that those who do teach may not have a very clear understanding of the faith themselves. In our churches many people are nearly illiterate in terms of both the Bible and the Christian faith, and yet many of them are urged to volunteer to teach. They may have no malicious intention of teaching false opinions, but the church needs to be aware of what is being taught and prepare teachers adequately.

These false teachers to whom 2 Peter refers created problems for the church, first, because they denied the Master by their lies, and second, because what they taught encouraged licentiousness and therefore brought disrepute to the church. In other words, they did damage both within the church and beyond it, harming the opinion the wider public had of the church. I mentioned earlier that by the late first century there was some unofficial persecution by neighbors reporting Christians because they thought they were a danger to society. The greatest protection Christians had was the good opinion outsiders had of them, because they were loving and helpful, even to those who were not part of the church. If outsiders changed their opinion because some Christians were acting badly, it would reflect on the whole church. Furthermore, it was precisely Christians' excellent behavior and hopeful attitude that made others think of joining them. If the false teaching lessened either good behavior or hope, the witness to the world at large would be less effective in terms of evangelism. What Peter says is that those outside the church will look at the immoral actions of these Christians who have been led astray, and this will bring disrepute upon the church. The world will be confused as to what the church really teaches. If Christians believe what these false teachers are saying, they are ruining the reputation of the congregations.

The text says these teachers were motivated by greed. Exactly what this means is not clear. Were they charging for their teaching? Did they expect to occupy significant places in the church? Were they seeking power in the church rather than money? Some teachers may have been paid, but even that is not clear. If they wanted power, they might create quite a following if the catechetical classes were large, and once baptized these people might look fondly at their former teachers.

For the first time in this letter, we have at least a partial picture of what these false teachers were saying. Evidently, these teachers were telling Christians that the strictly moral life the church required was not really necessary. You could be a Christian and still live according to the standards of the pagan world. There was no reason to be so concerned about behavior. We know that the orthodox catechetical classes were very concerned about behavior, and lessening the standards there would make it easier for Gentile converts to combine their old way of life with their new beliefs.

If there are always false teachers who arise to challenge the truth of the gospel, does that mean that contemporary churches also need to be aware of false teachers? In the midst of a culture that assumes each person has a right to his or her own beliefs, and questioning them is inappropriate, it is difficult for some churches to say that certain interpretations of the gospel are outside the bounds of what is legitimate. Other churches find heresies even in slight deviation from a very narrow interpretation of the gospel. It has probably been difficult in every generation to make such distinctions, but in a culture such as ours that does not grant much authority to anyone, assuming individuals to be their own authority on matters of faith, it is particularly difficult.

For the writer of this epistle, the false teachings are not simply intellectual matters. The proof of their falsehood is in the behavior they permit. In our own day, there is little agreement among Christians as to what constitutes unacceptable lifestyle or behavior. For the early centuries of the church, it was impossible to imagine a Christian in military service. Soldiers could not be baptized because they were under orders of people who did not hold to the tenet of loving your enemies. No one who was involved in the theater could be baptized, because the dramas were accounts of the pagan gods. When the church became the dominant religious institution in the empire, all of that changed.

Our churches have been divided on many issues, some of which have been resolved, only to have even more difficult ones take their place. At one time it was thought impossible for Christians to divorce, and even less possible for those who were divorced to remarry. Pastors who were divorced were removed from the ministry. But after several decades of confusion and discussion, most Protestant denominations found it possible to permit divorce, and the church rejected the idea that anyone had to stay in an abusive marriage. Gradually, the acceptance of divorce even for reasons other than desertion, abuse, or infidelity became the norm for many Protestant denominations. The Roman Catholic Church has had even greater difficulty deciding what marriages could be annulled, since divorce was not possible. The Vatican has moved from few annulments to easy annulment and back again. Now some question the ease with which marriages in the church can be entered into and then dissolved. On questions of homosexuality the churches are divided. The issue of premarital sex is not so much discussed as simply ignored.

In other words, contemporary churches have difficulty knowing what are legitimate changes in attitudes brought about by a better understanding of the implications of the gospel itself and what are false teachings that should be rejected. We know that there are new understandings of the implications of the gospel in the church throughout history. The ending of slavery came because of such a new awareness. The status of women both within marriage and in society has altered because of the work of the Holy Spirit in the life of the church. We face the same questions as did those early Christians: What should be the legitimate difference in our own day between the Christian life and the life of those outside the church? Are there any hallmarks of the Christian life? Does the church bring disrepute upon itself if it differs in no clear respect from the rest of the world? Do people flock to a church because it does not require much in the way of amendment of life, or do they look for a congregation that does show transformed lives? Are there "greedy teachers" who proclaim a false gospel in order to prosper financially or to have a large following? These are questions each church needs to consider. It is not so much legislative bodies of denominations that can make such distinctions; it is even more the task of Christians who live together at the congregational level, who know their neighbors outside the church are watching them.

The epistle warns that all such false teachers will be destroyed. God judged them and found them wanting long ago. Their judgment is sure, even if it is not visible at the moment. It would be easy to decide who is a false teacher and who is true if fire and brimstone were to fall on all the false ones. But that is not the case. Though judged, that judgment has not yet been made manifest. The writer assures us judgment is not asleep but is on its way. That means that for the present we shall have to use our understanding as to who are false and who are true teachers.

2:4–10a

The Necessity of Judgment

Already in these opening verses of chapter 2, the author has begun borrowing from the writing of Jude. Both letters agree that the false teachers were condemned long ago, but now their preaching has disrupted the congregations. These teachers preach licentiousness and deny the Master by their actions and their words. The copying from Jude continues in this next section.

In a brief rehearsal of how God rescued the godly from the clutches of the unrighteous who by their behavior dishonored God, the writer begins with the angels who fell. God kept them in chains, and they will be so kept until judgment. This may be based on non-biblical sources that extrapolate from Genesis 6:1–4, the account of the angels or "the sons of God" who had children with human women. Or it may be a more common understanding that some angels fell and became the demonic host. That will be discussed further in regard to 2 Peter 3:13. There is a similar passage in Revelation 20:1–3, where Satan is bound with chains in a pit for a thousand years. The list in 2 Peter goes on to Noah and Lot. Both were brought safely out of the destruction that punished the evildoers among whom they had lived. Noah and his family were rescued when the rest of the world was covered by the flood. Lot was brought out of Sodom and Gomorrah when fire destroyed those cities. These are proofs that God is able to save the righteous even while bringing judgment upon the wicked, especially those who are licentious. Jude is more interested in examples of God's judgment upon the wicked, whereas Peter is also concerned about showing that God rescues those who are righteous. If these Christians to whom the letter is written oppose the false teachers in their midst, they also will be rescued by God when the time of judgment comes.

The stress on judgment is important since a major concern is that the false teachers doubt that there will be judgment and therefore behavior does not matter. Again, many in our own age deny any judgment or at least any final condemnation by God. The thought of a final judgment is relegated to "cleverly devised myths" of a less scientific age. For many Christians today, God is not interested in judgment but in showing unconditional love, regardless of what we do. The corrective to this should not be trying to scare people into proper action. What is needed is the restoration of a sense that God is indeed concerned about how we live. That is obvious throughout the biblical record. Christians often make a false dichotomy between the Old Testament and the New, so that the Old Testament is concerned about behavior because it is legalistic, whereas the New Testament is about grace and forgiveness and therefore not particularly concerned about our actions. One could come to such conclusions only if one did not read either Testament. The Old Testament is filled with God's loving and gracious acts of forgiveness, and the New Testament is filled with expectations about behavior. It is the same God in both Testaments, a God who is interested in forming a people who will be a light to those outside, showing who God is and what God desires for human life.

What God wishes is for us to agree with God on what constitutes true human life. Both creation and redemption are for the purpose of having a human family that is truly human, not superhuman and not inhuman. We are less than human when we do not live the way God has created us to live. Our communities do not work, our relationships are warped, if we do not pay attention to what we are created to be. Judgment is necessary in order to alter the fallen world and have it be God's good creation. Judgment is not for the sake of punishment but for the sake of redemption. Parents know that with children. Sometimes children have to learn the hard way that certain behaviors do not lead to the happiness and joy they thought, no matter how much their parents warn them. Will there be some who are condemned forever? That is God's business, not ours. But one thing is clear: if we do not change our minds about how we should live, if we continue to go our own way rather than God's way, we are condemned to live in a less than human world, a world that has not yet reached the goal for which God created it. God's concern is for the whole creation, not simply individuals. The law is a description of how human society should be, without covetousness, without disrespect for parents, without stealing and murder, and so forth. God is obviously concerned with individuals, and will rescue those who are righteous in the midst of an evil society. But God's ultimate concern is for the creation of a truly human society. For that, judgment is necessary. Even for individuals, judgment is part of the process of sanctification. If we do not understand what it is we have done wrong we will be unable to change.

2:10b–22

The Character of the False Teachers

This section is filled with strange images, many of them taken from Jude, and not all very clear. The opponents in Jude may not be the same as here, but many of the phrases of condemnation are used. The author of 2 Peter probably saw in Jude a good description of those who teach false doctrine and appropriated it here. We will discuss more of this when we study the Epistle of Jude. Obviously, here there is some concern about what the false teachers were saying about the angels, but exactly what they were saying is not clear. The diatribe against these teachers is that they are greedy, irrational, leading lives of excess and licentiousness. This author agrees with Jude that such teachers are "creatures of instinct" rather than of thought, but adds that as such creatures they are "born to be caught and killed." These are strange words indeed and may simply mean these teachers are like subhuman animals. There is another charge, not in Jude, that these people find it pleasurable "to revel in the daytime." This may mean that they do not do a day's work, perhaps because they have earned enough by their teaching to enjoy themselves during the daylight. They evidently participate in the Christian love feasts, but because of their debauchery they turn such feasts into something shameful. The phrase from Jude is also used, that they "slander what they do not understand." This may mean that they make fun of parts of the theological tradition they cannot comprehend. Probably chief among these is the return of Christ and the judgment to follow.

From verses 18–19 it is clear that these false teachers' major victories have been among recent converts. This is one reason to assume they may have been working with these recent converts even before the converts were baptized. Those people who had just begun to change their lives, leaving behind pagan ways, now are told by these teachers that in Christ they have the freedom to return to those ways without condemnation. It would make the transition easier if there were little or no difference between their former lives and the new ones in Christ. These converts would have less problems if they could join in the pagan feasts, make offerings to the gods, and so forth. These are behaviors 1 Peter was urging Christians to continue rejecting, even under the threat of persecution.

Verses 20–22 make clear that those who have once tasted the true life in Christ are in greater danger if they fall from this than they would have been had they never heard of Christ. The question that is raised here is the possibility of returning to faith if a believer once rejects Christ after having become part of the church. These words seem to be about the false teachers and not necessarily those they have influenced. These teachers once had the true knowledge that they were given in the church. They are baptized full members of the church. But they have left that path and now seek to have others follow them. They therefore show themselves to have turned their backs on Christ. Can they ever be returned to the church? Perhaps, but it evidently will be even more difficult than their original conversion was.

A quotation from Proverbs and another saying close the section. The second, nonbiblical proverb speaks of a pig that was washed and yet returned to the mud. If these teachers were baptized the connec-

---

A synod of African bishops made this decision after one persecution before the beginning of the next:

We had indeed decided some time ago, . . . having mutually taken counsel one with another, that they who, in the fierceness of persecution, had been overthrown by the adversary, and had lapsed, and had polluted themselves with unlawful sacrifices, should undergo a long and full repentance. . . . But now, when we see that the day of another trouble is again beginning to draw near, . . . we have decided that peace is to be given to those who have not withdrawn from the Church of the Lord, but have not ceased from the first day of their lapse to repent, and to lament, and to beseech the Lord; and *we have decided* that they ought to be armed and equipped for the battle which is at hand.

—Cyprian

"Epistle LIII" 1 (*ANF* 5:336–37).

tion would be very clear. Once they were washed clean in baptism, but now they have returned to the licentious ways they had before baptism.

A few places in the New Testament point to the difficulty of restoring believers who turn away from the faith. The clearest is in Hebrews 6:4–6: "It is impossible to restore again to repentance those who once have been enlightened . . . since on their own they are crucifying again the Son of God." In Luke 12:10 Jesus says that those who blaspheme against the Holy Spirit cannot be forgiven. The early church, particularly in the West, had some difficulty with those who weakened during persecution, made the sacrifices to the emperor, and then, after the persecution was ended, sought to return to the church. Is this a description of how the church ought to act—that is, not allowing such a return? Or is it a statement that those who have actually lived within the community of faith and have experienced the power of the Holy Spirit in their lives, and then turned away from that, will find it almost impossible to return to that life, since they evidently did not find in it the satisfaction that it promised? It would be difficult to think that the church should give up on some people, rather than offering another chance, even though recognizing that it may be impossible for the person to make the transition to faith a second time.

The false teachers are thus condemned. The congregations are urged to reject these new teachings. So far the major concern about these teachings is that they promote sinful behavior on the part of Christians because they deny that there is any day of judgment coming to condemn such actions.

3:1–18

The Crux of the Matter

The major concern of the epistle so far has been that these false teachers deny there is judgment coming for all people. The coming judgment is an essential part of the gospel, however, and the behavior of Christians, those who acknowledge God's coming judgment, should be as moral as possible. Those who deny there will be judgment are also supporting sinful behavior. The hearers of this letter should remember that the prophets, Jesus, and the apostles have all warned that there will be scoffers, those who do not believe the truth. That these false teachers do not believe there will be a judgment, however, is tied to an even more important element of the gospel.

3:1–4

The Return of Christ

The author addresses the readers as "beloved," and assumes they are still part of the faithful. Since the letter is written as a prophecy about what will happen in the future with false teachers arising, the congregations who receive this letter would still be faithful, and need to be forewarned and therefore forearmed so that they will not believe these teachers. In reality, the letter is probably sent to congregations that already have the problem. Since the letter is written in Peter's name, there is a reminder that this is the second letter. The first evidently is 1 Peter, though there are few actual links between the two letters.

The authority of this letter is backed up by reminding the readers that the prophets in Israel, the words of Jesus himself, and the teachings of the apostles all agree and they will disprove what these false teachers say. The listing is interesting: the ancient prophets, Jesus, and the apostles. This corresponds to the writings that were already authorities in the church or were gaining authority: the Old Testament, the Gospels, and the writings of Paul, Peter, and others. There was no official canon of the New Testament at this point, and it would be a few generations before it took shape. But the beginning of the process is clearly reflected here.

The false teachers mentioned in 2 Peter are claiming there will be no judgment because they doubt that Jesus will return. Everything has stayed the same, and therefore what difference does it make what Christians do? There will be no change, no full redemption of this world. This is a very basic question: What difference did the life, death, and resurrection of Jesus make if nothing has changed? It is clear that the earliest Christians expected his return in the very near future, and had to deal with the question of why the delay. If that was true even in the time of Paul—and we can see reflections of this in some of his letters, especially 1 and 2 Thessalonians—then surely a few generations later it was an even more serious question. It is not clear if the "ancestors" or forefathers meant here are the entire human race back to the beginning or the first generation of the church, the apostolic age. If it is the latter, then the reason for the questioning by the false teachers is that the whole apostolic generation is dying and the end has not come, which appears to negate the words of Jesus that the present generation would not pass away before his return (Matt. 24:34). At the same time, the argument of this letter

---

Jesus Christ's coming again for judgment, His ultimate and universal manifestation is often described in the New Testament as *the* revelation. He will be revealed, not only to the Church but to everyone, as the Person He is. . . . In full clarity and publicity the "it is finished" will come to light. For that the Church is waiting; and without knowing it the world is waiting too. We are all on the way to meet this manifestation of that which is.

—**Karl Barth**

Dogmatics in Outline, trans. G. T. Thomson (repr., New York: Harper & Brothers, 1959), 134–35.

goes back to creation, showing that there have been changes, which suggests that the issue was whether anything had changed since the beginning of human history.

There could then be two different issues here. First, did anything really change because Jesus lived among us? Second, will Jesus return? These two are somehow connected in the false teachings. What is not clear is what these false teachers, part of the Christian community, believed to be the value of being a Christian. Was Jesus a savior who took us out of this creation rather than a savior who has an impact on creation? If so, then the false teachers might be heading in an early gnostic direction. They seem to accept that Jesus is a savior of some sort, and yet his salvation does not have moral implications.

It is at this point that we can see one of the great differences between the letter called 1 Peter and this second letter. It may be a matter of when they were written. First Peter is not long after the first generation of leaders; it reflects a much earlier understanding than 2 Peter. As we saw in 1 Peter, those early Christians believed that something quite new had begun in Christ. They were living in what can be termed the down payment, the foretaste, of the new creation. They lived both in the new and in the old creation. They had to practice the life of the new creation in the context of the old. Only when they met together as the church, especially when they gathered at the Lord's Table in the presence of their risen Lord, were they able to be fully themselves as new creatures. The rest of the time they had to negotiate living their new lives in the midst of an old world that did not recognize the new, and that could lead to conflict and persecution. Their moral behavior was part of the new life. Judgment was expected, but they were already undergoing judgment in the context of God's love for them—a judgment that led to increased holiness and was part of the process of sanctification.

Here in 2 Peter the situation seems quite different. Little is said about their already living in a new creation. They seem to have been left a list of behaviors to follow, and judgment will come for them as for everyone else: at the end of history, the Day of the Lord. There is little sense that the new creation has broken into the old, even in a hidden fashion. The new creation is awaited, but only at the end.

And now there are false teachers denying that even that will come about.

We can see, then, a contrast in the eschatological character of these two letters. In 1 Peter there is a sense that the end has broken into this world, though the fullness of the new creation waits until the final day. We live, as Christians, in the beginning of the end. For 2 Peter this does not seem to be the case. Christians as well as the rest of the world wait for the coming of the new creation, which involves both the return of Christ and judgment. Christians are able to do what is necessary in order to be part of that new creation when it comes, and this involves the moral life. Others, who do not know or practice the life that is necessary, will be judged at the end and found wanting. Second Peter is written to encourage those Christians who thus must wait to keep believing that the coming of the Lord will truly happen, and with that day, the judgment of the whole world. Evidently the false teachers have told them the Lord is not returning, there is no judgment, and so they can lessen their struggle to lead a morally good life.

FURTHER REFLECTIONS
Eschatology

It is quite true that the church lost its sense of the new creation breaking into the old. It was not a uniform process, but it definitely had changed by the fourth century, when Constantine supported the church. Most of the church now assumed that there would be no more persecution, and as much of the new creation was present as there would be until the end of history. Christians were to lead morally good lives, since this was necessary in order to enter the kingdom, but until that end time, there would be no changes in the world. The world had changed enough by the government support of the church and almost everybody being part of the church; but other than that, we should not expect any further changes until the end. The end, however, was not expected any time soon. Each individual met his or her own "end" at death, and judgment would be at that point.

Such thinking amounts to a loss of an eschatological view of the Christian life now, in the midst of history. Everything is postponed to after death, with the final end of history left to some ultimate future that has little bearing on the present. The church becomes the teacher of what must be done now in order to inherit the kingdom after death, but does not really see itself as the inbreaking of the new creation in the midst of the old.

Most of us, as Christians in the twenty-first century, are probably more at home with the thinking of 2 Peter on these matters. That has really been the norm for centuries. At the same time, within the last generation there has been a recovery of the earlier understanding. This has been true particularly in the liturgical renewal that has affected many churches in the last forty years. There is more interest in seeing the church and ourselves as part of the new creation, with all of the struggles this means for us.

Part of the reason for this new interest in eschatology is not academic. It is not simply due to the recovery of ancient documents that help us to understand parts of the New Testament better. It is also because the great loss of an eschatological view about the church was tied to the increasing support by the Roman Empire, begun by Constantine, and then continued in various ways in the whole Western world. Since we now live at the end of what has been called the "Constantinian Era," the significance of an eschatological perspective on our lives as Christians, and particularly on the role of the church as the inbreaking of that new creation, is greater now than it has been for centuries. During the Constantinian Era we could assume that we lived in a Christian society. Granted it was still affected by sin, but it was generally Christian. Now, with an obviously increasing secularism, we live in a society that has more in common with the world around those early Christians. The difference between the church and the world is clearer, and therefore the newness of the Christian life is also clearer.

To the question, Has anything really changed since the beginning of creation until now? the contemporary answer, like that of 1 Peter, is increasingly likely to be, yes! In the life, death, and resurrection of Jesus, God's new creation broke into history. Its fullness is still to come, but we who are part of the body of Christ now live in the foretaste of that new creation, and the church itself, the congregation in its life together and the life of the one church all around the world, is a witness to that new creation. We know that there will be a time of final fulfillment because we have already experienced its beginning. We try to lead moral lives because that is the nature of that new creation, not because we must if we want to be admitted to that kingdom later.

3:5–13

Why the Delay

The author continues with his own answer to the question, Has anything changed since the beginning of creation? The world was destroyed by the great flood. Surely that was something that had changed from the beginning! But just as the world was once destroyed by water, and with Noah's family there was a new beginning, the earth will eventually be destroyed by fire, which will usher in the end of history, with judgment and the return of Christ with a new creation. The time for that final event has not yet come, but the fire is being stored up even now for that final judgment.

It is by God's word that the world was created, and later flooded, and will be judged and destroyed. Note the emphasis on the power of God's word. The same divine word that accomplished all of this in the past can be trusted to accomplish its purposes in the future. What the true prophets, Jesus, and the apostles spoke was the Word of God. Jesus himself was the word of God. Therefore, that word will happen, and that word includes the final judgment and the return of Christ. What the false teachers speak is not the powerful word of God but the weak, human word that is false.

One could argue that not much changed after Noah. The earth may have been purified by the flood, but sin found a foothold with Noah's family, and now, millennia later, there is as much sin and lawlessness as there was before the flood. Nothing really new has happened. For Christians the really new is the new life in Christ that is hidden from the world. But that idea is more at home in 1 Peter than here. It may be that the false teachers here in 2 Peter believed that forgiveness had been given in Christ, and therefore believers were free from the restraints of the law.

The author gives the reason for the delay of the coming of the end. It is a delay only from our perspective. God's time has a far longer perspective than human time. The author quotes Psalm 90:4, that in God's sight a thousand years is but a day. God has far more patience than we have, and God's patience is for our good. By delaying the end and judgment, God is giving people time to repent. God wants everyone to come to repentance and newness of life. The longer the time, the more who will be able to repent. This statement is directed to the Christians to whom he writes: they should be glad God is patient with them. (God's patience may allow future generations to repent, but a thousand years is no great extension of time for individuals to repent if their lives are more like sixty or seventy years!)

God's patience is a very important theme, and one that has often been used to explain why the end of history has not yet arrived. It is also very helpful to remind ourselves that God's concern is for the whole of human history, as well as for each individual. God's purpose in creation was more than individuals. God wished a society living together with the rest of creation as its stage. God intends to bring to completion the purpose that was there already at the beginning. The incarnation and the work of Christ are part of that whole—an essential part. Our individual salvation is of concern to us, and we can well believe it is of concern to God also, but God's plans include far more than us, even far more than only the human creation.

In verse 12 they are told to continue waiting for the Day of the Lord. They are to have an attitude of expectancy even though not anticipating the end at any particular time. It is difficult to wait for something when you have no idea when it will arrive. The expectant mother has a clear idea when the pregnancy will end, with the birth of the child. Children wait for Christmas or their birthday with a sense of the amount of time they have to wait. It is much more difficult to wait for something, keeping the expectancy alive, when there is no due date, no estimate of time given. The false teachers had given up on the waiting, but the epistle urges these Christians to continue the expectant waiting, and to do so with patience. In some translations they are told to "hasten" the final day, and it is difficult to know what that would mean. Would their improved behavior hasten it? We pray in the Lord's Prayer that God's kingdom would come on earth, and perhaps if we are transformed by our prayers we hasten the day of its coming. Other translations read that these Christians are to desire earnestly the day of God. It does make sense that if we truly desire the coming of God's full reign, then we are hastening to it, hoping that it will arrive. However, if we have a relatively good situation in this world, though we may pray the prayer, we may be hoping that the end will not come during our lifetime.

The end of history is coming, and destruction of this world will be by fire. This is in accordance with the understanding that God promised never again to destroy the earth by water. The next time judgment will be by fire (Luke 3:16–17). In verse 13 there is a familiar phrase: God has promised a new heaven and a new earth. This is a promise that may be difficult to believe. We are so familiar with these words that we often overlook how strange they are, how contrary to the way we usually think. At least three times in Scripture these words appear: here in 2 Peter 3:13; in Revelation 21:1; and in Isaiah 65:17. Two things should surprise us here. First, the promise is of a new earth. Much of Christian thinking assumes that the world to come is "spiritual," whatever that means, and the earth is obviously "earthy"! Scripture, however, does not have a problem with physical reality. It is good because it is from God. The new earth will not be exactly like this one, partly because it will be a habitation fit for righteous people, a creation in which justice and righteousness are at home. Paul deals with the question of what the new world will be like when, in 1 Corinthians 15, he says that God can provide the kind of bodies we will need in that new creation, and they will be spiritual bodies. Even that combination of words may be strange to us: "spiritual" and "bodies" do not go together. Bodies are by definition physical. On that new earth, we will have the bodies we need.

The second surprise here is that there will be a new heaven. For us, heaven is the place of goodness, perfection. Why must there be a new heaven? For both Jewish and Christian thinking, evil must have its origin in God's good creation. All things were created by God, and there can be no independent origin of evil. The usual way of understanding the source of evil is that some of the angels fell, that is, turned away from God and sought to be their own powers. One of these angels was Lucifer, or Satan, and others were spiritual beings who followed Satan. Thus there arose a reign of sin, by which the human creation was captured when it yielded to temptation in the garden. The fall of humanity also involved the fall of creation: pain, domination, thorns and thistles, and all the other negative things that mark our world (Gen. 3:14–19).

The work of Christ was to free humanity from the bondage to sin and decay, to overpower Satan, and to lead humanity to a new life. We see overtones of this belief throughout Scripture, and in this letter in 2:4. But if some of the angelic host did turn away, then not all is well even in the heavenly places. Hebrews 9:23–28 speaks of the death of Christ purifying the heavenly sanctuary once and for all, whereas the earthly sanctuary was repeatedly purified with the sacrifice of animals. Now that Christ has purified the heavenly sanctuary, he has purified us as well, and our sins are forgiven through his death. He will come again to receive his own. In Luke 10:17–18 Jesus tells the seventy whom he had sent out preaching that he saw Satan fall from heaven because of the preaching of the gospel. In Revelation 12:7–9 there is a vision of a war in heaven, and the archangel Michael fights with Satan, and throws him out of heaven onto the earth. It is for this reason, John of Patmos says, that conditions are becoming worse on earth.

These may seem very strange passages, but they all point to the fact that heaven needed to be changed so that no new sin could arise, leading a new earth back into bondage. Therefore, the promise of God is for a new heaven as well as for a new earth.

FURTHER REFLECTIONS
Changes in Creation

Much of the Western Christian tradition has viewed creation in a rather static fashion. That is to say, God created the world, and it was perfect. Then there was the fall, sin entered, and all was changed into the world we now know. Jesus came to save us from this sinful world. Granted, modern Christians manage to combine this view with some understanding of evolutionary changes within the creation. But there still remains a sense that creation was completed and then was corrupted by sin.

Within the Christian tradition, however, there are other options. For instance, the second-century theologian Irenaeus spoke of the first chapters of Genesis as describing the *beginning* of creation. Always there was the intention that creation would grow and develop. There was no sense that humans were expected to stay in a garden. God assumed that when the population grew large enough, cities would be founded. Always there was the understanding that human beings would invent new things, civilizations would grow, science would discover, even computers and airplanes might have been on the horizon. In other words, God began creation, and it was intended to develop from that beginning, with God's involvement.

Irenaeus says that it was always expected that Jesus would come, that God the Son would become incarnate and enter into our history. That did not mean that the cross would have occurred, because if there had been no sin, there would have been no need for the cross. But there would have been a need for the incarnation, because there were levels of human growth, stages of human history that could not occur without the incarnation. Irenaeus assumed that certain understandings about justice could not have been understood without the incarnation—perhaps dealing with justice when there are large populations that do not see one another face to face and have to deal with justice in regard to people they never meet. (We have those issues in ecology—what does justice mean in relation to future generations, or to people who live in another part of the world and yet our actions affect their seas or their air?)

This understanding of creation is dynamic in the sense that it is always growing and developing. Granted that sin has entered human history, and therefore all these scientific and cultural advances have been used for evil as well as for good. But God is not only the Creator. God is also the one who shepherds this creation, leading it toward the future God intends. Not everything that has happened on the way to that future is good, nor is everything evil. Always our history, like our work, is mixed, and we need God's help to see what is good, what can be used for good, and what is sinful. Take nuclear energy, for instance. Did God intend for human beings to discover this? Bombs are an evil use of it, and war is not what God intended. But could it have good uses? How do we determine this? We cannot simply look up in Scripture to see what it says about atomic energy, but does this mean it is totally evil? What about various discoveries and interventions in regard to conception and birth? Did God intend that human beings discover all these things? What is the good use of such discoveries? What is an evil use? How do we decide?

From the perspective of Irenaeus, such discoveries could be expected, and God continues to guide us in the good use of these discoveries. Many discoveries and inventions have the purpose of bringing human beings together, as in the areas of communications and transportation. Can we see in these things the hand of God guiding creation toward greater unity? What does Scripture tell us about God's ultimate purposes for all of creation? It is in discerning God's ultimate plans for the human creation as we find them throughout Scripture, from the beginning of Genesis to the end of Revelation, that we find clues to understand what in our own world leads to those plans and what takes us away from them. As Peter says here, the world God intends is one in which justice and righteousness are at home.

3:14–18
Final Words

The epistle closes with words of encouragement to these congregations. It has urged them to ignore what false teachers are saying and therefore continue to wait for the new heaven and the new earth that have been promised at the return of Christ. These congregations are to live at peace, to prepare themselves for the judgment that is to come, seeking to live righteous lives now. Even more, they are to practice now the virtues they will need in that promised future. They are not to concern themselves with the fact that the end has not come, but to view the time given them as a sign of God's patience and therefore time given to them to get themselves ready for that future, which includes judgment.

The author says that Paul has said the same things to them. This probably means they have read his letters, which were circulating by the end of the first century. He evidently wants to make sure that they realize the apostolic witness is one, that Peter and Paul agree on these things. But, he cautions, Paul's writings are not always easy to understand, and some have twisted his words. The comment that Paul wrote "according to the wisdom given him" sounds as though there is some question about exactly how much wisdom that was! Some ignorant people have misinterpreted his writings and led themselves and

> Look how Peter says that there is much to be admired in Paul's writings. Yet in his letters, Paul criticized Peter. Peter could hardly have said what he did if he had not read Paul, but when he read him he would have discovered criticism of himself in them. Thus the friend of truth was able to praise even the fact that he had been criticized, and he was happy to do so because he realized that he had been wrong.
>
> **—Gregory the Great**
>
> Quoted in *James, 1–2 Peter, 1–3 John, Jude*, ed. Gerald Bray, ACCSNT 11 (Downers Grove, IL: InterVarsity Press, 2000), 161.

probably others to destruction. We can assume this refers to the false teachers mentioned earlier. The issue, when we look at the whole letter, seems to be that these teachers have used Paul's words to assure some recent converts that in Christ they have been given freedom from the law, and therefore they do not need to be concerned about changing their behavior. They have been assured that they have forgiveness and the whole issue of following the law is for others, not for them. The law is not essential for Christians.

Throughout the second century several heresies developed, some of which pitted the law against the gospel. Marcionism was chief among these, although there were also some libertine gnostics who did the same. Since we are not sure of the date of this letter, we cannot tell if the false teachers mentioned here were influenced by them. There is no dualism here, pitting spirit against matter, which would be a telling characteristic of these heresies. But always the church has the problem of keeping together the freedom we have in Christ, the forgiveness of sins that comes by grace, with the desire for righteous living that is sanctification. If there is too much stress on the need to live a righteous life, then it seems we are saved by

following the law, and Christ has little to do with our salvation. If we
stress freedom and forgiveness, then we are in danger of preaching
what Dietrich Bonhoeffer called "cheap grace." It then appears that
God has forgiven us because of Christ and we can keep on with the
same sinful life because that forgiveness is readily available. Neither
of these alternatives is good.

Some in the late Middle Ages tried balancing the law and the
gospel by saying that we needed to do the best we could, with the
understanding that we could not be perfect. We had to try our best,
and after we died, if God knew that we had done our best (limited
though that was), then, on the basis of Christ's sacrifice, God would
give us enough grace to allow us to be saved. Luther was raised on
this theology and discovered that such a theology is impossible for
a sensitive person. Luther could always think of more he could have
done. He could have fasted more; he could have prayed more; he
could have been sorrier for his sins. On that basis, he was always
sure he was going to be damned. "Doing your best" is an inadequate
measure because we can always imagine more we could do, even if
it might not really have been possible to do all that we could imagine. It was against this theology that Luther discovered the biblical
understanding of salvation by grace through faith.

The loss of eschatology mentioned earlier has a lot to do with this
false choice of law or gospel. If we truly experience and believe that
we are living in the beginning of the new creation within the life of
the church, then the law is seen as a description of the life for which
we were created rather than a burden that if not obeyed denies us
the future kingdom. If we actually believe that in the law God has
given us the directions for an ultimately satisfying life, then we will
be eager to follow this way as closely as possible, both as individuals and as a community of faith. But our salvation does not hinge
on doing our best. Peter wants his readers to be stable in their faith,
not easily thrown off course by false teachers. They have stability if
they cling to the gospel that was preached to them. Stability is an
interesting choice of words here. We do not think of stability of faith
as something to strive for, but the word is helpful. Those who are stable, who have a solid foundation for their faith, are not easily swayed
by the latest thing they hear.

There are people in the church today who are quite unstable, who are likely to pick up the latest book, the latest fad, whether it is reincarnation or certain prayers that will bring success if one repeats them often enough. Without stability they cannot tell the novel from the true. At the same time, stability does not mean that one never learns anything. The epistle wants these Christians to be stable and at the same time to increase in knowledge. Christians should be open to learning more about their faith while not forgetting the solid foundation of that faith. The foundation includes the return of Christ and judgment. The early baptismal confession of faith seen in the Apostles' Creed affirms that Jesus will come again to judge. That was part of the earliest gospel proclaimed by the apostles, and it is still part of the firm foundation of our faith, a foundation that gives the wanted stability. Stability contrasts with the negative things said about these false teachers, taken from Jude, to be found in 2 Peter 2:17, that they are "mists driven by a storm." It is hard to imagine anything less stable than such mists.

The false teachers are losing eschatology totally. They deny that there will be a future judgment; they deny that Jesus will return. What is left is the end of history, and we are not sure what follows that end in their minds. But Christians are warned not to believe these teachers. They are to amend their lives, do what is right, seek to grow in the knowledge of Christ, and not worry about when the end of history will come. The letter closes as it began, with a prayer that they would grow in knowledge. Then they would be able to tell true teachers from false ones. The last verse includes an ascription of praise to Christ, our Lord and Savior. It is not as Trinitarian as 1 Peter is throughout. Glory is to be to Christ's now as well as in that final day and the world that comes with it, throughout all eternity.

Final Thoughts

Second Peter was relatively foreign territory to me, whereas 1 Peter was well-known and a favorite. This letter showed what it was that threatened the communities, what challenges they faced from within the church itself—and they were different challenges than those faced by the congregations to which 1 Peter was written. It is clear that the late first and early second century was a difficult time for the church. From those within the church they faced many teachings that contradicted the heart of the gospel the first generation knew. With the growth of the church in Gentile areas, there were combinations of the gospel with cultural elements quite foreign to a movement that began in Jewish territory.

There also were few structures of authority. The Old Testament was used as an authority, but exactly what Christian writings were authoritative had not yet been decided. First Peter was evidently known in the churches, and its authorship is claimed by the writer of this letter. Paul's letters are mentioned here, and we know that they circulated as a collection near the end of the first century, but the author warns the churches about easy misinterpretations of Paul that were apparently a serious matter. The apostles had authority, but most likely they had all died by the time this letter was written. It may be for this reason the letter uses the authority of Peter to counteract what are viewed as the dangers in Paul. There is no mention of church officers, whereas 1 Peter speaks of the elders.

Two things were particularly surprising. The first, as mentioned above, is how different the atmosphere and the purpose of 2 Peter are from 1 Peter. It is not simply that the writing is different; clearly the situation is quite different. The dangers are internal rather than external. There is little sense that there might be persecution. Relationships with those outside the church are not an issue, whereas they were a major concern in 1 Peter: how Christian slaves should relate to non-Christian masters, Christian wives to non-Christian husbands, all Christians to the state. These issues are not the concern of 2 Peter. This does not mean they had ceased to be important, only that 2 Peter has a different agenda.

The second surprise is how many verses—even partial verses— are well known, and yet that they are in this letter is probably not well known. Think of, "no prophecy of scripture is a matter of one's own interpretation" (1:20); or "with the Lord one day is like a thousand years" (3:8); or the Lord does not want "any to perish, but all to come to repentance" (3:9). It is helpful to understand the context within which these phrases first occurred.

Though the writing of 1 Peter may be more congenial, we probably live in a situation more like that of 2 Peter, where many strange things are taught in the name of Christ, including teachings that stress forgiveness more than amendment of life. Particularly Protestants have a difficult time stressing sanctification, the process of becoming holy, without falling into a theology that looks very much like salvation by works. Second Peter has that problem. In counteracting a view that sees little need to cease sinning, the emphasis is very strong on the need to obey the law in order to be welcomed into the heavenly kingdom after death.

Our culture has problems with judgment—judgment is so negative—and prefers only the word about grace. It is helpful to read this letter partially as a cautionary tale about our own lives as Christians. We may see ourselves reflected in this strange letter that we rarely read.

PART 3
JUDE

Introduction:
Why Jude? Why Now?

Why now? may be the easier question to answer. A major reason is that the discovery and study of a great deal of Jewish writings in the first century of the Christian era have shed light on this epistle, an epistle that could rightly borrow the title of a novel by Thomas Hardy, "Jude the Obscure"!

Once the letter has been deciphered through the use of such early material, it is easier to answer the question, Why Jude? Jude is dealing with a situation in which some church members are luring other Christians into bad behavior. They seem to be doing this by assuring the others that, though such behavior is prohibited to Christians generally, they have moved beyond that stage and are mature enough that they can engage in this behavior as a holy and not sinful act. This may well have meant sexual behavior, since it is considered licentious. Such claims are common in our own day—and many church leaders have been discovered using similar arguments. Whether it is male pastors with female church members or priests or youth ministers with young boys, the issue of this letter is relevant to our situation as well as to Jude's. What is interesting in this letter is how the situation is addressed, as well as the measures recommended to deal with the problem.

Though the issues are relevant, the language and references in the letter are extremely difficult to understand without constant reference to commentaries. It is this that makes it so obscure. Yet the study is well worth the effort.

There is another reason we need to read this epistle today. We are so familiar with Paul's writings that we do not really hear minority views that were common in the first century and are enshrined in the New Testament. Second Peter shows the dangers largely Gentile congregations saw in Paul. Jude is the reaction of a largely Jewish Christian congregation that also had problems with teachers who took Paul to extremes. Difficult as the writing is, it provides a window into the diversity of the earliest churches and how they dealt with such diversity. One thing they did was preserve all of these voices in Scripture, not silencing them. We have effectively shut out these other voices simply by ignoring them. We would do well to recover that plurality of views the early church did so much to preserve. The church today has great diversity, even within denominations. There is always the tendency to try to unify them and dismiss the weaker voices. Obviously, there are interpretations of the gospel that are simply wrong. That said, there are varieties of interpretations that the church can and should tolerate. It may help us in our own church life to recover the non-Pauline—and to some degree, anti-Pauline—voices in the New Testament.

Some Necessary Background

As mentioned in the discussion of 2 Peter, it is most likely that Jude preceded 2 Peter and was used extensively by the author of the latter. It is necessary to try to erase from our minds what 2 Peter did with the material from Jude, and try to see what is here in Jude rather than being influenced by the use made of it later. The circumstances may not have been the same. In fact, the general scholarly opinion is that, although 2 Peter probably originated in Rome, in a circle influenced by Peter, Jude may have come from the Palestinian area in a Jewish Christian circle influenced by James, the brother of Jesus. This would make some sense out of the names attributed to the authors of the two letters.

The letter presupposed a knowledge of noncanonical Jewish literature as well as traditional Jewish interpretations of biblical material that most contemporary Christians who are not scholars of the period do not understand. By using commentaries by such scholars, however, we can come to appreciate the value this letter had for the congregations to whom it was written. It can therefore help us as we deal with similar issues today.

Precisely because of the obscurity of much of this little book, a pastor cannot read it simply with possible preaching in mind. It needs to be approached for its own sake—seeing what lessons it has for our own congregations—and then, after discovering that, thinking about how a study of it might be approached within the congregation. Pastors do tend to think about how a text could be the basis of a sermon, and this letter would present quite a challenge.

1–25

The Letter

In reading this letter, we need to put ourselves back into a church very different from the ones to which Paul wrote. It was most likely a Jewish Christian congregation, or a group of such churches. They have a background in first-century Judaism and therefore appeal is made to its literature. They may know the letters of Paul, but they do not represent the same milieu.

1–2

The Greeting

The writer begins in the usual fashion, identifying himself. The names, however, may be confusing. Jude is another form of Judas. That name was ruined for Christians when one of the Twelve by that name betrayed Jesus, and therefore in English and in some other languages, others of that same name are usually called Jude. The claim here is that he is Jude, the brother of James. Two of the twelve apostles are named James, but neither is said to have a brother named Jude or Judas. In Mark 6:3 two of the brothers of Jesus are James and Jude. In Acts 1:13 there is a James listed among those at Pentecost, and with him a Jude, whose exact relationship is not clear. In Acts 1:14 we are told that Mary, the mother of Jesus, was present, along with his brothers. Most scholars think that it is this brother of Jesus who is meant here. Yet this Jude calls himself a servant or slave of Jesus. This could be a sign of humility, not claiming a particular relationship to the Lord except that of servant. All of the fol-

214

lowers of Christ are on an equal footing. No blood relationship to him, no position in the church, no long years of study give anyone a role higher than that of servant. With one another, however, we are brothers and sisters, whether by blood or by faith.

We know that the brothers of Jesus did have considerable authority in the church in Jerusalem. James may have been martyred there. The Jerusalem church moved to Pella, a city northeast of Jerusalem, across the Jordan. In the same way that a circle of Christians formed around Peter in Rome and continued his influence, writing in his name to other churches, this church in Palestine may well have continued the influence of its leaders by writing this letter in the name of Jude.

The letter is to Christians, those who have been called by God. In this calling God has kept them safe in Christ. Since the letter is to speak about the dangers they face from heretical teaching, they are reminded that in Christ they are safe from such dangers. Their task is to remain "in Christ" so that they will not be led astray.

The greeting concludes with a blessing, asking that God give them three things: mercy, peace, and love. These three go together: if they have mercy from God, then they know that they have been forgiven and have God's love. With this relationship to God they have peace. Out of the abundance that God has shown to them, they are able to love one another as well as God, who has given them so much.

The letter tells us nothing of the intended receivers. It seems a very general letter about a specific problem, and may simply have been intended to apply to all churches that find strange teachers among their number.

3–4

A Call to Faithfulness

The writer indicates that he was already planning to write, perhaps simply to keep contact among the churches. Letters from those who have some authority in the church to congregations far from those over which they have direct responsibility show that their authority is really over the whole church. The first generation of leaders, which included the Twelve and Paul, along with some relatives of Jesus such as James and Jude and some others, did have an undefined authority. Therefore when they wrote, their letters carried weight, which increased after this first generation died, and all that was left was their letters. Paul's letters were gathered from the various places to which he had written, and began to circulate among the churches by the late first century. His authority continued long after his lifetime through his letters. It is because these first-generation letters had such authority that later writers used the names of that first generation when they composed their own letters.

The letter Jude intended to write had been a treatise on the meaning of salvation in Christ. However, reports of problems in the church—whatever church or group of churches were his addressees—caused him to write a different sort of letter, one that would warn them of dangers to their faith.

What is perhaps the best-known passage in this letter reminds them that they had been given "the faith that was once for all entrusted to the saints." One of the reasons for assuming this to be a fairly late letter is the concept that there is a definite body of doctrine that Christians know and believe. Clearly by fairly early in the second century churches had developed a statement of faith that was required of candidates for baptism. (See above, pp. 47–49, "Further Reflections: Early Baptismal Practices.") This was a basic statement with some variations, of which the early form of the Apostles' Creed is an example. This understanding of the faith as a list of doctrines to be believed played a very important role in the life of the church, not only at baptism. Irenaeus, writing in about 185, related that he had evangelized many of the Celts in Gaul; and, though they had no written language, and therefore could not have a Bible, there was no danger of their falling into heresies, because they knew and believed the confession of faith, what was called the "rule of faith."[1] In that writing, *Against Heresies*, Irenaeus quotes the rule of faith several times, never twice alike, and yet always the same essential elements are present.

21. Irenaeus, *Against Heresies* 3.4.2.

However, deciding that "faith" here means an actual body of doctrine may be reading too much into it. As the letter progresses, the issue is not so much doctrinal as moral behavior. The two cannot be totally disconnected, but the faith delivered to the saints here has a great deal to do with lifestyle rather than with items contained in the typical rule of faith.

Jude has written because some people have intruded themselves into these congregations. The dangerous people in 2 Peter are referred to as "false teachers." Here, however, they are not so designated. Perhaps they were Christians from another place who had entered these churches, and it may be their lives and their conversations rather than any formal teachings that are in danger of corrupting the congregations. Clearly these are not people who were catechumens and then baptized into this congregation. They may be itinerant preachers or members of the church from other areas. These people have denied Christ, perhaps by their behavior rather than by specific words. They evidently have been baptized, because they are permitted at the love feasts, but their lives have perverted the grace of Christ that was given to them. Their behavior is licentious. This may be a general condemnation or mean more specifically that they are libertines in sexual matters. God has condemned such people long ago, and their ultimate condemnation is sure.

Nowhere in the letter are the intruders addressed directly. They are a clear group that can be distinguished from the churches into which they have inserted themselves. The letter assumes that the rest of the congregation has the ability to remove them or at least condemn them and their teachings. All of the advice is to the nonintruders. The goal of the letter is to strengthen the faith and the resolve of the church to counter these intruders and perhaps get rid of them.

5–13

Relevant Late Jewish Traditions

These verses are complex and use Jewish traditions current in the first century to support the argument of the writer, traditions that are merely mentioned without much explanation. The thought that the recipients of the letter were Jewish Christians is based in part on the fact that the references used to prove a point here would have been very obscure to largely Gentile congregations. In order to have some idea of what is meant here, we need to imagine ourselves as Jewish Christians, reasonably well versed in noncanonical Jewish traditions. If the letter is from the middle to fairly late first century, a sense of exactly what constituted a Jewish scriptural canon may not yet have been clear. Second Peter does not use all of these references, either because his audience would not understand them or because the author wanted to use only canonical material to bolster his argument against the false teachers. Since 2 Peter is later, either is possible.

The first reference is clear: God chose a people, Israel, and saved them from Egyptian slavery. Those who did not believe were destroyed. The destruction may refer to the fact that those who had been disobedient were not allowed to enter the promised land. The second reference is somewhat more obscure, though 2 Peter 2:4 also uses it: the fallen angels were put into chains until the judgment comes. The sin of the angels may refer to Genesis 6:1–4, when the angels mated with human women. That probably would have been the traditional understanding in the first century. If so, the next reference to Sodom and Gomorrah makes more sense. Second Peter uses this one as well, but not specifying the evil the cities did. In 2 Peter these cities, destroyed by fire, are an example of what will happen to the whole world at the judgment. Second Peter also stressed that the righteous, namely Lot and his family, were spared from this destruction. In Genesis 19, however, the issue is more the sin the people of these cities committed. Most have thought that this sin is homosexuality. However, the way the reference is used here, the interpretation probably picks up on a different theme in the Jewish tradition of the time—the sin was that the men of Sodom wished to have sex with the angels. This was the reverse of the sin of the angels who wished to have sex with humans. In either case, however, God's creatures, angels and humans, desired to leave the place in which God had created them, as angels or as humans. These human beings suffered the same punishment as the fallen angels.

Verse 8 returns to the sins of the intruders. First they are called "dreamers." This probably means that they base their activities on revelations they had received in visions, and use them against the traditions of the church. They are not only licentious and disobedient. They also are saying evil things about the angels. Angels played a great part in much Jewish theology of the time. They also played a role in early Christian theology. Paul refers to angels many times, but one of the most interesting is 1 Corinthians 6:1–4, where he speaks of lawsuits that Christians have taken to secular courts. He writes that if in the world to come human beings are to judge angels, then in this world Christians ought to be able to deal with difficulties that arise among themselves. In 1 Corinthians 11:10 women are told to wear a head covering, in part because of the angels. It appears some angels may still be tempted by human women! In Hebrews 2:5–8 we are reminded that dominion over this whole earthly creation was not given to angels but to human beings. Then the author of Hebrews quotes Psalm 8, that human beings were made a little lower than the angels for a little while, but clearly, in the future, human beings will be superior to the angels.

Humans and angels each have their stations, and they are not to confuse them. The intruders are moving out of their sphere when they challenge the angels—evidently angels are meant by "the glorious ones." Who these angels are is not clear, but one tradition at the time would have angels as guardians of the law of Moses. If so, speaking evil of the angels would be denying the present validity of the moral law given to Moses.

Then comes the next strange reference—a fight between the archangel Michael and the devil as to who had a right to the body of Moses. One Jewish tradition held that, since Scripture said that no one knew where Moses was buried (Deut. 34:5–6), it was God who arranged the burial. God sent Michael to bury Moses, but Satan argued that he had the right to the body, either because it was composed of matter (which sounds rather gnostic) or because Moses had murdered an Egyptian, and therefore was a sinner and subject to Satan. The point of the story here is that, even though Michael was an archangel and carrying out the mission of God, he did not directly curse Satan, the devil, who was also an angel, although a fallen one. Michael respected the angelic character of Satan. He called on God to judge Satan rather than judging and condemning

Satan himself. Now these intruders, though human beings, are judging angels and saying negative things about them. If Michael did not directly condemn an angel, neither should these humans.

This argument may not make a lot of sense to us, but to those who heard these references and understood them, it was clear that these intruders did not recognize the tradition of the church, and part of their heretical view may have been what they said about angels. If their behavior was corrupt, it may be that they felt that, in Christ, they were free of the tutelage of angels and now could begin to judge them. They may have based their words on Paul, misinterpreting him just as the false teachers in 2 Peter did. These intruders do not understand what the church teaches in this regard, and they are therefore a danger to the rest of the congregation. Again, the main concern will be the behavior that results from this judging of the angels and the law that they protect.

Evidently, these intruders are lawless—they do not recognize that they are still expected to be moral and increase in holiness. They simply live by following their instincts, their lusts, and are destroyed by them. They do not act as rational human beings, but rather like the lower animals. They are thus to be condemned.

The issue here seems to be that the intruders believe that the time has already come when the redeemed will be the judges of angels, and, since that time has come, the old moral law does not apply to those who have already passed through to the new situation. The church, in contrast, claims that the time when humans will be superior to the angels has not yet come, and will only come with the return of Christ. Until then, the moral law and the tutelage of angels remain in force.

We may be tempted to discount all of this as strange ideas from the first century that have no relevance to today's church. However, there are examples today that show just how easy it is to distort the gospel message in order to follow one's desires. An article appeared in a newspaper recently that spoke of male church leaders who had affairs with women in the congregation, assuring them that those who lived now in the kingdom were no longer bound by the morality of lesser Christians. Much abuse in a wide variety of churches, both against children and against women, has stemmed from a sense that some leaders are so holy that whatever they do is no longer sinful. When they are able to convince their victims of this, it becomes easier for abuse to occur and to be hidden from others who are not thought to be able to understand because they are not so holy.

The intruders in Jude's letter evidently are saying that the law does not matter for them because they are beyond the stage of needing it. They may have based some of their ideas on Paul's words about the law no longer being binding, but they discount what he says about sanctification.

The author then gives another series of examples, now to show that such people are to be condemned. They are condemned just as Cain was. Cain had chosen envy and hatred of his brother, and that is what the intruders have chosen. Balaam, who took money to prophesy falsely, points to the false words and greed of the intruders. Korah, who rebelled against the leadership of Moses, parallels the intruders' rebellion against the tradition and the leaders of the church. Again, the mention of these names and the traditions about them were understood in first-century Judaism, and therefore little more has to be said about them in a Jewish Christian church. (Second Peter uses only the example of Balaam and then explains what is meant.) The intruders are jealous haters, greedy, and rebellious. That is the import of these examples. Evidently, these intruders are gaining something by their actions. Are they teaching for money? Are they abusing the hospitality of some members? It is not stated.

Jude also reminds us that the grace of God can be perverted when the moral precepts of the gospel are disregarded, especially those pertaining to sexual conduct. We can delude ourselves into thinking that sexual libertinism is compatible with salvation, when in reality it is a concession to the flesh and cultural attitudes and practices that are incompatible with a faith commitment. We may not be perverting the grace of God with any *teachings* that denigrate the value of moral behavior. However, our *behavior* may be perverting the grace of God, presuming that grace easily covers behaviors that we do not desire to submit to the scrutiny of the gospel because we do not want to forsake those behaviors and let Christ be Lord.

—Duane F. Watson

"The Letter of Jude," in *The New Interpreter's Bible*, ed. Leander E. Keck (Nashville: Abingdon, 1998), 12:486.

They are joining the congregation's love feasts—which probably means Communion meals—and that is a great shame. These intruders have nothing good to give to the church. They bear no fruit; they are those for whom condemnation has been reserved. That they are called "wandering stars" may indicate that they were traveling preachers.

14–16

The Coming Judgment

Jude quotes from *1 Enoch*, another noncanonical writing that would have been known to a Jewish Christian audience. In the genealogy of Genesis 5, Enoch is listed in the seventh place. But the book of that name was very popular in the church of the late first century. What Jude quotes is the prophecy that the Lord will come to execute final judgment, and he will be accompanied by ten thousands of angels. Since the intruders are negative both about a future judgment based on traditional morality and about angels, this is a double attack on their teachings. Part of the judgment will be on those who have spoken negative things about the Lord. In this context, by "the Lord"

The book of Enoch, from which this quotation is taken, belongs to the Apocrypha, not because the sayings of that prophet are of no value or because they are false but because the book which circulates under his name was not really written by him but was put out by someone else who used his name. For if it were genuine, it would not contain anything contrary to sound doctrine. But as a matter of fact it contains any number of incredible things about giants, who had angels instead of men as fathers, and which are clearly lies. Indeed, it was precisely because Jude quotes him that for a long time his letter was rejected by many as being uncanonical. Nevertheless it deserves to be included in the canon because of its author, its antiquity and the way in which it has been used, and particularly because this passage which Jude takes from Enoch is not in itself apocryphal or dubious but is rather notable for the clarity with which it testifies to the true light.

—Venerable Bede

Quoted in *James, 1–2 Peter, 1–3 John, Jude*, ed. Gerald Bray, ACCSNT 11 (Downers Grove, IL: InterVarsity Press, 2000), 255.

Jude probably means Jesus, whereas that would not have been the case in *1 Enoch*.

The final judgment will show that God still is concerned that human beings keep the moral law, and there is no exception for those who think themselves holier and not needing to pay attention to it. Godliness, or at least growth toward godliness, is still expected of Christians. Godliness here means righteousness. Speaking against the holy angels also will be punished. These intruders evidently complain, perhaps about the challenge they receive from church leaders. They are also flatterers, which could be the means by which they seduce the weak, telling them that they really are superior to ordinary mortals and the law no longer has meaning for them.

17–23

Closing Remarks

As the letter closes, the writer turns from showing the sins and condemnation of the evil ones and speaks to the congregation he is urging to remain faithful. If this letter was read in the midst of the gathering, which is what was normally expected, the intruders would also hear it. Yet the way it is written they would understand that it was written about them but not to them. The reading itself would increase the separation of the faithful congregation and the intruders.

The word to the church is the reassurance that such false teachers are to be expected. The apostles predicted such things would happen. They are therefore not to be surprised. In fact, the presence of such people is a sign that the end is near, along with the judgment that will accompany it. One of the reasons for thinking this letter to be at least a second-generation product is that it speaks of the apostles as in the past. That may be true, but it does not mean that the letter has to have been written a long time after the apostolic period. In the same vein, there is the stress that the congregation should build themselves up—edify themselves—in the "most holy faith." This again, as in verse 3, can be taken to mean that faith is a series of doctrines, which would indicate a later rather than an early date. But it may also mean that their faith, including the words about Christ returning in judgment, is to be the basis of their growth as God's people.

There cannot be a total division between doctrine and behavior, as though what we think about God and Christ is an intellectual matter and has no relationship to our behavior. That thought is totally opposed to the teachings of the entire New Testament: Gospels, Paul, and all the rest. Indeed, much of the catechetical training of the early church seemed to be focused on behavior, using a change in behavior as an entrance into understanding the doctrines that the church taught (see above, pp. 21–25, "Further Reflections: The Catechumenate").

The intruders are described as not having the Holy Spirit. We need to remember that for the early church, it was the gift of the Holy Spirit that gave them community. They shared jointly in the Spirit and this brought them together. The gifts of the Spirit were given to individuals, but for the sake of the whole. The Spirit tied them to Christ. The Spirit led them into holiness. The intruders did not participate in the Holy Spirit and they therefore caused divisions rather than unity. They were worldly rather than holy. They based their opinions on their own visions and dreams rather than on the inspiration of the Holy Spirit.

The true members of the church, however, were not to be like them. They were to keep themselves in the Holy Spirit in prayer, in the love of God, and in the hope of the future when they would receive mercy from Christ and participate in eternal life. They therefore were to have faith, love, and hope. The intruders had none of these things.

What should the faithful members do about those who have been influenced by these intruders? The last part of this section speaks of this. It does not say how they should treat the intruders but rather how to save some of their own members who may have fallen for the flattery or the easy life the intruders offered. These are the weaker brothers and sisters who need to be rescued. The letter tells its readers that they are to have mercy, and treat these wavering ones with love and concern. They are to rescue them from the fire to which they have come close. This may mean that there are some in the congregation who have listened to these intruders and thought that maybe they had a better message than the church did. Others might have begun to live the false lifestyle, and were therefore already in the fire and needed to be pulled away. But rescuing such people needs to be done with fear, lest the faithful themselves be corrupted.

The imagery in verses 22 and 23 reflects Zechariah 3:1–5. This is the passage quoted by the archangel Michael in *1 Enoch*, asking that God rebuke Satan, the passage Jude had referred to in verse 9. Zechariah's vision is set in heaven. Before the throne of God stand an angel, Satan, and the high priest Joshua. Joshua is clothed in filthy rags. Satan is there to accuse Joshua, but God rebukes him, saying that Joshua is "a brand plucked from the fire." Then the angel orders that the filthy clothes of Joshua should be removed, and he should be clothed with clean ones. The angel says to Joshua: "See, I have taken your guilt away from you, and I will clothe you with festal apparel." Jude uses this imagery to show that those of the congregation who have been influenced by the sinful intruders should be treated as Joshua was. They should be pulled away from the fire, and then, with their guilt forgiven, they can be rid of their filthy clothes. But Jude adds that care should be taken that the rescuers are not themselves contaminated.

There are two very interesting points in this passage in Zechariah. First, the role of Satan as the accuser of the saints. The image is that Satan is still in heaven, able to argue with God's angel about the salvation of someone. Satan, the accuser, has a long history in both Jewish and Christian literature. In the beginning of Job, 1:6–12, Satan is pictured as challenging God, arguing that if the good things in Job's life were removed he would no longer praise God. God allows Satan to remove all these things from Job. In Revelation 12:10, where the archangel Michael throws Satan out of heaven, a loud voice in heaven says: "the accuser of our comrades has been thrown down." (Traditionally, in the Roman Catholic Church, when a person is being proposed to be named officially a saint of the church, someone is appointed, called "the Devil's Advocate," to try to disprove the saintliness of the person. The term, "the devil's advocate," simply means one who tries to show that the good person is not as good as is thought.)

The second point is the imagery of new clothes as a sign of the forgiveness of sins. It is clear that the early church used this imagery in the baptismal services at least in the second century, and it is not known how early that might have happened. It does not mean that Jude reflects a contemporary baptismal practice, but it could be part of the basis on which the church soon after Jude's letter began to give new robes to those who had just been baptized.

24–25

The Ascription

The concluding ascription is one of the most famous in the New Testament. We are so used to the words we may not see how they are connected to the whole letter. The whole letter has been about keeping the faithful from falling for the false ideas of the intruders. Now it is God who is called the one who can keep them from falling. This parallels the words in verse 1, which calls the faithful those who are "kept safe for Jesus Christ." No amount of urging can keep them faithful. But God is able to do so. Those who do not fall will, at the final judgment, be presented before the throne of God, and there they will be able to rejoice in the midst of his glory. This is true, because they will not fear the judgment. Just as Joshua was able to stand before God, even when Satan tried to accuse him, so believers will be able to stand before God without fear of condemnation. God is our Savior, through Jesus Christ, who is our Lord. It is God who has authority, and through the Holy Spirit that authority has given the church the knowledge of what God desires. The visions of the intruders have no such authority. They cannot save, nor can they give us clean clothes that signify forgiveness. They themselves are the ones in filthy clothes, and they deny the need for forgiveness.

The ascription sums up the faith of the church: in spite of our sin, because of Christ, we can appear before God without fear. Our sins will be removed, and the mercy of God will be shown to us. We will rejoice eternally in the presence of God.

Final Thoughts

Jude is indeed a strange book, and yet well worth the study. It puts the reader back into a time early in the church's history, in the midst of Jewish Christian congregations. Such congregations had a totally different flavor than the more Gentile ones with which Paul was concerned. It also is quite different from 2 Peter, even though that author quoted much of this epistle in his own task of opposing false teaching. This writing reminds me more of Revelation than of any other book, in the sense that there are constant overtones of Old Testament passages and frequent typological use of Jewish tradition, woven together in such a way that the full meaning would not be understood by a largely Gentile church.

This means that this epistle, more than most others, gives us a glimpse into a church that had some problems with Paul. At least some of the people the letter opposes may be taking Paul's word about the law to an extreme, far beyond what Paul intended. (In 2 Pet. 3:16 there is a specific reference to this in a different context.) The newness of life in Christ at a minimum gives us strength to be more holy, and holiness is defined in terms of the moral law. That is, true holiness may exceed the moral law by loving enemies and laying down one's life for others, none of which is required by the Ten Commandments. But it is not less than the holiness seen in the law. No matter how filled with grace we think we are, we do not grow out of the guidance of the law. Our salvation does not depend on fulfilling the law, that is clear. Even saints need forgiveness and mercy from God.

We may think that such libertine views were only an oddity of the early church. But in our own day there are church leaders who have a view of themselves that allows them to exploit others by telling them that sexual relations with them—the leaders—are holy and approved by God. We need to arm congregations against such views, as well as making sure church leaders do not hold them.

The frequent references to unfamiliar literature and traditions make Jude difficult to read, and a preacher would have difficulty with much of the material, since most of the sermon would have to be taken up with explanations of all the strange references. It is no wonder that the lectionary does not include any readings from this book. At the same time, the general thrust of the letter—opposition to those who claim their faith makes them superior to mere morality, and how the church should deal with those who are tempted to follow such people—is a message worthy of the congregation's hearing.

Jude might work very well as a Bible study, and would certainly provide a solid basis for serious discussion. Such a study would require much more input from the leader than is usually the case, but it could be very satisfying for a group really interested in how the early church faced difficulties to which we also are subject. If a pastor wished to preach on a passage from this book, the most likely section is the last few verses, 20–25, on how to treat those who have fallen, especially if one includes the final ascription as part of that advice, showing that we need God's grace to remain faithful. It may be an ancient book, written to a very different congregation, but it holds an important place in the church's Scripture for those who spend time and effort with it.

Selected Bibliography

Bartlett, David L. "First Letter of Peter." In *New Interpreter's Bible*, edited by Leander E. Keck, 12:227–319. Nashville: Abingdon, 1998.

Davids, Peter H. *The First Epistle of Peter*. NICNT. Grand Rapids: Eerdmans, 1990.

Davids, Peter H. *The Letters of 2 Peter and Jude*. Pillar New Testament Commentary. Grand Rapids: Eerdmans, 2006.

Elliott, John H. *A Home for the Homeless: A Social-Scientific Criticism of 1 Peter, Its Situation and Strategy*. 2nd ed. Minneapolis: Fortress, 1990.

Green, Joel B. *1 Peter*. THNTC. Grand Rapids: Eerdmans, 2007.

Harrington, Daniel J. "Jude and 2 Peter." Pages 159–299 in *1 Peter, Jude and 2 Peter*, by Donald P. Senior and Daniel J. Harrington. Sacra Pagina 15. Collegeville, MN: Liturgical Press, 2003.

Jobes, Karen H. *1 Peter*. BECNT. Grand Rapids: Baker Academic, 2005.

Perkins, Pheme. *First and Second Peter, James, and Jude*. Interpretation. Louisville: John Knox Press, 1995.

Senior, Donald P. "1 Peter." Pages 1–158 in *1 Peter, Jude and 2 Peter*, by Donald P. Senior and Daniel J. Harrington. Sacra Pagina 15. Collegeville, MN: Liturgical Press, 2003.

Watson, Duane F. "Letter of Jude." In *New Interpreter's Bible*, edited by Leander E. Keck, 12:471–500. Nashville: Abingdon, 1998.

Watson, Duane F. "Second Letter of Peter." In *New Interpreter's Bible*, edited by Leander E. Keck, 12:321–61. Nashville: Abingdon, 1998.

Index of Ancient Sources

Index of Subjects